The Chronicles of Shannyn Casino

CONTENTS

CHAPTER 5

The Spirit Of Moreland Street

CHAPTER 6

Middle School

CHAPTER 7

The Community Center

CHAPTER 8

Soul Ties

CHAPTER 9
Fame & Torture

CHAPTER 10
Before Graduation

CHAPTER 1

"Mikey"

— From The Start —

TJ was born in Cocoa, FL, in the '60s.

When she was four years old, her mother packed up her two siblings Nellie and Bryce, and moved to Boston, MA. TJ's mom decided to leave the sunshine state in the hopes of finding better work and giving her children a better life away from racial tension and small town heartbreaks of the south. Years later, TJ's Mom met a man and soon after had another baby, Breena.

TJ became a typical inner-city girl in Boston with strong roots from the south. Church on Sunday, chores everyday, and a traditional southern style of grooming and well-taught manners. Yes Ma'am, No Sir's, Please, and Thank You's were expected of TJ and her siblings.

But, despite that good nature, life proves that nine times out of ten, we become our environment. So, TJ grew up curious about the fast life. That sweet foreign sound of the ghetto right outside her window. Fights in the street, timely, never-ending public transportation in route, police sirens, blowing horns, and numbing music blaring at any time of day or night.

As that sound became a new normal, TJ started to fall off in her school grades and find childlike mischief to get into instead. One time, TJ gathered and motivated a group of her neighborhood friends to help her burn down a man's auto body shop for hitting her sister Nellie.

Another time she was chased into a Bodega where she realized that she could only back down but for so long. It just wasn't in her nature to run from anybody. TJ took off her sock, put a can of peas in it, and beat up the girl who had been bullying her for weeks. TJ wasn't a troublemaker, but if it wasn't one thing, it was another with her. Some years later, her mother even sent her to live with her dad three and a half hours away in Newark, NJ, in an effort to keep her on the right track. As if Newark was any better.

Being that TJ's dad was a career man who had very little patience and his own struggles with compassion and the understanding of proper parenting, that union wasn't the best idea and was not very long-lived.

So not feeling the love that she maybe hoped to find with her dad, at the age of thirteen, TJ ran away. She came up with just enough money to get her a one-way Amtrak ticket back to the City that she fell in love with. Boston.

Although she had a good heart and a mother who often prayed for her obedience, TJ somehow, was already on her way to skipping high school altogether. Without even knowing that she was already on the right track to SIDEWALK UNIVERSITY.

— Orientation —

Well-endowed for her age and a before her time maturity, TJ's attractions to the older crowd was magnetic. She met a woman twelve years her senior by the name of Mikey.

Mikey was an "IT" girl; a part of the in-crowd that TJ was so attracted to. Mikey had it all! She was tall and slim, beautiful and sexy. Elegance was her middle name.

Her whole spirit was that of grace and style with a touch of gangster. From Connecticut, Mikey was a glamorous hippie woman. She had a decked-out apartment with the latest furniture and pricey whatknots. Incense burning over the aroma of weed, and two kids running around as she was a single mother. She worked at Filene's. An upscale department store right off the Orange Line (MBTA) at Downtown Crossing.

Mikey knew how to flip hats very well and was stunning to see. Even the white women adored her. Mikey and TJ were together So often that the known rumor around the city was that they were lovers.

But things were good then. Running smooth as TJ was being swooned to be the next best thing. Relearning how to talk, walk, and carry and handle herself if she was going to be affiliated. But ultimately, how to catch the attention of men. Especially men of Status.

In a club already by the age of 16 when ID wasn't as important as associations and clout.

With heavy pours of cognac, cigarette smoke, slight ratchet conversations under the booming sounds of 70's music that keeps the spirits grooving every other night of the week.

TJ's mom became more and more concerned with the duo's relationship. But nothing or no one could break what has now become a sisterhood.

TJ dated a few guys her age but just didn't feel the connection she was looking for. She was way too dominant and wise for young boys and childish neighborhood dating. Especially since the crowd she was in had enough men to choose from that fit the criteria she really wanted.

It wasn't too long before TJ put her spotlight on a young man. Still, he was ten years older than she was. He was this, he was that, he was like no one she had ever met. He had the best afro in the place. Muscular, well-spoken, chocolate bronze complexion, dapper, yet a very stern demeanor about him. A real alpha male. Needless to say, TJ just could not deny her immediate feelings toward him. His name, "Doc Holiday," Also known as Randall Johnson. He was a featured Disc Jockey at Lanes Lounge on a typical night out with Mikey.

His baritone voice over the music was full of demand and excitement. Women of all shapes, styles, ages, and backgrounds were all over him—a real magnet for the opposite sex.

But that wouldn't stop TJ from going after what she wanted. This was more of a priority to her than going to The Burke High school as she had already dropped out in the 9th grade, two years earlier.

Although Mikey always advised her to go back to school, TJ felt as though she had the best professor in the world and life experiences of Mikey to guide her.

TJ was confident and ready to get what she believed was hers. Needless to say, TJ & Holiday started casually dating. At this point, they knew nothing of each other's past. TJ didn't even tell him she was only 16. The age difference could be cringeworthy, but the '70s was a different time. So the honeymoon days were full of newness and bliss.

TJ was in love, but Holiday not so much in the beginning. He's been down this road quite a few times before. So this was nothing more than a fling that he thought for sure would come to pass. But this wasn't the mindset that TJ had at all. TJ had a common issue known to young girls growing up in a household without a stable dad around. "Daddy Issues". So she grew attached to him and began to tag along with him as if she was his closest buddy. Mostly helping him load and unload his car with all of his crates filled with vinyl records, turntables, speakers, and other equipment needed to set the mood for a night of partying. She enjoyed that, the spotlight he had on him. His fast-paced lifestyle. The acknowledgment he got from some of the Cities most popular and street high-profiled. As if she wasn't already, TJ was growing up quickly.

Mikey knew all about Holiday. She had seen him around before. She knew just what TJ was getting herself into but also thought they would just be another fling for one another and move on quickly. As time went on, TJ learned more about Holiday's lover boy ways and multitasking women. This grew a fit of jealousy and competitive spirit within a young and insecure TJ. Being that she was just a tad bit younger. The women were more of Holiday's age and, of course, had more to offer mentally and intellectually. This started to make her grow more aggressive, with Holiday all the while stepping up her game to even be considered a threat to the next dame. Every issue the new couple was going through was reported back to Mikey. But TJ's complaints had become a new normal, and Mikey didn't have all the answers. Mikey had her own trials and tribulations in her life to deal with. She was single and had two mouths to feed. A son and daughter. Her kids were her world, so she kept them sheltered and didn't want them to even try to understand what was happening in the streets. So her standards were high. She would rather do it all on her own than to settle for what the inner city dating scene had to offer.

Yet, still Mikey had met a man that really liked her. He tried and tried repeatedly to get her to take him more seriously as the man in her life as he promised her a great life with him. He was a Boston Taxi Cab driver named Curtis and always had money. It was a very popular and honest way to make a lot of cash back then without education. He became Mikey's Beck & Call. No matter the time, day or night. If Curtis wasn't working; whenever she needed a ride, she would call him, and he would be right there to take her to and from wherever she wanted. He always complimented her and flirted as much as he could, as he could not resist her beauty and sweetheart nature. There was nothing that could stop his mission to get her: Rain, sleet, shine, or snow. After a year gone by, finally, it was working. Mikey began to give in and start to confide in the Cab Driver. Giving him a test here and there to see how he would handle some of the things she had been through in her life. He had some of the greatest answers, and then there were times you could tell he was trying to impress her and would fail miserably. Mikey would laugh a lot of it off and move on to another topic. She thought he was cute! She was quick-witted and charming. One night, the cab driver got up enough nerve to ask her out on a date while taking her to her destination. Even though he was picking her up and dropping her off all over the city, she wasn't comfortable being alone with him just yet. So Mikey called up TJ & Holiday at his Franklin Hill apartment and asked them to double date with her and Curtis. Of course, they were more than happy to oblige.

The weekend comes, and it's now time to do what they all do best, Party! Holiday had his own car and decided to be the driver. He and TJ went to pick up Mikey from home and then met Curtis in Grove Hall, Roxbury near his home. When they arrived at the Blue Hill Ave/Warren Street split, he was there waiting. He hopped in, and Mikey introduced him to Holiday. TJ already knew who he was. She traveled with Mikey quite a few times before in his Taxi Cab. Mikey can already feel like this is going to be a great night. She was excited to finally give someone a chance.

Holiday asks, "Where we Goin"? Nobody had a solid answer, so Holiday continued driving towards downtown. They found parking, and they began their late afternoon date with a walk through the Boston Commons, talking and jiving. To help the mood, of course, Holiday had a flask of Brandy. "who's down"? Holiday asked while dangling the flask in everyones face. He knew just how to set the mood, and they all sipped from it. They stopped here and there as spectators of street performers singing, dancing, playing instruments, and even wowed by street magicians.

The night was young, and the spring night breeze was nice. The leaves on the trees were just beginning to bud. The Cab driver was starting to feel accomplished as his confidence grew with every passing minute. He tried to hold her hand, and she did a couple of times but felt the energy to let go. Mikey didn't feel the need to show any type of PDA. It was too early for that, she thought. TJ & Holiday, on the other hand, had never-ending smooches and light petting. But Mikey, she didn't feel like the cab driver was the one for that. She started to realize that Intellectual boundaries were arising as the night went on. But she didn't let that stop them from having a good time.

They ended up back at Lanes Lounge in Mattapan Square to end the night. They served food before the party-goers got started. They dined on Fried Chicken and Pork chops, With some Collard Greens, Mac & Cheese and baked beans, and let's not forget a tall glass of Pepsi. After everyone was good and full, Mikey asked TJ to step outside while she smoked a cigarette. TJ didn't smoke. Right away, she asked Mikey, "What's up Girl? You having a good time"? Mikey replies, Yeah, girl, you know I have a good time with everythang' I do". But TJ Knew that was just Mikey being Mikey and not wanting to be negative. So TJ asked, "Do you like him?" Mikey slowly replied, "Not really, but he is nice and good-looking. But kind of quiet tonight, right"? TJ said, "Yeah, he's not as talkative as he usually is when we in the cab". Mikey had a lot of respect for Holiday, so she asked TJ, "What does Holiday think of Him?" TJ replies, "Well, he's been getting a little upset because he keeps noticing him looking at my butt". They laughed, and Mikey says, "Girl, who can stop looking at that ass, you can't miss it". There was more laughs and then an awkward silence. TJ said to Mikey, "Just give him a chance. He could be just what you need for you and them kids"! Mikey turned and looked at her young friend and said, "He has a lot of money, and I do need a man with money, But I need more than that, like a soulmate, a real connection ya'know? So Naw, I'm sure I can do better. I'm sure we both can". Mikey went on to say, "Babygirl, as long as you keep your head on straight and not get swallowed up by this crazy city, You and Holiday could have something really special". Mikey wanted to go on in the moment as she usually does mentoring TJ but was interrupted by Curtis.

It was getting late, and he had to get up early to start his Taxi Shift. TJ excused her self and went back in the Lounge. Mikey and the Cab Driver Curtis stood and talked a little while longer out in front of the Lounge. He told her how he had a good time and would love to do it again. She replied saying, "We'll talk about it". Before he walked to the 28 route bus stop, he accomplished a hug and kiss, ending the night.

— The Good News —

TJ Called Mikey, excited with some good news, "Girl, Girl.... I have something to tell you," Mikey Replies, "What is it, what's going on?" TJ, a young and dramatic type, says, "I can't tell you over the phone, But I don't know what I'm gonna do". "Are you ok?" Mikey replied. "I don't know. What did I do?" a seemingly confused TJ says, screaming on the phone. Crying and laughing at the same time. Mikey had a good guess what had happened but wanted to hear it from TJ, so she scheduled to meet with her at Woolworth in Dudley Station later on that day. They arrived 15 minutes apart, and TJ was there first. When Mikey got there, she sat at the diner bar. TJ had the biggest smile and tears flowing down her face. Mikey looked over at TJ and started to laugh aloud, confidently knowing what was about to come out of her Mouth. "What,... What did you do, TJ"? TJ wiped her face and said, "I'M PREGNANT!" Mikey laughed even louder and said to TJ, "I knew it was coming wit'cho country fast ass". With open arms leaning in for a hug, Mikey says, "Congratulations, Babygirl, you're going to be a mommy"! Mikey lit up a cigarette, ordered them both some food, and cried and laughed and cried and laughed some more. TJ had so many questions about motherhood and what to expect. Mikey had all the answers she was looking for at the moment. Then she asked TJ if she had already told her mom. She told Mikey that she was a little nervous about telling her but figured she wouldn't be too mad and would understand. Because TJ's mother was 17 when she had her as well. So, no big deal. The one TJ was most worried about telling was Holiday. They must have sat there talking for about 3hrs.

Two days go by, and TJ finally musters up the courage to tell Holiday the latest. It was a Wednesday, and she got up early with this already on her mind. It was Dreary and cloudy that day, with a weird silence outside like nobody lived in her neighborhood. For some reason, she wasn't as excited to tell Holiday the news as she was with telling Mikey.

So she took her time getting over to his apartment. She could've got anybody to give her a ride this day, but she decided to take the long way. Still, she left around noon on a mission to finally get the news out and began her nine month experience. She walked two blocks to the nearest bus stop and waited. She looked good too. She had on a spaghetti strapped romper with a pair of clothed strapped wedges, a few pieces of Zulu accessories, a clutch, and her umbrella. A childhood neighbor even stopped to ask her if she wanted a ride, but she unusually declined. She stood out because her hair was died red. The girl had some style!

The route 14 bus finally came and took her up Columbia Rd. She got off at Franklin Park Zoo and walked to Holiday's project apartment. As she was walking, she came up with so many different ways to tell him the good news. But nothing carved into her mind as to what she'd end up saying. Emotions were running high as she draws nearer to her destination. A few more tears would flow and a few encouraging words out loud to help keep her composure. But still nervous. She finally arrives at the front of his building. She realizes that it's now time to put on her big girl panties, shake it off and get on with it. She walks into the building and up one flight of stairs to his second-floor door. But, startling to see, his door was cracked open. No sound or as usual his music booming on his day off from work. She slowly pushes the door open. She skeptically walks in slowly and notices the smell of familiar cleaning products. But that's not out of the normal for Holiday. Everybody knows he's a neat freak. She walks through the house, passing his bedroom, thinking he's in the bathroom. She calls out, "Holiday....Holiday...." But no reply. Suddenly, she heard movement coming from his room. At times he also was a prankster. So she smiled, put down her clutch and umbrella, and got herself set to barge in on him to counter prank him. But with everything good comes something bad. She grabbed the door knob and finally burst in. TJ said "Boo" with all excitement. Only to catch her first glimpse of Holiday in a full Nod from a heavy dose of heroin. He didn't even flinch. The sight stopped her high joy dead in its tracks. It was like time stood still. She didn't cry out loud at all. Just an immediate flow of heartbroken tears. The strongest man she knew thus far in life, an addict. TJ didn't know what to do. She backed out slowly and took a seat on the couch in the living room. She must have sat there for about 40 minutes, confused and sobbing, until she finally got up and left. TJ never got the chance to tell him the great news.

A week goes by, and the weekend finally comes back around, and TJ is back at Holiday's place. She wanted to bring up what she saw, but placed it in the back of her mind as a minor issue for the sake of love and embarrassing him. At the same time thinking that if she did, it would change the night's mood since they were back to normal. All day Holiday had his eye on TJ, watching her every move. He had a high intuition that something was different about her. It was a variety of could-be guesses and thoughts.

TJ noticed his eyes and the quiet demeanor that he had all day. A few times, she thought that maybe this is a good time to tell him the big news. But she digressed every time. She wanted to know for sure what his quietness was about.

Being that it's a Sunday, the day started to wind down early, and TJ figured she'd just stay overnight. He was cool with that. As Holiday was sitting on the barstool at his in home fully stocked bar. The sound of The Whispers playing lightly in the background set a mild vibe. As TJ was walking by, he says "Hey, come here". She slowly turns and walks over to him. While still sitting, he grabs her hand, holds it high over her head, and spins her around. She giggles and says, "What are you doing?" Guessing that he was feeling a bit "mannish" since he had already guzzled a 6pack of Private Stock and a couple of shots of brandy. All signs were there. But he started to laugh and shake his head. He got off the barstool and walked over to the window. TJ is still standing at the bar with a slight look of confusion. She says, "What's wrong with you?" There was a 5 second silence, and Holiday, without, any doubt in his mind, confidently told TJ, "Yo ass is pregnant"..... She burst out into laughter and tears of joy, saying, "How did you know, Who told you?" Holiday immediately was confirmed of his intuition. TJ never had to tell him. They laid in bed all night talking about what to do next and shared thoughts of the great parents they'd be.

The next day TJ told her mother, and she was right. Her mom gave her a bit of an argument but ultimately gave TJ her blessing and was also excited about a new addition to the family. The Journey now begins.

A few months go by, and things look promising. It's like the whole city of Boston now knows the news of TJ and Holiday's new bundle of joy coming. TJ's younger siblings are doing their best to come up with the coolest names for girls and boys. Nobody knew the gender at this point. But TJ's mom and aunts were already planning a baby shower. This will be the first baby born into this family starting a new generation.

As the weeks pass by, here comes yet another bomb. Interrupting all that is going so well.

Holiday's Promiscuous playboy days have caught up to him. TJ was getting evil stares and the worse gossip you could think of being smeared about her. The jealousy of other women became intense. But the natural fighter in TJ was at full obedience and joy of her pregnancy. She insisted that nothing broke her spirit. But it seems like, "With everything good comes something bad". TJ was out shopping when she noticed a woman watching her on every aisle. She didn't work there, so TJ got suspicious. Just when she got the idea in her mind to ask the woman if she knew her from somewhere, the woman slothfully walked up to her and said, "Is your name Tara?" Her street smarts told her to step back and place her hands over her stomach as she replied, "Yes, and who are you?" The woman seemed upset but not so much at TJ and said, "Don't worry bout it and Girl, ain nobody gon'do nothin to you". A young TJ held her ground and said "what do you want then"? She asked TJ if she knew who Holiday was and what he was about. TJ gave the woman a few answers and then concluded that this might be his ex-wife. So she let down her guard a bit. In the middle of the grocery store, TJ was getting an ear full of information about the man she thought she knew everything about. The things said were disappointing but still nothing that would make her let him go. Until the end of the conversation, TJ was unbothered and started to feel like the woman was just scorned because Holiday didn't want to further their relationship. Before the conversation ended, the woman had worked up enough courage to tell Tara what was most important. Most condescendingly and sarcastically, she goes on to tell TJ that her name is Janice and when you have the baby be sure to come by and let them meet each other. TJ was taken off guard and puzzled. So she asked, "Let who meet?" The woman then told her that she had just had a baby girl with Holiday 4 months ago named Sade. This was the straw that broke the camel's back. ,"A US navy ship full of atomic ammo of words, ready aimed and fired, disturbing other shoppers with the debris of loud and sharp language. Both missing the target, in which whom is nowhere to be found. They both were kicked out of the store.

TJ does the first thing that comes to mind when she's in a jam and finds the nearest payphone to call her girl, Mikey. Her first instinct was to have Mikey come to handle the woman Janice since she was out of commission to do what she thought she could do herself. Heavy breathing on top of an irate tone and a lot of "should'a-could'a-would'a,"

Mikey is entertained by the young puffed up scrappy TJ. So just like a mother, Mikey told her to bring her swole ass to her house so she could calm her down and get to the bottom of things.

Well, once TJ told her what happened. It must have set off an alarm within Mikey too. Because this situation has pissed her off to the point that now TJ is looking at her strangely like this is not her usual approach. Maybe this is something she went through herself. Mikey started yelling and saying things that weren't as positive as TJ knew her to be. She said, "F*ck Him" ..."and f*ck that ole scallywag too" "I'm so sick of these MuthaF*ckin men". TJ is now sitting there silently, watching and listening to Mikey go deeper and deeper in a rage about the issue. She takes a couple of drags from her joint and exhales. She looks TJ straight in the eye and told her that she don't have to worry about anything. Telling TJ that she'd be damned if she let a n*gga get over on her like that. Expressing her empathy toward TJ being young and knowing what it's like to have her first baby. Mikey then took another drag from her joint and said with frustration, "This ain the way no woman should bring her firstborn into the world. So I'll be the baby's damn daddy then". Then a quick chuckle from TJ relayed a slow forming smile on Mikey's face.

From that moment on, It was understood and known that Mikey is hands down the new baby's God-mother.

Mikey started to do all the things that Holiday missed doing. But mostly there for emotional and moral support of the mother to be. She genuinely loved and cared for TJ despite what she was going through with Holiday. Mikey felt like she was going to be ok when she grew up. That's why she stuck by her side and stayed in TJ's ear about going back to school. She knew she was smart. As for Holiday, He had his own demons to deal with. But he wasn't, so they surely became what he was used to; a love bipolar relationship. He was in and out. When he could provide, he was there, glowing of a stand-up family man. But when he couldn't, he was not. The pattern As a SIDEWALK UNIVERSITY STUDENT, Holiday was making the grade.

— Unprepared —

The countdown has begun. The due date is upon us. The anticipation is rising and driving everyone crazy with excitement. TJ has slowed down and doing a whole lot more eating and sleeping. The baby shower has come and gone, The crib is built up, The bassinet is already by the bed, Pampers are stacked high to the ceiling, and an endless amount of new & used baby clothes. This family was ready!

TJ was sitting up late and getting last-minute jitters about the baby coming. She got up off the bed, went to the wall, and called Mikey to get her head back together. But, No answer. No big deal. TJ laid back down and fell fast asleep. The next day she got up and ran some errands with her mom and little sister Breena. The day went smooth along with that New England chilly spring breeze. They paid a couple of bills; the most important ones. They washed a few loads of clothes at the neighborhood laundry mat. Then quickly went to pick up a bucket of Kentucky Fried Chicken, and they laughed and gossiped about people they knew, didn't know, and men. They even stopped by their favorite auntie's house, Aunt Linda. Just what TJ needed, a girls day out with the family.

TJ was in high spirits and ready to pop. They made it back home about ten that night. TJ got showered and ready for bed. But before she did, she realized that she hadn't spoken to her girl in a couple of days, so she gave her a quick call to say what's up and get the latest with her. But yet another failed answered call. No sweat to TJ, Mikey is an It girl and always on the go. But this is in a time without cell phones or beepers. So TJ just had to wait until the next day to talk to her. She was exhausted so she went to bed as her other sister Nellie was sneaking in after curfew.

The next morning, there's an aggressive knock on the door. TJ's mom hurries herself to the door to answer it and to see what the urgency is about. She slings open the door and is shocked to see The Boston Police department. "Good morning Miss, sorry to disturb you so early, But does Tara or TJ live here"? She immediately was cooperative and said, "Yes, she does. But Why? What's going on Officer"? The officer replies with "She didn't do anything wrong we just have some questions for her". Before she could call her name, TJ was already walking as fast as she could toward the front door. The officer looked at TJ and became concerned with her condition. But he still went ahead and asked her if she knew Mikaela Cardova. TJ's heart sunk, but it didn't break her. Because in the back of her mind, she was thinking, maybe she got caught up in a credit card scam or even stealing a few items out of that Filene's department store she worked at. TJ also thought maybe her and Mikey were finally busted. Even at 9 months pregnant TJ was still a rider for her friend. The officer told her that they would need to ask her more information down at the police headquarters. So TJ and her mother threw on some clothes, and the officers escorted them to the squad car as the whole neighborhood looked on in suspense.

They got to the station and made them wait for about an hour. A detective finally comes in and introduces himself. He asked TJ when she is due, and she told him at the end of May. He went on to attempt to make small talk, but TJ's mom cut him off swiftly and said, "Sir, with all due respect, I've never been to jail, and I'm nervous. I need to know what is going on here". The officer was hesitant but said ok and asked TJ, When's the last time you spoke to your friend Mikaela? With a loyal tongue, TJ told them, "I don't know, you the Detective"

He didn't crack a smile. Her mom gave her the famous "Mother Stare". He continued by saying, "Tara, I know you're young and pregnant, but this is very serious. The family of your friend "Mikey" made a missing persons report a couple of days ago. Her kids have been home for three days alone until they went to their neighbor's house in search of food. They're the ones that called Mikaela's family. Now all I want to know is, do you know where she might be"? In that moment, TJ instantly grew up. She knew for sure that this wasn't like Mikey at all. This was out of code. TJ wasn't sure what Mikey's master plan was, but she told them enough to keep them working, but until she spoke to Mikey, she wasn't gonna give her girl up.

They finally sent her and her mom home. As soon as they left out, TJ started to sob out of confusion and being left out of Mikey's plan. She even said out loud, "Mikey tells me everything".

2 days roll by, and the detective is again at the door. When everyone is supposed to be filled with glee and joy, nobody could release the thought of where Mikey could be. So with everything good comes something bad. The detective gives TJ and her family a devastating blow of information. "Tara, I'm sorry to inform you. But we found your friend". May 5th, 1979 They found Mikey, dead in an open field behind the Roxbury YMCA with her skull cracked by the blunt force of a sledgehammer, hands bound by wire, and set on fire.

They immediately wanted to start the investigation but held off due to the high-stress levels of the case. It just wouldn't be healthy for the baby.

In the end, he was caught. Mikey was the 10th woman of 11 who was found dead that year. A local serial killer who both TJ & Mikey knew of; "Osbourne (Jimmy) Shepherd." They've only seen him around the town at different clubs from time to time. Needless to say, there was no more taxi rides to give, no more taxi rides to take. Curtis, never got a second date.

Rest In Peace, MIKEY!

Chapter 2

Happy Birthday

— The Coming —

It was a quiet spring day. The sun was shining and not a cloud in the sky. TJ just finished eating some leftover soul food cooked the day before. It was Sunday's dinner. When she finished, she wobbled from room to room, looking out the window and looking at pictures on the wall. She was bored and totally exhausted from this pregnancy. She would randomly shed tears in the thought of her friend who had just passed away a few weeks ago. She certainly had a lot on her mind.

At this point, TJ was ready to get it over with, but her calendar due date was still about a week away. She turned on the TV to watch her favorite sitcoms and daily shows. After about an hour, while lounging on the living room sofa. SPLASH.... TJ's Water Breaks! She immediately screamed out to her mother, "Ma....oh my god, oh my god.... Maaaaa...I think my water broke".

In an instant there was an uprise of excitement from her mom and siblings in a panic rush to get to Boston City Hospital. TJ picked up the phone to call Holiday to let him know it's time. But there was no answer.

Right behind her, TJ's mom called her sister Linda to meet them over at the hospital for support. They quickly loaded up the Chevy Nova and sped off.

Along for the ride was TJ's baby sister Breena. She was so excited about being an auntie. She looked up to her big sister a great deal. Once TJ felt her first contraction, it became real to her that she was finally going to be a mother. Her contractions were about 16-20 minutes apart.

They finally pull up to the emergency door of the hospital. TJ's mom told Breena to run in and tell the front desk that they needed some assistance with a wheelchair for a pregnant woman going into labor. So she did. Once they got TJ into a room, she tried once more, calling Holiday. But again, no answer.

The doctors checked on TJ and concluded that it would be a little while before the baby came. She wasn't yet fully dilated. So they just made her as comfortable as they could until it was time.

Meanwhile, Breena started to get a little bored as it fell into the evening. So she started walking the hospital halls as if she was at school, peaking into other classrooms as she passed. Asking random doctors and nurses questions about their duties to pass the time. She finally gets a little hungry so she asked her mom for some money to go to the hospital's cafeteria to grab something to snack on. She gets on the elevator and goes. While she was eating she noticed a man sitting at a table by himself. He appeared to be whimpering and talking to himself, but then she realized he's just drunk. He looks over at her, and they make quick-breaking eye contact. The man turned his head as if he might have been a little embarrassed. She could tell by how he was dressed that he wasn't a homeless guy or a wino. But he obviously was going through something. When Breena finished eating, she skeptically walked over to him. She simply asked him what was wrong. The man looked around and said to her, "I ain happy". We all know that when drinking, we tend to tell the truth. Even though Breena was only twelve-years-old, the man began to talk about what was going on with him in his life. He was very straightforward and honest in telling her he had problems in his marriage, his kids not doing right, and admitting that he drinks too much. But he never did mention why he was at the hospital that day.

After about 10 minutes of talking, the man suddenly asked Breena where her parents were? She told him that her daddy was at home and her mom was upstairs with her big sister, who was about to have a baby. Feeling a bit sorry for the drunken guy who seemed to be a nice guy overall. Breena invited him up to the maternity floor. She wanted to introduce him to her mom. She thought that maybe she could help him with his issues. Once they got up to the lobby of the paternity floor, she told the man that she'd be right back and went to get her mom. When she got there, she was met by her Aunt Linda who was also a heavy drinker and her daughter, Monique. After saying hello to them, she turned to her mom and whispered, "Can you come with me down the hall? I think this guy needs your help"? Her mom replied, "What man, and what kind of help does he need? He's already in a hospital"? After some light pleading with her mom, she finally went. When they walked up on him, he was sitting in a corner seat with his head on the wall with his eyes closed. Breena walked over and tapped him on the knee. He opened his eyes and immediately stood to his feet. He was quite bashful at the moment as he was gaining his composure. Breena went to introduce the two, but the man cut her off and said hi, followed by telling "Ma" his name, Frank. From there, they began to talk. But back then, kids weren't allowed to sit in grown folk's conversation so Breena's mom excused her. As they conversed, they learned that they had a few things in common. They both were hard workers and had relationship issues. Not feeling appreciated in relationships where they both were the better half. It didn't take long before they were smiling and laughing at the vibe of one another. That quick, they enjoyed each other. Periodically, Ma would go back to the room, check on TJ, and return to the lobby to continue their acquaintance.

A few hours must have passed before it was time for the man to go. He asked her if it would be ok to see her again, and she said it would be fine. She wrote her number down on a torn-off piece of a TIME Magazine with Robin Williams on the cover. She then walked him over to the elevator and told him to give her a call when he could. When the elevator door opened, he stepped in and turned around. They said goodnight, and she walked away. As the doors was closing she looked back once more only to catch a smirk on Franks face and blushing eyes staring right back.

Meanwhile, back in the room, TJ was getting more and more uncomfortable as her contractions were getting closer. Her Aunt Linda had asked TJ what she was going to name the baby? TJ told her with a doubtful tone that since Holiday already has 3 girls, she thought it would be good to name the baby after him. Making the new baby a Junior. Her aunt took another sip of her Seagrams and grapefruit juice and sat back in the chair, and simply said, "Okay". Along with a fun devilish, smirk and giggle. Aunt Linda asked TJ right then, "Well, where is he anyway?" TJ told her that she really didn't know and then tried once more to call Holiday. But this time, TJ's mom grabbed the phone to make the call instead, and it was to Holiday's mother's home. After about 4 rings there was an answer.

TJ's mom said hello and asked if she could speak to Randall? She Replied with, "Who's calling?" TJ's mom went on to tell her who she was and her reason for the call. She asked her if she knew where he was? Holiday's mom was very protective and loyal with her kids, so even if she did know, she wouldn't tell it. So Randall's mother told TJ's mom that she didn't know where he was tonight but that she would let him know when he came in the morning to give them a call. It was a normal routine that Holiday brought his mother a newspaper and a coffee every morning.

After telling Holiday's mother that TJ was in labor, TJ's mom couldn't tell if Holiday's mom was excited about the new baby coming. But before they hung up, she told her that she hoped this one was a boy.

After the call, aunt Linda immediately chanted out, "He probably out there wit some other hoe". TJ's mom told her sister Linda to hush and keep quiet, but the spirit had taken over, and she went on for about ten more minutes. It was a moment to remember. Even the nurse and midwife were laughing.

A little while after that, the room got calm. Nothing but the sound of the air conditioner and heart rate machines was going. TJ's mom had dozed off only to be awakened by the sound of TJ crying and asking why? So Ma got up and walked over to her bedside and knew just what she was asking but had no answer to give her. She knew that even though she was there as her mom that TJ still felt alone without either Holiday or Mikey there with her sharing this moment. All she could do was shed a tear with her.

At about 4:45am, TJ gets a strong contraction. Just 3 minutes later, there was another one. The Doctor comes in to check on TJ and say's, "It's time". TJ's mom leaves the room to run down the hall to the family waiting room to wake her sister Linda and tell her to come. By the time they get back to the room, the doctor is all set and ready for the procedure. There was a Jamaican midwife lady in the room that was so sweet and helpful throughout the whole night.

The Doctor finally starts telling TJ to push. She grabs onto the bed rail and gives it a go. The baby's head is beginning to crown but keeps going back in. After about an hour and 40 minutes, the Baby is born. It's a Boy! With his eyes wide open along with his little fingers spread wide on both hands. The midwife grabs the baby and begins to chant a few Jamaican blessings as she seems to be in shock by something peculiar with the delivery. The midwife turned to TJ and her mom, both with tears streaming from their eyes, and said in her Caribbean accent, "Wow, with all of the years I've been bringing babies into the world, I have never given a birthday to a child with its eyes wide open and hands so free". The midwife then laid the baby on TJ's chest and whispered a few more prophetic words to TJ about the baby. TJ was more than happy. Where there was just hurt and pain in her heart a few hours before, she now hasn't a care in the world about anything else. This was an immediate love affair with her life.

As protocol, they take the baby away to measure and assess. Aunt Linda goes out to get Breena and Monique to come in to meet their new family member. TJ's mom leans over the bed rails and gives her a big hug and kiss and tells her how proud she was of her and how good she did in labor. The doctor yells out from the far corner of the room and says, "It's Tuesday, May 29th, and the time was 6:43am. Happy Birthday kid, Welcome"!

The Asian Doctor then asked the question that everybody wanted to know. But there has never been a solid answer. "What's the baby's name"? TJ finally said it, "Lorenzo". In Unison, TJ's family repeated with heavy discouragement in their voices, "LORENZO?" TJ's mom quickly told her that making the baby a Junior was way better than

24

that name. TJ was very upset with Holiday at this point for not being there. So for about two hours, the baby's name was "Lorenzo". But her mom eventually talked her out of it. So, of course, the baby will be named after his father.

— Name Calling —

TJ was exhausted and finally fell asleep. As the hours ticked away, still, there was no call or show from Holiday. When she woke up, it was now noon. Aunt Linda had left to drop off her daughter Monique at home. When Aunt Linda got back, TJ's mom was now napping. So TJ and her aunt got a chance to talk. Mostly about the good stuff. But then they got on the topic of the baby's name again. Her Aunt slowly started instigating the ideas and possibilities of why Holiday wasn't there—making TJ's temper heighten. Her tough-loving, underlining way of welcoming her into single black motherhood, perhaps. You know, finessing the young girl in the moment. Aunt Linda looked over at the baby in the clear plastic Bassinet. She walks over and picks him up. She played, hugged, and kissed on the baby. She walks over to the window and looks out over the city for a minute or two. She then walks back to TJ's bedside and says in her most genuine loving voice, "Name him Shannyn. He looks like a Shannyn". TJ gazed at her baby for a few seconds and then began to smile. She decided right then, the baby's name would be Shannyn.

At about 3pm, you could hear a ruckus coming down the hall. The voices of men loud, talking and laughing. One of the voices was finally Holiday's. Here he is with his best friend Bones, and brother Dale. All three tipsy and with cigars between their lips. Although TJ was pissed, it was no time before she was at ease with his presence.

Holiday felt no immediate need to explain his absence at the time. He went right along with the joyous occasion. With his charming and dominant composure, he walked over to the bed and kissed TJ. He asked her a few questions about the procedure and if she was ok. She gave him a brief and quick watered-down re-run of the past 24 hours. He noticed that the baby wasn't in the room and was eager to meet him. Minutes later, the nurse comes in with the baby from running a few tests. With a great big smile, welling eyes, and a chest full of pride, the nurse hands over the new born and he gets to hold his first son for the first time. TJ, her mom, and aunt Linda, began to flow with tears. An emotional and powerful sight to see with so much meaning. Holiday's good friend Bones shouts out loud in the room. "Congratulations, my brother, Kings create Princes that become King's" Bones was touched at the moment as he reminisces of the day he had his first son. Holiday's Brother, Dale, right behind him, says in his very humorous and obnoxious loud voice, "Take his diaper off and let's see how his d*ck hang; I wanna know if my Nephew gon' be alright"? He was so loud that it was said that the entire maternity floor heard it and was in gut-busting pain from laughing so hard.

After that, everyone decided to leave and let the new little family have some privacy. They all said their goodbyes, and the door closed.

Holiday walked back over to TJ's bedside and sat down. There was a 20-second awkward silence in the room. Well, for everything good comes something bad.

But this time it falls on Holiday. Still, with the baby in his arms, he says out loud with 100% confidence, "Man, I have three girls and finally my Junior". TJ's face became paralyzed, staring up at the TV in the corner of the room.

Taken completely off guard by the comment. It never even crossed her mind as to how she would tell this man what the baby's name ended up being. Where is Aunt Linda when you need her? TJ asked Holiday to pass her cup of ice chips on the tray. Not that she was thirsty at all, but to at least buy herself just a few more seconds to get her head together. She even thought real quick to just let it flow. But realized that she already gave the doctor the last and final name to start the birth certificate process, and it was too late to change it. So TJ comes right out and says, "I have something to tell you". With a distinct contoured face, Holiday looked right up at her in a way that he might have thought she was about to drop the ultimate bomb on him. TJ shook her head and reassured Holiday that he would never have to worry or even think twice about this baby being his. She went on to tell him as calmly and straightforward as she could. "Randall, the baby is not a junior". He looked off and started to shake his head while slowly leaning back in the chair. He took the news better than she thought he would. But she could still tell he was pretty upset about it. Maybe it was a good thing he had the baby in his arm still. He then sat back up to the edge of his seat and said, "You know I wanted my first son to be named after me; how could you not keep your word on that? " TJ had an answer for that but before she could even try to give it to him he abruptly cut her off and said "What's his name then"? TJ took a deep breath and told him; Shannyn Abdul Johnson. Holiday stood up and shouted "WHAT," "You got to be Jivin," "You named my first son an Irish, African N*gga name"? He passed the baby back to TJ and walked out of the room to let off some steam.

About 15 Mins pass by and Holiday came back in the room. He seemed to have pulled himself together.

He steps to the foot of the bed, leans down, and puts both hands on the foot rail of the bed. He told her how happy he was about the baby and that he loved them both. But again made it very clear as to how upset he was with the baby's name amongst other dissatisfactions with her. TJ cut him off sharply, right in the middle of his spill of reprimand and superior emotions. Dead silence quickly became the sound in the room. TJ just couldn't take it anymore. She was in utter disbelief at the arrogance and audacity of this man. She looks at him with a face of disgust and scorned eyes. When she finally opens her mouth, she tells him off with such a nice & nasty tone yet noticeably trembling with a battle within to keep her composure and anger tucked away. "How could you,... just how could you even be as pissed as I have been for the last two damn days? You walk up in here like you God almighty. Like you can never do any wrong. You couldn't even look my mother and me in our faces and say sorry or even try to explain where the hell you were". Holiday quickly said, "I don't have to explain myself to no damn body". TJ begins to cry and said, "Oh really, what makes you think you don't have to check in with your kids? I just gave you your first son. Remember when I was pregnant, and you said you wished it was a boy? Well, here he is, you selfish bastard. All you care about is what you want and could give a damn about how and who you get it from". TJ struck a nerve with this. Holiday got even madder and yelled at her, saying that it wasn't true and that he loved all of his kids. Telling her how he just wishes he could do more. As they went on, they got louder. So the nurse came in and told them that they would have to keep it down. They did but kept up with the back and forth tug-o-words. The baby started to cry, so TJ began feeding, interrupting their feud. But at this point, she was furious and done with the conversation. Holiday could tell that nothing he was saying was phasing her, so he just stopped talking. Their lips were sealed for quite some time and all three eventually fell asleep.

The nurses periodically would check in on them and get the vitals of TJ and the baby. After that, back to sleep, they go. Holiday was on the cushioned reclining rocking chair while the baby was back in the bassinet. TJ was lying on her side facing Holiday. About 3 am he opened his eyes slowly as if he was awakened by the feeling of being watched. He was. TJ couldn't sleep anymore. She was disturbed by the missing information that she desperately needed to know from him. She calmly asked, "Where were you last night?" Holiday sat up and wiped his face in his hands, and sighed with submission to her question. He said, "I was arrested yesterday". TJ had no faith in the answer he just gave, but he explained what had happened. With his hot tempered and "back down to no man" policy, Holiday got into an altercation with an uncle of one of his daughters; her name is Latrice. For a matter involving him and Latrice's mother. The police came and saw Holiday as one of the aggressors in the situation, and they arrested him. Holiday was known to be a bit of a hell-raiser when he wanted to. What ever the situation was, it was known to be the very reason Latrice's mother packed up and moved her and her two kids to the other side of the country to live in Compton, California.

TJ was still skeptical until Holiday got up and pulled out a sheet of paper from the Boston Police station that was folded up in his back pocket. It had his arrest date, charges, and release date on it. It also showed an upcoming court appearance date. She looked at the paper. Then, without another word, TJ rolled over and fell back to sleep.

The next morning the new small family was awakened by the doctor. He had some questions to ask about the medical history of both TJ's and Holidays families. After getting a few answers from the couple. The doctor goes on to tell them not to be alarmed, but he has found a medical issue with the baby. They both take a deep breath and become instantly astute. Holiday asked the doctor with deep concern what the issue was. The doctor explains that about 1 in 13 Black African-American babies are born with sickle cell traits. TJ begins to worry as she knows that Sickle Cell is a trait that runs in her family. The doctor tells them that the information is not final but just a start to a series of many different possibilities. The Asian doctor was well educated and passionate about getting to the bottom of this. Test after test and eight days later, the doctor finally concludes that the baby had nothing more than an uncommon blood bacteria, which could be cured with the proper medication before the baby even has his first birthday.

They were released and finally got to take baby Shannyn home. 154 Seaver St was the new home address. Where endless family and friends stopped by to congratulate the couple and welcome the new baby. Shannyn was ready for the world with a head full of hair and an already noticeable lazy eye.

— Holiday Surprise —

This is TJ and Holiday's first apartment together. Holiday took charge as the man of the house and had two decent jobs. While TJ stayed home and enjoyed her new motherhood. One of Holiday's jobs was at a Juvenile Detention Center, and the other, he worked part-time at a liquor store down in Dudley Square.

They started decorating and buying new furniture. An afrocentric vibe and decor to entertain their continuous guest as they were both popular among their friends. The summer of "79" was in full blaze, and the relationship was getting better. Almost like they finally started falling in love. Things are looking good. They were always out and about. They got acquainted with most of their neighbors in the building. There were cookouts and family gatherings almost every weekend. Holiday even started to bring TJ around his family more often even though TJ thought his family might have been bougie and judgmental of her. Overall, It was a great summer. The couple even spoke of marriage as a future plan.

It's now August and also TJ's birthday month. Holiday decided to give her a birthday party. He figured she deserved it with everything she's been through in the past year. He did everything he could to make it all come together. He reached out to everyone to make a specialty dish for the occasion. He planned to decorate and invite everybody he could think of to make this night special. Since he worked part-time at a liquor store in Dudley Square, he had the hook-up for the booze and, of course, planned to be the DJ for the night.

Finally, it's the morning of TJ's Birthday. He planned that this will be a night that she'll never forget. TJ's mom picked her and the baby up for the day. They went back to her mom's house, and her mom made her and her sister Nellie a grand breakfast. TJ and her sister Nellie shared the same date birthday. All of her siblings are talking and laughing at the table just like old times. The only difference, TJ is breastfeeding Shannyn in the midst of it all. She spent the whole day with them. She even left the baby with her younger sister Nellie while she walked to the corner store for some laundry detergent and other needed household items. Even though TJ had her own place, she fell right back into the traditional Saturday morning house cleaning mode that her mom had instilled in them all. The music from the radio gave a spirit of ambition throughout the house. Everybody was cleaning, Dancing, Singing, and enjoying each other while W.I.L.D (Boston Radio Station) played all the latest hits like; "I WILL SURVIVE" by Gloria Gaynor, "HOT STUFF" by Donna Summer, or "SHAKE YOUR BODY" by The Jacksons was the tone. But the day moved by pretty quickly, leading up to the festivities. It was finally time for TJ to go and get herself ready for her party. She had already worked out a plan with her mom to babysit for the night. This will be the first time TJ has ever left her baby overnight with anyone. She laid across the bed with her Baby Shannyn and played and kissed all over him for about 20 minutes. Promising him she would be back the next day and expressing her tremendous love. It took her a while to leave. She went through what most new moms go through when leaving their child for the first time—that "innocent guilt" of leaving their side.

TJ's mom starts to laugh yet tells her to get out and go have a good time. Reassuring her that the baby will be fine and that this is not new to her. She has been through this four times. TJ looks back at her mom and says "OK" and "thank you, I will see you tomorrow". One last kiss, and she was out the door.

TJ makes it home and starts prepping herself for the party. She realizes that Holiday had been home but must have gone back out. He left all the groceries on the kitchen table still in bags except for the refrigerated items. He is always in a rush. So she quickly put everything else away. On the way to her bedroom, there was a knock at the door. She opened it, and it was her neighbor from down the hall, Jo'Ann. Jo'Ann was young and vibrant. Full of personality, attractive, and street-savvy herself. She was a North Carolina girl. But she was a hustler.

Jo'Ann saw TJ coming in and just wanted to say Hello and see if she needed anything else for the party. The whole building knew about it. TJ invited her in and told her that they got everything taken care of, but she just didn't know what to wear for the night. The two girls go into the room and start pulling out everything she had. They started to mix and match her clothes collection. After 2 hours of girl talk and multiple wardrobe changes, they finally came up with the right combination. Thanks to Jo'Ann, TJ is ready for the night.

Holiday finally got back with everything he set out for and all of his errands complete. He was in such a great mood and seemingly excited about having guests for the night. He turned on his music and began freshening himself up while dancing, cooking, and singing all over the house. Every now and then, he'd invite TJ for a quick private dance. She loved that about him. The charm and that charismatic confidence he had. Even when no one else is looking. That night, it didn't even matter that she named the baby Shannyn, as this had been an off and ongoing conflict between the couple for the past few months. So this is going to be a good night.

The doorbell rings, and over the intercom, TJ says Hello. It was her first guest of the night. After that, it wasn't long before they all started to pile in—one by one and group by group. Drinks are being poured and mixed. Miller and private stock as a chaser. Everybody is socializing while eating, dancing and enjoying the occasion. Oh yes, there was a party going on up on the 5th floor At 154 Seaver Street. Holiday would play a song that he really liked and let the spirit move him to turn on the mic and serenade his guest. He was quite the entertaining host. Most of TJ's family liked him a lot. Overall, they thought he was good for her.

This was when Holiday revealed his love for TJ in front of everybody. Letting them all know that she was his. A night of celebration. A night of the second coming.

As the night was winding down. The music tempo and vibe slowed down as well. Songs like "Cause I Love You" by Lenny Williams, Heatwave's "Always & Forever" and, Blue Magic's "Spell" just to name a few. The living room lights were turned dim, and the lava lamp and black lights were glowing. The mood was set. All the couples that didn't leave yet got closer. Letting the spirit take over them and step into the middle of the living room floor to slow dance. Or, shall we say; grind their bodies together like magnets. Setting themselves up for a pleasurable nightcap once they got home.

After all the goodbye's, Hugs, Thank You for coming, and doggy bags of food to go was done, it's now just Holiday and TJ. They sipped on the rest of their drinks, started a light clean up and talked a little more while laughing and highlighting the party. As the night sky was becoming dawn, TJ says to him "I think i'm going to go lay down now. I have to get the baby in a few hours or so". Holiday with a drunken speech, told her, O.K. and give him a minute, and he will be right there. TJ goes in the room and begins to get undressed. Right before she was about to lay down, Holiday came in the room with another demeanor about himself. As if he was angry with her. She asks him, "Are you alright?" He replied, "Hell no, I ain alright. I give you a damn birthday party to show you I love you and you can't give me what I want"? TJ is puzzled and thought he was just drunk. So she giggled a bit, which increased his sudden change of mood. He walks over to the other side of the bed where she is, and he grabs her aggressively and starts to kiss her. He pushes her down on the bed and gets down on top of her. She's confused. Because he seems upset but very sexual. She asks him again, what's the matter, baby? He told her to shut up and don't ask him no questions. She's too tired to argue or fight with him, so she doesn't. He gets up and takes off all of his clothes. He then grabs her leg and yanks her body to the edge of the bed. Where he is usually gentle and the captain of foreplay, this night, it doesn't exist. He lays down on top of her and stares at her for a few seconds, and says, "You gon'have my Junior".

Nine months later, Shannyn has inherited his first responsibility. Happy Birthday, Randy Jr!

CHAPTER 3

Footprints

— A Family Bond —

It's now 1982, and the young couple couldn't be happier and more in love with their new little family. Everywhere they went, everybody knew Holiday, TJ, and those two boys, Shannyn and Randy Jr. Being that they weren't even a full year apart, the couple used to dress the boys up like twins. Same outfit yet different colors. They would attend every event the city had to offer, especially in the summer. From family cookouts to birthday parties, park events, and more; They were there. They were happy babies, and everybody wanted to hold them and love on them constantly. But Randy Jr, didn't particularly like people smooching on him. TJ noticed this characteristic about him early, so she began to teach the boys not to let people touch them when she wasn't around. That stuck with them, and they didn't have a problem curving the random incoming lipstick stamps and cheek smooshings. TJ used to get a kick out of that as she use to tell them "that's my sugar" and not give it away to anybody.

As for Shannyn, if you wanted his attention, all you had to do was play music, and he would start dancing. This kid had a natural rhythm and could imitate all of his favorite entertainers of the time.

The two boys established a bond very early in their lives as siblings would. They were very protective of one another. One time, Holiday was play—wrestling and rough housing on the bedroom floor with the boys when he accidentally hurt Shannyn, making him cry. Randy didn't like that, and to the rescue was his little brother to risk his own safety and jumped off the bed down onto their dad's head to avenge his brother. A heart of gold and very protective, a characteristic Randy Jr. was born with.

Randy couldn't quite get the proper annunciation of his elder brother Shannyn's name, so he just called him "BROTHER" for many years. That name was carved into Shannyn's mind so deep that he actually thought that was part of his real name.

They were real little boys. They played hard and could be really mischievous at times. Even at just two and three years old, you could already tell they were each other's keeper.

Up until this age, life was good for the boys.

In fact, the brother's first Christmas that they could remember was great. They woke up to fresh new snow on the ground that fell the night before and more gifts than they needed. Pac-Man & Smurf Big Wheels, Clothes, Cowboy boots, Superman, Batman & Robin bed sheet sets for their twin beds, all types of toy figures, and most of all, a bunch of love. Holiday and TJ did good. It was a day well spent as a family and what looked like the beginning of a great start to life for the boys.

— A Weekend With Sistah —

While Holiday was working, TJ would stay home with the two boys. All day she would play and sing songs with the boys. Answer all of their curious and sweet nothing questions, feed them, and even discipline them when she had to. She loved every minute of it. But what they loved the most was when she would take them to the playground across the street. It was also the backside of Franklin Park Zoo, on the Seaver Street side. It was heavy traffic all the time. One of the main crossroads that took you from Dorchester into Egleston/Roxbury. Sometimes TJ would even knock on Jo'Anns door to get her son to go along with them; Corey. They all had become like family. So much that Jo'Ann trusted Holiday to take Corey with him and the boys to the Disney ice capades at the Boston Garden. Shannyn and Randy has always embraced Corey.

After a few hours of ripping and running on the playground with the boys, TJ decided to get them back to the house and get them cleaned up and ready for bed all the while cooking dinner. She had a schedule to keep. As Holiday didn't like to come home to dinner not being ready to eat, and the boys not being bathed and ready for bed.

Holiday finally gets home and it's a usual night. He talks about his day at work, get an updates on the boys, and gives small critiques to TJ about her duties around the house. But on this night, Holiday adds that his oldest daughter might be coming to hang out and stay the night with them the coming weekend. He told TJ not to tell the boys until it was confirmed that she was really coming because the boys would get too excited. Shannyn and Randy loved their big "Sistah," Kayla. "Sistah" is what the boys called her. But Holiday didn't want them to be disappointed if the plan changed. As for TJ, she was all for it.

The weekend is finally here, and while Holiday was at work, Kayla was dropped off by her mom to spend the weekend as planned. She spent the day with TJ and her little brothers that she adored. She played with them all day. But TJ realized that Kayla was the same age as her younger cousins and little sister Breena, who all looked up to her. She thought it would be a good idea to have them come over as well to hang out with Kayla. About an hour or so later, they all showed up. TJ's cousins were a part of a very popular local dance group back then. They all were very close friends with a few members of New Edition. Even a young Bobby Brown showed up for a short time that day. He was dating a friend of TJ's little cousin. TJ knew a little bit of everybody.

The girls all kicked it off well but began to practice their latest routines in the living room and even low key trying to see if Kayla had the moves enough to join. Breena could dance but was way too bashful to get on stage in front of anybody, anywhere. Double Dutch was her thing. But they all were having fun. Shannyn & Randy loved the excitement and started imitating all the latest dance moves they could catch on to. Just barely walking, Shannyn caught the vibe.

TJ began prepping to cook as all of her young company were beginning to notice the sun going down and had to make their way home before the street lights came on.

An early childhood responsibility learned by most inner city kids. Usually the first lesson came with a consequence if you disobeyed the order.

When they all left, Kayla began helping TJ cook. They were getting to know each other in the process as well. Kayla seemed to like her dad's girlfriend. She would go back and forth from the kitchen to the boy's bedroom to play some more until dinner was done and her dad got home. But on this night, Holiday came in a little later than he usually would. That wasn't really a big deal. But with everything good comes something bad.

Holiday came through the doors and wasn't in a very good mood. This was nothing new.

But unfortunately, she noticed it was a little more intense than his usual.

Holiday was going through withdrawals and in need of his "Fix". At the moment, TJ didn't catch on and was trying to get him to watch his temper as his daughter was excited to see him and unaware of his struggle. He gave her a quick faint hug and a nonchalant "hey, how are ya"? Not quite the greeting Kayla was looking for.

Holiday focused his attention on TJ and began knit-picking at her every move and word. Out loud complaints about the stereo being on, why the coffee table was moved from in front of the couch, why aren't the boys asleep; and how long does it take her to fry some damn chicken?

TJ is on her best behavior, trying to deescalate whatever angle he is coming from, trying not to let things get out of hand as they sometimes do when nobody is around. She especially didn't want anything to get too crazy as this is the first time his daughter has been around them since Holiday and TJ moved in together. It wasn't like Kayla's mom was thrilled with her being there in the first place. But Holiday; he's was on a mission. He is in and out of every room in the apartment except the boy's room. His daughter is sitting in the living room in silence, waiting for him to do or say anything that lets her know that she exists in the apartment. He begins to sweat and becoming angrier and angrier as he is looking for something that seems to be very important. A 12-year-old helpful Kayla asked her dad if she could help him find what he is looking for. His answer was edgy with saying, "No. go back in there and sit down until the food is done". So she did. Suddenly, The phone on the wall rings, and it was TJ's mom checking on her and the boys and also to see how long it was after Breena had left the apartment. Because the street lights had been on for about 30 minutes, and she hadn't made it home yet. As TJ is on the phone with her mom, Holiday yelled out TJ's name and told her to come in their bedroom. She said, "OK, gimme a minute". He was already dominant and had some control issues, but this withdrawal has changed him into a whole new kind of beast. One minute must have felt like an hour to him. He came out of the room in a silent raging storm, went to the wall, and pushed down the hang-up lever on the phone. He hung up on TJ's mother in mid-conversation and said, "Didn't I tell you to come here," and before she could spill out an answer, Holiday reached out and slapped TJ across the face. She ducked her head in submission to his strength, not knowing if he was going to continue. He snatched her by her clothes, yanking and pulling her out of the kitchen back into the bedroom and slammed the door. Meanwhile, His daughter is still in the living room with tears flowing because she has never seen him this way.

He must have gone on for about 20 minutes shouting, scolding, emotionally and physically attacking TJ. Kayla then goes into the room where the boys are and try to turn their attention from the chaos. While at the same time doing her best to console herself as she didn't know how long these types of events lasted. But what stood out to Kayla in the midst of the chaotic moment. She notices that her little brothers are unbothered by it all, as she knows they're hearing exactly what she is hearing in the other room. Yet she stays in the room with them, hoping the commotion would stop soon. Well, Kayla would need a lot more than hope to change what comes next.

TJ had decided that this would be her last night going through this. She was never really the submissive type, but she was in love with Holiday, so she let a lot slide.

TJ got out the room, and now what was an attack on her had turned into a full-out brawl in the apartment. Kayla even stepped out the room, leaving her brothers and screaming, "Stop it, Stop Fighting".

But that held no weight in the matter. By now, you would have thought the police would have come. But in the hood, every other door in the building had similar problems of some sort. So people overall minded their own business, and even then, (early 80's) in Boston, there was a NO SNITCHING policy that everybody abided by.

There was a lot of vicious talk and deliberate breaking of each others belongings and valuables.

The young couple were destroying the apartment.

Then it happened, for the last time, they interlocked like Hogan and Savage and rumble back toward the kitchen. There was a slap. There was a punch. Even a Seagrams gin bottle smashed over TJ's head. Then; there was the moment that everything changed.

TJ had grabbed the kitchen knife that she was just using for cooking and now has cut Holiday with it across the back of his hand. When she realized what she had done, she ran toward the front door. This ultimately enraged Holiday. So he ran behind her with a force and the mindset to now do total damage. But as he grabbed her, she turned around and impaled Holiday with the knife, stabbing him twice. From the bedroom, Kayla and the boys heard a screaming cry out from a sudden excruciating pain. Holiday fell to the floor, bleeding out so profusely that it started looking like his white T-shirt was purchased in red. "Sistah" was so scared to come out of the room cause she knew from the sound of it that it couldn't be good. But she couldn't resist. She comes back out of the room. And there, right in front of Shannyn & Randy's bedroom, was their dad laying in a pool of his own blood. "Sistah" Immediately starts to scream and cry even more. Now totally devastated, she is no more good for helping out with the boys. She runs into the living room scared and afraid of both her dad and his girlfriend.

The boys come out of the room next out of curiosity as their mother is standing there also in total shock of what just happened. The boys were not crying but had never seen their dad lying on the floor crying. One of the two brothers said, "What's wrong, daddy" as they walked around with bare feet stepping in and out of his blood, leaving their "FOOTPRINTS" on the hardwood floor.

From the floor, Holiday was still aware of everything that was going on. He told his daughter to call a taxi cab and go home. So she did. He then told the boys to go back into their room and close the door, and they did just that. TJ was numb to it all but still walked the boy's sister down to the cab. TJ never made it back up the five flights of stairs. The Boston Police had just pulled up along with the ambulance. It got live pretty quick. Literally, even the local news was there and had set up their cameras outside of the building to catch the story. What they caught was TJ on the middle island of the street screaming and crying. Right in time for the 11'O'clock news.

The boys didn't really understand the seriousness of what was going on at the time, but because kids are not stupid, they knew it was bad once they saw the authorities inside their apartment. Something that they have never seen before. Because all they knew before this was that Officer Friendly could only be seen outside. Never where they live. Holiday was rushed to Boston City Hospital.

The Boys didn't see it, but their mom was arrested and charged. Shannyn & Randy fell asleep in the midst of it all. They woke up the next day at their grandmother's house in Uphams Corner. But unfortunately for the brothers, this was just the beginning.

— Backtracks —

Three weeks later, and after major surgery and overcoming a coma, Holiday wakes up. In the room by his side is a few of his siblings. They all love on him and welcome him back into his right state of mind. He asked for his mother right away, but truly knew already that she wouldn't be there. Holidays mother didn't support his ways and the mischief he seems to get himself into. After the tears have fallen and dried. Holidays oldest brother started to mentor him in the moment about his life and all the turmoil around him. Holiday is trapped under medical equipment, staples, and stitches. So his brother took advantage of the moment and asked him a question that he thought he'd get the most logical answer. He asked him what he was going to do now? Holidays' very straightforward answer was, "I'm gonna Kill'Her" without any hesitation. Very swiftly, the family became upbeat with concern, consoling Randall Sr. Letting him know that they understood why he would be angry. But also giving him more level-headed suggestions.

One of Holiday's sisters was there as well, Iris. She told him to focus on the word of God and that he will fix this. They knew how bad of a temper Randall had, so they said all that they could think of.

Holiday was so angry and full of emotions, and he couldn't properly release it. Just boiling inside. Everything they were saying went in one ear and out the other. Then, his oldest brother Harold bent over the bed rails and whispered in Holiday's ear, "You have to think about those boys Randall," "God spared your life, and no matter how pissed off you are, you can't take their mother away from them". Holiday told his brother he didn't want to hear that sh*t and stuck with his original mindset of retaliation.

It's late now, and Holiday's family has left the hospital. He laid there for hours in silence. Thinking about everything that happened that night, and since then, hasn't heard a word from TJ and the boys.

The pain is still throbbing as he is getting familiar with his body again and some battle scars that he'd have to live with for the rest of his life. Yet, he still wants some type of revenge. Holiday was a man of principle and don't let nothing slide.

Another few weeks go by, and the doctors finally clear him for release to go home and do the rest of his healing. Holiday called one of his closest friends "Tick" to pick him up. He had a one-track mind. He had his friend drop him off at the apartment. But he told "Tick" to let him out down the block from the building on the corner of Seaver and Elm Hill. He called the apartment from the payphone that was outside. He was checking to see if anyone was home. But he got no answer. He didn't have his keys, so he rang a few random door bells hoping that someone would buzz him in. They did. Holiday got in the elevator and went up to the fifth floor. He crept to the door and put his ear to it to see if he heard anything or anybody. But heard nothing. Holiday then left back out of the building and went through the alley to the back of the six story building. He sized up the balconies from the second floor to the fifth. He then began scaling the balconies until he reached the fifth. Once he got there, he looked around to see if anyone saw. Not a soul was watching. Full of adrenaline and still riddled with pain, Holiday kicked in the back door like a firefighter. The back door opened into the kitchen, and the first thing he saw is the flipped-over kitchen table and what looked like a tornado just passed through. He knew right then that nobody had been back at the apartment since that night. When Holiday walked through the door and turned to go into the living room, he saw his dry blood everywhere. What came over him was un-describable. He started to weep. As he got closer to the front of the house. Randall stopped at the sight of the FOOTPRINTS of his two sons' little feet in his dry blood on the hardwood floor. He immediately thought back to what his oldest brother Harold had said to him weeks ago back in his hospital bed. He then broke down and cried by himself.

Randall Sr did something that you wouldn't expect right then. He got all of the cleaning products the house had and began cleaning and mopping the entire house. Because he knew that the boys would come back at some point and still had to live there. Even though he knew he would never again.

CHAPTER 4

Mama'..... Is That You?

— Passing Time —

It's been almost two months since Shannyn & Randy last been at the apartment. They've been staying at their grandmother's house all that time due to all the drama. The family thought it would be best for the brothers.

TJ and Holiday, on the other hand, were going back and forth to court to get the matter resolved. She was facing fifteen years for attempted murder. But surprisingly, the case took a turn. Randall took the stand and admitted to the abuse that night. TJ's Lawyer took advantage of his clarity and his outspoken compassion for the mother of his boys and redirected the case to be a matter of self-defense. By the grace of God, TJ never served time.

It was a long time before Holiday ever returned to the apartment.

So now, TJ has realized that it's just her, Shannyn & Randy Jr.

She was doing her very best. With all the support she was getting from her family with the boys, it was like nothing ever happened in the first place. She returned to taking the boys to the park regularly, going to family functions and special occasions. But what she liked most was popping up at talent shows with her little cousins and giving them a guarantee that they'd perform. Most of the time, they did. TJ had something very special about her. She could never be denied her efforts with her bold and very direct demeanor. She even made Shannyn & Randy a duo dance group and entered them in every talent search that came to town, "The Jordache Kid & His Sidekick". Named after the popular clothing line in the '80s. It was cute, but that act wasn't very long-lived.

The boys are growing up, and at their tender young ages, they now can see and understand where and how they are living. It became clear to them that their Mama was struggling. But she tried as best she could. She took some cleaning jobs here and there and even at the new Burger King on the corner of Columbia Road & Washington Street, right next door to the Jeremiah E. Burke High School that she dropped out from. The Boys grandmother would stay on her constantly about applying for a position with the public transportation authority (MBTA). Because then, that was considered a great paying job with benefits. TJ's mother just wanted what was best for her and her grandsons and didn't want to see TJ fall down a black hole and give up. Because despite whatever else the rest of the world knew about the city; The Tea Party, Paul Revere, JFK, The Celtics, the prestigious colleges, and believing there were no black people in the state of Massachusetts. This was the hood of Boston. A playground for drug dealers, killers, scammers, pimps, and hoes.

The area they lived in was tough, and not too much has changed since TJ was a little girl. But still, it's a new day. Heroin was nothing new. But, the crack epidemic has caught on. Around that time, Jo'Ann, who had become one of TJ's closest friends, was already involved with the neighborhood happenings and became a dancer in the strip club. Being that TJ was very outgoing and could dance very well, you would have thought that she'd already pick that up as a hustle. But that just wasn't her thing. She had more of a gift of gab and very dominant in her demeanor. She was well known, and nearly everybody liked her. Especially the way she freely spoke her mind and kept up with her boys. Even in her financial struggles and also depending on a welfare check. The brothers were always clean and well-mannered.

— Readjustment —

One day TJ was coming back from across the street from the park with the boys. As she walked toward the door, a familiar guy from the neighborhood said hello to her and the boys. Shannyn and Randy spoke and then were excused to go and play along the sidewalk with their friends. The guy and TJ stood out there and talked. To Shannyn and Randy, it seemed like a long time. The sun was going down, but they continued conversing.

Shannyn and Randy were beginning to think this guy was trying to date their mom as all kinds of men always pursued her. They were definitely Holiday's kids because they just knew how to block the incoming pursuits. They began to rudely interrupt and do something that TJ really disliked. They screamed out, "Mommy, we hungry. When you gonna feed us". That did the trick, and she cut the conversation short. She hated to be embarrassed in that way. But the boys heard her say on the way into the building, "I dig it, we will talk more about that later". The boys could tell by the look on their mother's face and the look of desperate help on the guy's face that they'd be seeing him again, soon.

About a month went by, and TJ walked toward Shannyn & Randy's room. She stood in the doorway and watched them play hard, jumping from one bed to the other. In their element, just being typical high energy boys. Usually, she'd tell them to stop and sit down before they hurt themselves, but this night, there was a new vibe. She had been quiet all day. But there was a look in her eyes that said everything would be alright. She sat at the end of the bed and told the boys to sit next to her so she could talk to them. She asked them if they knew that she loved them. They said yes. She assured them again that she did with all of her heart and began to teach them that nothing in this world is more important to her than them and they should always feel the same for each other. Don't let anyone hurt your brother and if someone touches you or hurts you in anyway, you better come and tell me first was her spill. The Boys were very understanding but still didn't know why she was talking this way. She then told them something that would stick with them for the rest of their lives. A lesson that ultimately taught them how to further build a solid bond. She told them, "Whatever happens in this house, stays in this house, and it's nobodies business what goes on here". She asked them if they understood, and before they could answer, Randy quickly replied with a question asking, "Even if it's Ma?" She looked at them with that look that all mothers give when they mean business, and with a straight face she replied, "Even if it's Ma". The boys knew then that whatever was going on with her was extremely serious because up until then, Ma was the authority, even over her. This was when Shannyn and Randy began their first semester at Sidewalk pre-school. Learning the fundamentals of trust & loyalty.

A few nights later, there was a knock at the door. It had to be about 9:30 pm. TJ opened the door, and it was that same guy that she was talking to that day in front of the building. TJ welcomes him in and introduces him to the boys. He said his name was Winston, and he had a noticeable accent. The boys instantly got curious about what looked like a fat suitcase that he had with him. But from the beginning the boys didn't believe that was his name because he had a pack of cigarettes in his upper jean jacket pocket sticking out. Of course, they were Winston 100's. He told the boys that if they needed anything to let him know, he'll make sure their mother would take care of it. He had a good vibe about him, but Shannyn and Randy knew he was some type of hustler by his quick talking and upbeat personality. As he was talking the boys could see a few more people coming in the door, walking past the living room where they were, going towards the kitchen. Whoever they are, they never spoke at all. They just kept walking with a couple of bags and boxes, never even looking in their direction. At that moment, the brothers knew they were trying to distract them with talking and standing in front of them. Winston told the boys that they'd be seeing him around a little more and that if anybody ask who he was, just tell them simply that they didn't know. After that, he picked up the fat suitcase and joined whoever those people were in the kitchen.

TJ took note from what Winston said and told the boys that if anybody asked who she was, to tell them, her name was just "Mommy". She then told the boys to go into their room and from there without any further coaching, they knew not to come out. All of a sudden, the apartment had a new vibe. TJ and her company were in the kitchen all night long. Talking was to a minimum, and when it was, it was light as if everybody was whispering, trying to keep a secret. Every 20 to 30 minutes, TJ would check on the boys until she found them sleep. But usually by the time Shannyn and Randy woke up, then house was clear of any guests.

As time went on, it became more and more often that TJ had company. It was so many different people, in and out all the time. TJ just stopped introducing the boys altogether. She just kept them occupied with whatever they wanted to pacify her motherly duties. Coloring books, toys, clothes, and even cash. The boys quickly got used to that.

Approximately about two months later, the boys noticed that their mom all of a sudden had money all the time, and a lot of it. TJ tried her best to keep the boys from knowing what was going on, but they were far from stupid and caught on. They already knew. TJ got to a point where she would come in the room and throw a large stack of money at them and tell them to count it and let her know how much it was to keep them busy. Often she'd tell them if they could tell her the correct amount, then they could have it and split it amongst them. This is one of the ways the boys learned how to count money. Sidewalk Mathematics.

It was a Saturday morning. The two boys woke up early like they usually do in time for cartoons. Before they get to the box of Apple Jacks and milk, they were all of a sudden sidetracked by the fat suitcase that was sitting on the side of the sofa. The same one that Winston carries with him all the time. They were eager to know what was in it but still wanted to be good boys and not touch it. But these are TJ's kids, and they couldn't resist. They crept over to it and discussed what they thought might be inside. It wasn't long before they grabbed it and put it on top of the coffee table. In their little minds, they thought they were going to find large stacks of money or even a gun. They go to the window to check and see if anybody is coming. They don't, so anxiously they unzip it, flip the cover back, and they find out that it was a cell phone to their surprise. They were so excited because they only heard that rich people had that type of technology at that time. It had a detached antenna that they had to screw on, and an on/off switch. They must have played with it for about 20 minutes and even figured out how to call the only phone number that everyone in their family knew by heart, Aunt Linda's. It was a very easy number to remember. Somebody answered, but they hung up quickly. The Boys ended up backtracking how they opened it and putting the fat suitcase back where they found it. But they were impressed and suddenly, to them, Winston is the coolest dude in the city.

Shannyn and Randy had another surprise waiting for them that very same morning. The brothers discovered that their mom was in deep with what was going on in the neighborhood.

Two hallway closet doors were directly across from one another. One was the pantry, and the other was the linen closet. Both doors opened outwardly into the path going into the kitchen. Those doors were always open, crossing the doors to make a barricade. If the doors were closed, you could see straight from the front door right into the kitchen. These doors always blocked the boy's sight. They were never closed.

But on this morning, they still tiptoed to the barricade. That was like a mission impossible adventure to them that morning. They'd rather be caught messing with the fat suitcase than to be caught on ground zero, aka the kitchen. The boys finally made a break to go through the doors. When they did, what they seen put the excitement of the fat suitcase to shame. Shannyn and Randy were in awe by what they had seen. Stacked high was 100's, 50's, 20's and 10's of US currency. So much cash that you couldn't see the brown wooden surface of the table.

Shannyn and Randy would hear a sound that continuously flickered and beeped in short time increments from their room at night. Although they tried, the brothers couldn't figure out what that sound was. But now, they've found the answer. It was a money counting machine on the floor right under the table. And of course, they had to turn it on, and when they did, the same beep that they heard almost every night sounded. The two boys were growing up and didn't miss anything that was going on around them. Everything that was going on was raising their awareness. Collecting and adding up to the street smarts they would need in the years to come.

— It's Showtime —

Later that morning, TJ got back home with shopping bags of groceries and new outfits from Robelle's. She told the boys to get in the tub so she could get them dressed to go out with her. As she always did, she'd dress them alike matching her and made sure their faces was shining with cocoa butter.

It was the annual Kite Festival in Franklin Park. They get to the park, and it's a couple thousand people out there enjoying themselves. The boys loved it! It was said that there would be a special guest performing about 3 pm. But it was unknown who. This was also promoted on W.I.L.D's radio station. So the crowd was ready. Over the PA system, they tell everyone to start gathering in front of the stage. TJ grabbed the boys and moved them up to the front near the stage so that they could get a better view. Then a tall man stepped out onto the stage. He was very popular in the city for his Talents, showcases and creating local musical acts. The crowd immediately applauded and chanted as he wore a shiny military suit and hat. He was also known around Boston as the Lieutenant. He opened his mouth and said, "Ladies & gentleman, I bring to you, Michael Jackson". The crowd uproar in excitement. The superstar's music began, and everybody started bopping their heads and grooving. But still holding their breath until the first glimpse of the international superstar. But by the time he went out onto the stage, it took no time before the crowd recognized that who was supposed to be Michael Jackson was an impersonator. The crowd laughed and tried to give him a chance, but they could see he wasn't believable. The man was trying to get through his act but the energy of disappointment intensified. Quick thinking TJ was an acquaintance of the shiny suited guy, and she had made eye contact with him. She hurried over to the security line and made a suggestion to him. As she was talking to him, she looked back and pointed down at Shannyn, and told the lieutenant to put him on the stage. The man had a look on his face as if it might not be a good idea, but TJ kept insisting. The man finally gave in and reached down from the stage and grabbed Shannyn and placed him on the stage. The shiny suited man told the sound guy to play "Billy Jean" and Shannyn began to do his own Michael Jackson impersonation. The crowd reversed from upset to a total change of mood. Chanting Shannyn on as he did all of the latest Michael Jackson moves. The impersonator took this as a cue to exit the stage, never to return. Right then, a seed was planted in little Shannyn's mind that would never die.

Weeks and months have gone by and the apartment is even more popular than it already was. The boys already knew Jo'Ann very well from living on the same floor as them down the hall. But now there are other people the boys don't know, but seen around the neighborhood knocking on the door now. The door had a police lock and bar on it. The sound of the lock latching, unlatching, and the door opening all night was loud and constant. It was quite annoying to the boys considering their room was in the front of the house near the door.

One night Shannyn & Randy stayed up late listening to the in & out traffic and conversations that were going on. The lights were out in their room, and they were supposed to be asleep. But how could they with all that action. They got up quietly and walked over to the door with a crack in it to see what was going on. What they saw told them just what was going on all along. They saw a man they had never seen before sitting at the front door in a chair. He had one of the living room sets end table on his side with a bunch of small test tubes with different color caps. But what stood out to the boys the most was the nickel-plated long-nosed Smith & Wesson .45 on the end table next to him. Every time there was a knock on the door, the man never said hello. He just asked, "What you got," as he peeped through the peephole. The person on the other side of the door would say the amount. He would then grab the necessary tubes, pick up his gun and then open the door. Just enough for his hand to swap with the outside person. While all of this is going on, TJ is back in the kitchen with a few others. But whenever Shannyn and Randy called out her name for something, she'd stop whatever she was doing and come to their room door. It didn't matter what time, day or night, apartment 501 was officially a trap house.

The boys noticed that they hadn't seen Winston for a while now. But everything that was going on in the apartment was still happening. But now, TJ is going in and out of the apartment, leaving the boys behind with strangers in the house. Sometimes she'd be right back, and other times she wouldn't. The guy that sits at the door every night is always with her now everywhere she goes. Her personality started to change as she became more and more aggressive and confrontational in her personality. When she spoke, the people around her moved quick, about anything. Like when the boys room and the rest of the apartment got too messy. She always had someone to clean it up. As if there was a transfer in power. Because if not, there was some type of consequence. Or, she'd stop them from coming around. Tara was running quite the little operation for herself, and it was working out.

One late night she had the boys with her, and she was driving a car that the boys had never seen or been in before. Never minding the fact that she didn't have a drivers license. She was going from one house to another, 3 in total. Sometimes she'd go in, and other times she would sit in a parking spot for up to an hour. The boys would ask her if she was waiting for somebody to come out. She would never answer and tell them to go to sleep because they got to school in the morning. In times like those, she would first stop at McDonald's or something for the boys to eat because she never knew how long she'd really be. This was her way of distracting their minds for what the purpose of them sitting out there was. But for Shannyn & Randy, they knew in times like this, something was about to happen. At a certain time, randomly, people came out of nowhere, walking up to the car and dumping all kinds of plastic and brown paper bags into the car, each full with money. For each person who came to the car, she would ask if they saw somebody she seemed to be looking for all day. Nobody knew. After about a hour and a half, TJ pulls off and goes to another spot. She did the same thing and parked in an open blind spot. But when she got to the next spot, she must have seen who she was looking for. She pulls off and goes to the nearest payphone to use it and was back in the car in less than 3 minutes. She goes back to the same spot that she and the boys just left, and within 15 minutes, the guy that sits at their apartment front door almost every night pulls up in a car behind them. He gets out of the car and walks up to TJ's passenger side window. They had a quick discussion, and he walked away. But not back to his car. About 45 minutes go by, and the person she was looking for was going towards the door of a 3 family house. From the back seat, Randy is asleep, and Shannyn, wide awake, looks up and is familiar with a person walking by that he and his brother had seen at the apartment a couple of times. TJ rolls down her window and yells out, "you got that for me?" He was startled and looked to see where he heard the voice come from. When he saw it was TJ, he told her, "I already told you, I ain got sh*t and you ain gettin sh*t". Little did he know that the guy walking towards him was with TJ. The mouthy and arrogant man was took by surprise and viciously beaten with a steel pipe and then dragged to the back of the house screaming and whimpering. But by the time the "Door Man" came from behind the house, there was no sound at all. TJ says with a light tone and little emotion, "Shannyn & Randy, Y'all sleep?" Unsure if he should answer or not, Shannyn replies, "Yes". This intensity was non-stop.

A year later, Shannyn gets off his school bus in front of his door and right into the building. The elevator was broken. As he was going up the stairs, he heard some loud talk and arguing. As he climbed each step, every floor got louder and louder. By the time he got up to the 4th floor, he knew it was coming from his apartment. This has become normal, so this wasn't a big deal to him. Shannyn knocked on the door, and the arguing came to an abrupt stop. TJ didn't ask hello as usual because it had dawned on her the time, and she knew it was Shannyn. He walks in and drops his lunch box and school bag right inside the door. He takes his shoes off and begins his walk toward the bathroom to start his daily ritual. He happened to take a glimpse of who his mom was arguing with, and it was Winston. Shannyn was in shock but happy to see him and ran over to him out of respect to give him "Five". Winston asked Shannyn how he had been and if he was holding down the fort, charming and boosting his confidence. Shannyn answered with a yes but then asked him why he hadn't been around, and Winston replies with, "I was out of town taking care of my mother". But Shannyn somehow knew that wasn't true. He also could tell that Winston wasn't the same high-energy, fast-talking hustler that the boys once figured him to be. Shannyn continues to the bathroom. While he was in there, his mom and Winston continued their conversation. But they weren't as loud as they were before. But Shannyn could tell that it was a very touchy subject because he kept hearing Winston asking TJ about someone that Shannyn has never heard of up until then. Whoever it was, he was highly concerned with what the person thought of him and his absence. Also, how often TJ was in contact with this mystery person. Shannyn kept hearing Winston say things like, "If it wasn't for me"; or, "You didn't know shit"; and, "But I'm back now". Whatever they were butting heads about, Shannyn just knew that his mom and Winston were not on the same page. They returned to their heightened caliber tone of voice, and before Winston walked out, slamming the door, Shannyn heard his mom tell Winston, "Do whatever you gotta do M*thaF*#ker".

Shannyn became nervous because he had never heard his mother or anybody talk to Winston like that before. TJ had held her grounds as the queen in charge.

One Friday afternoon, she was in a good mood, cooking, cleaning, and for some reason, she was playing all the old vinyl records that Holiday had left behind, over 1,500 of them. She was singing and dancing, upbeat and dressed. She was radiant. All the while monitoring the street down below as the 5th-floor window had an overview of the block. This was something that the boys hadn't seen her do in a while. Shannyn even had a flashback of how she used to sit in the window and wait for his dad to get home from work. With the music being so loud, the neighbors didn't complain at all. Besides that, It's Friday, and Monday is a holiday. So it's going to be a long weekend. Even the neighbor directly across the hall wedged their door open to let all the oldie but goodies tunes chime through their apartment. It was like TJ didn't have a care in the world. But for some reason, the normal everyday customers would come to the door for their regular dose, but she turned them all away by saying, "Not today, we gotta do better than this". Shannyn took that as odd. Because she never talks like that or turned any money away. Some of them were old friends that she knew well and not so far gone into the life of addiction, so those were the ones she would let in. They were white-collar addicts. The type that has jobs and a family at home and somehow could be productive.

As the day turned to night she still had company, and she had moved the furniture so that when you sit down your facing the direction of the front door. But it was a night of conversation and no talk of drugs or even the unforgettable scent of cooking "crack" that the boys already knew so well. It was like TJ had a change of heart about the life she was living. The lights in the apartment are usually dim or off. But tonight, almost every one of them is on, and the two boys are not secluded to their room. Their door was open, and they ran from room to room freely, even the kitchen. As normal as that sounds, it was extremely awkward.

One of TJ's guests had left the apartment and confirmed a return by saying, "I'll be right back". TJ said that's fine, and the guest left out. TJ continued entertaining her remaining guests that were there. They all knew Tara was the boss lady and they seemed to be getting antsy as they might've been hoping she was going to give them what they want. To them this was another side of her that they didn't understand. But Tara never gave-in.

Then about 10pm, the unexpected happened. There was a dominant knock on the door and TJ says hello. Then there was a very loud voice saying, "SEARCH WARRANT, BOSTON POLICE DEPARTMENT" and then a big boom of impact made the front door come unhinged and wide open. The narcotics squad rushed in and there was complete chaos and panic. One of TJ's guests fainted from the commotion. The police are doing what they do by yelling and screaming, telling everybody to get on the floor. With their guns drawn they started asking if anybody else was in the apartment. TJ said no. Through it all, TJ and her two boys are completely calm. No emotions, not even one tear from either of the young boys. The Sargeant in charge already knew TJ's name. So he gets in her face and says, "If there's anything in this place that I might need to know about before I continue my search, now would be a good time to tell me". TJ replies sarcastically, "Well, it depends on what you're searching for, officer". The officer tells her, "I know you might think this is a small problem, or maybe you don't care, but I know if we walk out of here with these two little prizes of yours (while pointing at Shannyn and Randy) and take them over to DSS that would be very big to you now wouldn't it"? That tone straightened TJ out just enough for her to tell him to do what he came to do. TJ was smart enough to know that the police had just enough information on her that, if anything, they could take her kids away if they really wanted to. But she also knew they wouldn't find anything. She knew they were coming. She was tipped off by a friend whose cousin just so happened to be a female, Boston Police Officer. In fact, The same officer was the one who the sergeant ordered to shake down Shannyn and Randy to make sure that there weren't any drugs planted on them before they got to the apartment. Because it is standard in a raid that every person is to be pat down, even the kids.

The officers are moving and throwing everything in the apartment around. Within 10 minutes, the apartment didn't look like TJ cleaned up at all. All of the dresser draws were pulled out and tossed. The closets were all emptied out and scanned through. The Kitchen looked like a tornado touched down, and every cabinet door was opened and searched. Leaving all the items in it on the countertops, in the sink, or where ever they wanted to put stuff. But still they didn't find anything they were hoping to find, and it looked like they were going to leave. Until one of the narcotics officers went suspiciously to the corner of the living room. He picked up a grey jacket that was lying on top of one of the bar stools. The officer searched the jacket and in it found a crack pipe and a sandwich bag with a few rocks of crack cocaine in it. The officer got really cocky and confident and asked, "Who's jacket is this?" TJ's guests all said that it didn't belong to them, and they were right. But TJ knew exactly who the jacket belonged to. But she never came back like she said she would from earlier in the night. TJ was so angry and all of a sudden felt like she had been set up. The officer then told TJ that if she couldn't find the person the jacket belongs to, then he had to arrest her and everybody else in the apartment. TJ wasn't as concerned about getting arrested as she was about the police taking her kids. So she began to plead with the officers trying to assure them that it wasn't her jacket. She knew they believed her for some reason, but they still arrested her.

Her biggest issue with this was the boys well being. But the lady officer steps in one last time and asks TJ is there anyone else in the building that could watch the kids. She said yes, and they walked the boys down the hall to Jo'Ann's apartment. The boys stayed there until the morning. Their grandmother came to pick them up.

While in Nashua Street jail, TJ was puzzled by the jacket all weekend long. She couldn't figure out if it was a honest mistake, or if this was done purposely. Then it dawned on her. Hit her like a ton of bricks. The girl who left the jacket she met on the first night that Winston set up shop in the apartment. They were on again, off again lovers. That night in her cell, TJ learned a valuable lesson. "Keep your friends close, but keep your enemies closer".

After this ordeal was settled, it became quite normal that the police showed up to the address. TJ had been raided two other times.

One of those times, TJ had just cooked a meal for the boys while talking to her friend Jo'Ann in the kitchen. She came into the living room to bring the boys their food. Then back to the kitchen to finish talking. Then TJ realized that she had enough for one more plate, so she told Jo'Ann to go get her son Corey so he could eat too. She walks out the door leaving it unlocked cause she was only going down the hall; and just that fast as she walked out the door, a minute later a few undercover cops with another search warrant walks in the door, but this time without any boom. They walk right past the boys toward the kitchen. TJ wasn't even startled. The officer told her that he wasn't there for her or to give her any static, but they were looking for someone that they knew hung out there at the apartment. She told the officers that she didn't know where the person could be. But she asked them why did they come there looking? As the officer explained why, another officer, frantic and eager to find something to incriminate her, grabbed a canister off of the counter. As she's listening to one officer tell her what's going on, the other has gotten her eyes stuck on him and his every move, desperate to find something. He opens one of the canisters, and his eyes got big as bowling balls. Because he thought he'd hit the jackpot. In the canister was nothing more than All-Purpose flour, and he puts his dirty hands down into the jar, and

TJ giggled and belts out, "Well, he sure the f*ck wouldn't be in there now, would he?" TJ could tell he was an excited rookie cop.

After a while, Tara had begun to let the pressures of the lifestyle break her down.

The "Door Man" is nowhere to be found. Winston turned out to be a snitch, and her connect had stopped supplying her due to so much police presence.

So with every thing good, comes something bad. What was once a 40 thousand dollar-a-week enterprise is now a smokehouse. Just as fast as she got on her feet, it was even faster going down.

— Fourth Crack Commandment —

TJ made the most ultimate mistake of it all. She switched her role from seller to the customer and began her sophomore year at Sidewalk University.

This went on for just under two years in the apartment. Even other neighborhood legends are now coming in and out for their fix. One who stands out used to wear a cowboy hat and became a well-known preacher around the city.

It's quickly seeming like the boys are losing their mom. She would be up for 3 to 4 days straight and then sleep for 2. Or until the habit called.

But not only her, so did Jo'Ann.

One day, All 3 of the boys were playing in the hallway as they usually did. What they didn't know was that their moms haven't been speaking to each other lately. Somehow they both ended up at their apartment doors at the same time to tell the boys it was time to come in. But before you knew it, the two young mothers started arguing down the hall. The boys were clueless and didn't know what was going on. They'd never seen them act like this before. All of a sudden, they both stepped from in front of their door and started charging at one another. They locked up and fought like they hated each other right in front of all 3 of the boys. If it wasn't for the neighbors that came out into the hallway to break them up, there's no telling how bad it could have escalated.

But everybody got a story. Corey had one too. While one morning, he couldn't wake his mom up because of her crack-induced sleep comas. Corey was playing with some matches under his mom's bed and accidentally set the bed on fire while his mom was lying in it. If it wasn't one thing, it was another. Because a couple of months later, the father of Jo'Ann's new baby stabbed her up in her apartment. She survived. But it was a long time before we ever saw Corey again.

TJ's mother had enough and went to the apartment with the Boston Police and had them shut it down. When they came in, Shannyn and Randy had just thought it was another raid. But when they saw their grandmother come through the door behind the cops. They knew something was about to change. The phone was off. The house was filthy, and crack addicts were sitting around high with all the shades down, allowing no light in the house. The boys had been stuck in this condition for weeks and months. As TJ's mother went from room to room of the apartment, letting up the shades, the boy's grandmother began to preach and mentor at everyone there about getting their lives together. She wasn't a bible scholar at all. But she let it be known that God wasn't pleased with any of them. It wasn't a search warrant, but everybody had to go. Even the building management came with new locks and changed them as everything was going on.

The brothers wasted no time gathering their things to make it to their grandmother's car. As they were walking out heading to the elevator. They both looked up and saw one of the officers slap a big yellow sign on the door that read: "No Trespassing or Police will be Notified"; and they both knew right then, at the age of 5 and 6 that just like their dad, they would never see that apartment ever again.

It wasn't until years later that Shannyn thought back to a day back at that apartment that TJ's mother came to the door. But TJ wasn't home. Before she left that day, she had left the law laid down by telling Shannyn and Randy not to open the front door for anybody. Unfortunately, that meant their grandmother too. She pleaded with them back and forth through the door to open it. But the brothers didn't budge. She was hurt by that. Shannyn always wondered if that was the moment that made his grandmother come with the police and shut it down.

CHAPTER 5

The Spirit Of Moreland Street

— Crushing Fire —

All three Tara, Shannyn and Randy ended up living with Tara's mom
for about a year or so. She herself had a three bedroom apartment in
Uphams Corner. The Dorchester section of Boston, where diversity
met in the city.

Uncle Bryce had already moved out and lived with his Puerto Rican
girlfriend who just so happened to live around the corner, Ti-Ti
Carmen. Breena had just had a baby but was still living there with
her new baby also. The Brothers, Shannyn, and Randy were known
and had a lot of friends in their grandmother's neighborhood due
to them being over at her house a lot. Especially on weekends. So
the transition was smooth. Even the elementary school they were
transferred to was at the end of their grandmothers street and was
the same school most of their friends from the neighborhood went
to, The William E. Russell.

This is where I started 1st grade. Everything was good at that school except for one issue around Valentine's Day. I had a little crush on a girl named Marie from South Boston. She was my Valentine. We had a little party in class, and it was time to give out our Valentines Day cards. I only had one. It was for her, Marie. I thought she was pretty, even though she wore glasses. I asked her for her phone number to call her after school, and she told me that she couldn't. But she had a crush on me too. I could tell because we were always together at recess, and she even sat next to me at lunch time every day, her choice. But she ended up giving me her number after she had asked her mom for permission. I waited a couple of days, and then I called on a Friday after school and right after I finished watching Thundercats. The phone rang about 3 to 4 times, and then there was an answer. It was her mother. I politely said hi, and then asked if I could speak to Marie. Then really quickly and snappy, Marie's mother yells, "Is this Shannyn?" I said, "Yes," and Her mother said something to me that made me feel like I was different or something was wrong with me. She says, "Marie is not allowed to have black boys calling her at this house......", and before the woman could finish saying whatever else she was going to say; from the couch where my mother was napping, she must have had supersonic ears and heard what the woman had said and jumped up off the couch, snatched the phone out of my hand and shot an atomic bomb of words through the phone line at this woman in my defense. Overall she told her that she was dead wrong for talking to a kid that way and that she was part of the problem in this country. She also told her that she didn't raise her kids to even think or talk in that racist way to anyone. Going on to call the woman a "Racist B*tch," then hung up the phone on her. My mother was furious for the rest of the day. That Monday morning, Marie's mother went to the school and had the teachers separate us as friends by redirecting us from each other's paths. Marie and me never spoke again.

Another situation that comes to mind around that time was when me and my brother got cool with the Columbian boys that lived just on the other side of the alley. The alley courted the building block we used to play in. But they lived in a house next to it. They didn't cause any more mischief than we did except that it was 4 of them. They were tough, but they were cool. One Saturday morning, while my grandmother was house cleaning she told me and my brother to go outside and play to get us out of her way. So we did. We met with the Colombian brothers and began our pissy smelling alley way adventures. We loved it back there. We found an old mattress and boxspring and began jumping and playing on it. We must have played on it for at least 3 to 4 hours. When we finally got bored with that we moved on to something else. My brother Randy, at the time, was fascinated by lighters and matches. He found some. As me and one of the Colombian brothers found interest in something else we found next to the wooden trash house, Randy started striking matches and throwing them. But then he started dropping them in the holes that were in the dirty mattress. It had rained the night before so the match wouldn't live long and go out because of the dampness inside of the mattress. Before you knew it, he does it for the last time, and this time it didn't go out. I happened to look over at him, and he was desperately stomping on the mattress in one spot. But then all of a sudden the mattress started to glow from the inside of it from the fire. Me and the Colombian brother ran over to him and the mattress and started stomping on it too. But we didn't know that by us stomping on it, the pressure was breathing air into the mattress giving the fire more life. Before you knew it, one whole side of the mattress was in full flames. Of course, our bad asses panicked and instead of letting the mattress burn out in the middle of the cemented ground in the court. We all flipped the whole mattress over onto the wooden trash house. We for some reason thought that was going to put the fire out. But no, it caught on to the trash house too and burned the whole thing down to the ground. We all just stood and looked at it as it was burning for about 5 seconds, in disbelief that this is real and happening right now. Then, we all ran off in different directions. Me and my brother ran upstairs back into the house and sat quietly in front of the tv, Indian-style like nothing happened. All of a sudden, My uncle Bryce comes in the house with a smirk on his face. He gets something to drink out the kitchen. Then, he yells out, "Why y'all ain outside," and begins laughing hysterically. We told him with blank and clearly guilty faces, "It's nothing to do outside. It's boring". He laughed even harder and went to the backroom that views out to the alley. Right then I just knew he was going to tell on us. We watched him like a hawk every time he walked past my grandmother. We just knew it was over for us, especially when we heard the sirens coming up the block and saw the fire department. He told us to come to the window where he was and watch the firefighters put out the fire. He knew we were responsible for that, but he never told on us. We went back to the living room and sat down like good little boys. As he was going back out the door he gave us one last scare. With my grandmother standing there, he says, "Shannyn & Randy, who burned down that trash house out there?" Our answer was, "What trash house?" He shook his head laughing and walked out the door. Uncle Bryce never told on us.

— I Do Try —

My mother was overwhelmed by the transition and where life had put her. She was once the boss less than a year ago, now she is back under the same roof and rules of her mother's house. And let's not forget, a new habit that has now joined her life path that contributes to her already agitated spirit. She couldn't get along with anybody in the house. That led to the continuation of loud arguing and turmoil. At this point, Auntie Breena is all the way disgusted with the presence of my mom being in the house. Disappointed in who she is becoming before her eyes. Every interaction between them quickly became a snarl that sometimes escalated into vicious physical altercations. One time, early in the morning, while Breena was getting ready for work. Ma was getting on my mother about finding a job and regaining focus in her life. Breena had joined Ma and began adding her own adlibs. My mother took this as a double team threat, and what she couldn't say to my grandmother she was letting loose back at my aunt Breena. Before I knew it, Mighty Mouse wasn't the wake-up entertainment anymore. They locked up and became a careless tornado, knocking all kinds of stuff over and calling each other names that I don't even think existed. This was waiting to happen. Me and Randy knew we weren't going to be able to stop them, so we jumped up on the living room couch and called out for Ma. But she had heard them escalating, so she was up on them in no time to break it up. My Aunt ended up calling out of work out of being so frustrated, and my mother left for the whole day.

Believe it or not, my dad started coming back around again and a little more often. He even stayed with us some nights and weekends. But he never fully moved in at my grandmother's apartment. I think that in his mind he wanted to show his presence cause he understood the importance of a dad being around. Plus, I knew deep down he truly loved my mother, still. With him coming back around, I was happy but skeptical. Because I knew they couldn't get along. Especially now that both of them have that monkey on their back, but, I have to say, they tried! Letting bygones be bygones. They really made an honest attempt to make it work and even kick their habits together.

I remember going to many NA and AA meetings with them wherever they were held all over the city. I used to think that me and my brother were the only kids in the city who had parents on drugs. Because there were never any other kids at these 12-Step program meetings. But thank God I had Randy because we would make fun out of any situation or find a way to hustle. We used to stand by the vending machines and wait for a grown-up to come by. We would tell them that the machine just took our money. We even put the sad faces on. They would then either make a big deal out of it to somebody that ran the building, attempt to get it to work themselves, or simply just give us the money to try it again. It worked every time.

But there was this one place that I hated to go back then; The church in Grove Hall (Roxbury). They used to give away hot meals. Seems like the only people there were homeless people, wino's, Drug addicts, prostitutes, and us. I remember never wanting to eat there because I didn't want to eat off the silverware. Especially looking over at the people eating at other tables. Most of them looking like life has chewed them up and spit'em out.

Even though I was a kid and wasn't responsible for myself, I hated realizing that we were poor. But for me, overall, as long as we were all there together, no matter what we looked like as a family and even if it was only for a little while; I was happy.

But it wasn't very long before they began to argue again about their differences. I also believe my Dad still had a little underlying grudge about my mom stabbing him. So it became clear to me that they weren't going to work.

One day I overheard my mother talking to my grandmother saying, "I think I'm going to get the boys together and move back to Florida". My grandmother wasn't mad at that idea but didn't really coach her to go either. Because she knew that if my mother didn't get her life together here in Boston, she would be worse off in Florida. But my mother had convinced herself that she was going. So she decided to tell my Dad what her plans were. When she caught up with him, she told him what she intended on doing. This didn't go over so well with my dad at all, and the news broke him down. He pleaded with her saying, "No, please don't take my boys away from me". Because even though my dad had his issues, he loved my brother and I, and was very overprotective with us. I remember one time, while me and my brother was out with him, downtown Boston. We were all in a store and a white man called me and my brother "Knuckle heads". Dad didn't like that, so he jacked the man up and made him apologize to us in front of everybody. Then making the guy give us each $5. He was just passionate.

But TJ told him that she didn't know what else to do and was at the end of her ropes with the way she was living. They must've talked about this off and on for about 2 or 3 days. Going back and forth, weighing out their options. It didn't look like dad was going to get his way, and that fast, I have already accepted the fact that I was going to be moving to Florida. Maybe I was thinking anything would be better than the way we've been living.

But then, weeks later to my surprise. Me and Randy came home from school, and the phone was ringing none stop. By this time in our lives, we've already picked up the skills to read body language and eavesdrop. We asked her what was going on because she had a grin on her face, and we could tell while she was on the phone that she was talking in riddles. My grandmother told us that she would wait until my mom and dad got back to the house to tell us what she seemed to be sort of happy about. But we were kids, and our guess was that our parents had found another apartment, and we were all going to move back into our own place again, as a family. A couple more hours went by, and me and my brother was doing our homework at the kitchen table. Finally, in comes my parents. They were dressed up nice and noticeably happy. Sad to say, but this is not normal to me and my brother. So we knew something was up. They took their coats off and walked over to us giving us hugs and kisses. They sat down at the Kitchen table where we were smiling and grinning just like Ma was. I was so ready and excited to hear the news about us moving. But out of my mom's mouth comes something that every kid should be most happy about. She says, "Shannyn and Randy, your dad and I have something to tell you. Today me and your dad got married, and we are going to make everything better for all of us". Me and my brother jumped up from the table with the biggest smiles and showered them with the tightest hugs and kisses. The only way kids know how to say congratulations in times like these. I remember saying to them, "This is the best day of my life". But truly, up until that point in my young years of life, March 9, 1987, it was. Two weeks went by, and more good news came. Our Section 8 Voucher finally was approved for a new apartment.

So immediately, my mother and grandmother began shopping and putting new furniture on Lay-A-Way.

As the count down began to move, seemingly there was a shift in my Dad's energy. Like the happiness that he had a few weeks ago faded.

One night in the wee hour of the morning, Dad came to my grandmother's apartment where we were staying and both him and my mother were talking. They argued a little bit, but not like how I know they're known to do. They didn't want to wake anybody in the apartment, so they moved their conversation from the living room to the outside of the apartment into the hallway downstairs. They were out there for about an hour. It seemed like my mother was trying to get him to stay, but he insisted on leaving. But promised he'd be back before me and my brother woke up. He was acting kind of weird. The next thing I heard was the building door slam and my mother coming back up the stairs. Back in the room as I was dosing off, looking out the window. The breaking of dawn has just begun and I seen my dad riding up the street heading towards Dudley Street on a BMX styled, child's bicycle. He never came back that day. This was our move-in day. Sad but so, my mother and father had already broken up by April 9, 1987. Just 30 days after they said I do.

— Bienvenido Vecino —

The new place was a big yellow three-family house that sat on the corner of an intersection. But right in the center of our new street. At one end was Blue Hill Avenue, and the other side was Warren Street. It was an old house, and not only was it spooky-looking, it was. We moved in and lived up on the 3rd floor. It was an attic apartment. It was built back in 1890, and it looked like it. The bathroom was super small, and the tub was old fashioned but big and deep. It had small doors in each room. Randy and I was small enough that we would crawl from room to room in them. We found an old jar sitting ontop of an old dusty bible. We left it alone at first. But one day we opened it.

When you stood facing out of the living room doorway. It was a long narrow hallway, and at the end of it was me and Randy's room. Every door along the hall on each side there was a kitchen, a closet, the front door, and my mother's room. It was a small and tight place. We were happy to be in a new place, but for some reason, we had a feeling something wasn't right about it.

My mother was back up to her shenanigans in no time and had become even more numb to life. This is where she totally surrendered to the life of addiction. It didn't help that my grandmother just up and moved to Florida after we moved from her place, either.

On the first and second floor of the new apartment home we moved to, lived an entire Puerto Rican family. They were a huge family. Two brothers had married two sisters, and they all left Puerto Rico to come to the mainland of America for a better life. I don't know how things were back where they were from, but one thing that stood out to me about them early is that they all loved each other very much and had loyalty, laughter, and support between them.

Randy and I once again were transferred to another school, and it was good to have already made friends with the Latino brothers and their little sister that lived downstairs from us. While their mother was getting them ready for the new school year with new clothes and school supplies. Me and Randy were sorting out bags of hand-me-downs from our older cousins Ski & Wiz. We didn't like that very much but still found the good in it. We thought we were cool because we finally got a couple pairs each of stonewashed jeans that happened to be the new style at the time. And it didn't hurt that out the blue, my Aunt Nellie came by and bought us both shopping for a pair of new sneakers and school bags.

We ended up at The Paul A. Dever Elementary School out in Columbia Point. It was a little ways from the house, but luckily we were within the school bus zone. It was also cool that Manny and Julio went to the same school as well.

With my mom sometimes not being home or awake in time to get me and Randy up for school. Loud Latin music from downstairs became our alarm clock to wake us up. Almost every morning when we heard the music, we would get up, throw whatever we could find to wear on, brush our teeth, wash our face and out the door we went. We would meet Manny and Julio downstairs so we could all walk together. But never was it just us four. Their mother Olivia would walk all of us to the bus stop every morning. To be honest, I thought it was weird at first or not normal. Because we never had anybody to walk us that early in the morning anywhere.

It became quickly noticeable to the Delgado family that my mom was obviously on drugs, and with the motherly instinct that Mrs. Delgado had, she began to look out for me and my brother here and there. Through this, me and my brother got closer to her kids. Some days we would fight, and other days we were the best of friends, typical boys. Overall, they were true friends of ours.

The Delgado's were always having a party or gathering for some special occasion. I personally loved it because I knew there would be everything I liked there. Good food, Latina girls and of course loud music and dancing. This is where I learned how to dance Salsa Merengue. I also got my first french kiss from a pretty Puerto Rican girl that was at one of those parties.

One day they were having a cookout in the back yard of the house, and we were asked to come down to join them. As the day turned to night. Everyone could see that all the lights on the first two floors were on, but up on the third floor they could see that it was pitch dark throughout the window line of the third floor. I didn't know any Spanish. But I could tell, judging by all the grown-up's body language, talking and shaking their heads. With all eyes looking up toward our third-floor apartment, they were concerned. As they caught on to our living condition, Mrs. Delgado's husband, who didn't even speak English, asked me with a Budweiser in his hand, "Shannie, Where's you mother?" I just said I didn't know and ran off to go play. The very next day, we get a knock on the back door. It was Manny and Julio's mother with a long extension cord plugged in the wall from their downstairs apartment with a light at the end of it. She didn't say much. She didn't have to. We just pulled it in. Before we closed the door, all she said was, "Be ready for school tomorrow, and don't make me come to knock on the door, be ready". We had no gas or electricity for about a month or so at that time.

But that was normal. My mom wasn't concerned with paying a bill until she noticed that the service was off.

Just down the block was where the playground was. That park is probably where I began to learn who I might be in life. It had every-thing there from the swings and monkey bars to the sandbox and open field. Plus, there were kids from other blocks that would come there as well. This had become me and my brothers favorite place to be. The Moreland Street park. Manny and Julio wasn't allowed to come to the park, even though it was only one block from the house. It wasn't long before I understood why.

I was the dreamer type kid. I didn't need anybody to come to the park with me for me to have fun. I could be out there for hours without anyone to play with and be just fine. But that never lasted long. Especially on a Saturday morning by 11am, the park would already have at least 12 to 15 neighborhood kids running around. Plus, Randy was with me most of the time.

I had a lot of physical energy and was well versed with the obstacle and courses the park had to offer. At the park, I taught myself how to focus to achieve something. I use to focus on backflips. I got so good at it that I became a semi neighborhood legend. The older kids would always ask me to do a back flip. Then they started to dare me to backflip off of tables, benches, fences and I would. They started to instigate little battles between me and some of the other boys who could back flip. There was a boy named Kevin. He gave me a run for my money. He was really good, but he had professional gymnastics training, So he said. I believed him cause he was just that good. I remember being so intimidated by his form and how many continuous backflips he could do. So this is where I can remember my competitive side being born. I would go to the park every day after school and practice. Even on the weekends, I was focused. Then one boring day at the park, all the kids were sitting around talking and capping on each other under the permanent picnic tent. Like usual, one of the older kids was out there and said he would give $5 to anybody that is not scared to jump off the roof of the permanent picnic tent. Almost everybody said they would. But we had a little dilemma. We didn't know how to get on top of it. It was impossible to climb because of its structure. So collectively we grabbed all the tall steel trash cans in the park, dumped them all into one and rolled them over to the tent and stacked them on top of each other in front of the sandbox. I sat back and watched a couple of my friends go up, and each of them got spooked as soon as they looked down. George, the older kid who made the suggestion then up'd the price from $5 to $10, yet they still didn't jump. George was about 17 years old and was already a drug dealer. He was kind of shiesty, and for some reason, I thought he was bluffing about giving up the cash in the end anyway. He was good for siking us younger kids out like that.

I don't know why, but I shouted out, "I'll do it". The older kids said, "No little n*gga, you gonna hurt yourself, and I don't wanna hear ya moms mouth". Then Kevin said he'd do it, but midway up, he got scared himself and changed his mind. But I was determined to get that $10. So I said, If he doesn't do it, I will, just put me up on the second barrel. So George gave in and said, "If you don't do it when you get up there, I'ma get Steven to punch you in the face". Nobody wanted any problems with Steven. Once I got up there, there was no turning back. To make sure I didn't waste his time like the last three kids, he kicked the barrels over so I couldn't get down. Not only did I jump off the tent, I turned around and took a look back down into the sandbox over my shoulder. My heart was pumping, and it looked like I was jumping out of a 10 story window. I remember a man's voice across the street from the park screaming out, "Hey,...don't let that kid jump off of there". Time seemed like it went into slow motion. As scarred as I was, I closed my eyes and dove into a backflip off the tent, and landed in the sandbox.

As I landed, I remember all of the kids, including George, all screaming in excitement. They all ran over to me and gave me a bunch of compliments and high fives that came from everybody out there. George came over to me and told me that I was crazy. But only handed me over $5. I said, "What happened to the $10?" He told me since I did it so easy, he could only give me $5 while folding his wad of cash putting it back in his pocket. I was mad, but I did learn a lesson. "People will motivate you to do what they can't do and then tell you that your value is what they see fit". You forgive, but you never forget. So George still owes me $5.

But from then on, in the neighborhood, I was known as the "Suicide Kid". Believe it or not, nobody knows that I didn't even know what suicide meant at the time.

— Thank God, For Guest? —

Fall came, and Thanksgiving was coming up. By then, my mom had worked out a way to get the lights and gas utilities back on. But with everything good, comes something bad. We had no food to cook for the holiday that year. The refrigerator was bare, except for the opened boxes of frozen string beans. The string beans came from an organization in the neighborhood that gave away donated food for the homeless. My mother would send us down there to get in the line with a voucher every now and then. The boxes were opened because my brother and I sometimes had to resort to eating the cashew packs that came with each box.

Usually, my family would meet up at a designated family members house for the feast. Everybody would bring their special dish. But my mother, even though she had no shame in her game when it came to asking anybody for anything she wanted, had pride in some cases. She was always worried about what the family thought and didn't want to show up empty-handed. So She already made up in her mind that we would not be with the family this year. My brother and I didn't like that idea because we knew all of our cousins would be there, and we didn't want to miss out on our bonding time. But something came over my mother. The night before Thanksgiving my mother told us to come into her room with her to sleep for the night. It was late evening, like around 10 or 11 pm.

It was a chilly night, and as we were lying in the bed, an hour must have went by of complete silence in the house. Then right next to me, I heard my mother whispering something. It was the first time I heard my mother pray and ask God for anything. She must have gone on for about 30 minutes with this. I just laid there in silence until she asked me if I was sleeping. I told her I wasn't. In fact, by this time, I had already developed insomnia. I was used to watching the sun come up. She began talking to me while Randy was always fast asleep. She started to cry and explain how embarrassed and hurt she was about not having the food we needed for the next day. I didn't tell her this, but I felt the same way. But I remember telling her that I hated that she had so much company and was on drugs. But not forgetting to mention how bad me and my brother wanted to be with the rest of the family for Thanksgiving. At that time, telling her that was as bold as I could get. All she said was that she knew that and began to pray more. But I also didn't tell her that I knew what she had done with her food stamps that had just came the week before. Still I comforted her as much as a young son could, and then I got quiet. Then out of the blue, we heard a car pull up in front of the house. We weren't expecting anybody, so we didn't even get up to look out the window like usual. We just thought that whoever it was, they were probably going to the Delgado's downstairs. But then, the doorbell rang. It was obnoxiously loud and had awakened Randy.

Now my mother knew a lot of people. A lot of them were some type of street hustler and slicksters. But she did have a few good people scattered in the mix of them all. "Now who the hell is this"? She says to herself out loud. I just thought it was one of her crackhead friends who was lonely on Thanksgiving eve looking for a place to hide and smoke out. We all get up and start walking towards the front door. When we opened the door, It was my mother's good funny friend, Carl. He was leaning on the banister with a cigar in his mouth and a bottle of Hennessy in his hand. My mother said, "Carl?' What are you doin here"? His shocking and immediate answer was, "God sent me".

It was one of those moments that made me consider that a God really exists. My mother welcomed him in. He was already kind of tipsy. He came in loud, but he was real and straightforward with my mother. He really liked my mother but knew he couldn't be with her because of her lifestyle choice. Carl was a hardworking man and had some street smarts. He says to my mother, "Tara, I came because tomorrow is thanksgiving, and I know you ain got sh*t". "These boys are going to have to eat tomorrow and so do I". Carl was from down south and didn't have any family in Boston. He went in his pocket, pulled out the keys to his car, and told me and my brother to go downstairs and get the bags out of the trunk. Carl had already went to Stop & Shop grocery store to get everything we needed for a Thanksgiving feast. From the Turkey to the Cranberry sauce, cakes and pies, and even some pots and pans. It was all there. My mother was so thankful and immediately started to prepare to cook.

On this same night, while my mother was in the bathroom. Me and my brother went in the kitchen where Carl was sitting and sipping his Cognac. We always thought highly of him and knew that he was a good man. But what we didn't understand was, if he was such a good guy, why did he have a gun? He had it lying on the kitchen table right next to him. So, the kind of kids we were, we boldly asked him why he had it. He told us that it was for his protection cause he always got a lot of money. He said that one day when we get a lot of money, we might have to get one too. So my brother Randy says, "Let me hold it" Carl said no at first. But then we began to press him. We told him, "Well, if one day we will need one, then let us see what it's like". It worked. He finally gave in. He told me to hold my hand out. He placed it in the palm of my hand and let go. My hand felt the weight of it, and my arm dropped. I could remember the adrenaline pumping through me. He quickly grabbed it out of my hand and then did the same with my brother. We haven't seen a gun since we lived on Seaver St. But it all connected for me on this day. Either you had to take what you wanted or protect what you have in life.

We later learned that Carl planned to cook Thanksgiving dinner himself. But he ended up getting drunk before going grocery shopping and then realized he wasn't going to be able to cook. So he came to 56 Moreland St. Where my mother cooked it all. When I finally woke up in the morning, I smelt the food cooking while mom was napping on the couch, and Carl was gone. He never ate a bite of the food he brought, and we never saw him again. We made dinner time at Aunt Linda's and enjoyed our time with the family. That's all I wanted. Just maybe, God is good.

There was always something going on at that house. Although we didn't have much, somehow, we had something to offer to others in their time of need. Even if it was just our roof over their head.

Moreland street was where things got the lowest for us but where I could remember so many people lived with us. I could remember my Uncle Bryce and his Girlfriend Carmen staying with us for a short time. They used to argue and fight all the time. My uncle was a cool guy, but he was a smooth, low-key badass. One time my Auntie Carmen was at the house with us all day waiting for him. She waited so long that she just gave up waiting. They shared a room with my brother and me. We slept in the twin bed, and they slept in the queen-sized bed that we had in the room. In the middle of the night, about 3 am. My uncle Bryce finally came in and tried his best to slip in the bed with my aunt without waking her. But he failed miserably. As soon as he got settled, my aunt got out the bed and went to the kitchen. I heard the refrigerator open, but I figured she was just getting something to drink. She then comes back down the hall and back into the room. I was thinking, with how mad she was from earlier that day from wait-ing on him, she's taking this kind of good. But to my nosey surprise, she pulls out an icy 1-gallon water jug and pours it all over him, all while punching and cussing him out in Spanish. Then she ran out of the room. He got up, shook it off, and followed her into the living room, where they continued. I sat up and laughed my face off until I fell asleep. To be honest, up until this day, I have never seen anybody voluntarily beat on my uncle the way she did that night. Because his reputation was known to beat a man's ass first, then ask what's the problem later. Back around the time we lived on Seaver Street. Uncle Bryce beat up a man with his own 10 speed bike. Later that day, the man came back. They had a shoot-out; while uncle Bryce had me in his arms. Yet still, I looked up to him a lot. He was like a superhero to me. When him and my aunt moved out, they left the city and moved to Florida. They took their son with them; Francisco. But a year later, while they were there, they had another son; Mario.

Then we had my mother's very good and long-time friend, Georgina and her five kids came to stay with us on Moreland Street. She had gotten evicted from her place in Franklin Hill projects. She then went on the run with her kids because the state was trying to strip her of them. So it was crowded in our attic apartment for about two weeks. Me and Randy didn't mind them coming. As if we didn't already before, we had an even stronger bond with her kids after this. But now it's not just me and my brother left alone. It's all 7 of us. I have to say for the first time, I didn't feel the pressure of responsibility because Georgina had a son older than all of us and he had a few advanced survival skills up his sleeve himself. He figured out a way to feed us, and to keep the younger ones from crying. He would keep us laughing and playing made-up games all day and night.

To think that just one year before this, we were all in the Franklin Hill projects hallway fighting each other because our mothers were fighting. Until this day, none of us know why they were fighting, but that's the rule; when moms is fighting, you're fighting, even if we were outnumbered.

My mother was a little younger than Georgina, and neither had that mother thing quite figured out. But you become what you surround yourself with, and mom is passing with flying colors making the Dean's List this semester.

Although my mother was on drugs. She didn't look as if she was. My mother met a guy. His name was Ralph. He was Jamaican. My mother liked him a lot. He liked her too. He wasn't from Boston, but Ralph was a kingpin. He was young and flashy, but he was very mature and wise for his age. Me and my brother knew he was too young for my mom, but he was cool. Plus, he used to give us money whenever he came over. He always had this one guy with him. He was cool too, but he didn't talk much. But he use to get a kick out of me and my brother wrestling. He would laugh and tells us how we remind him of him and his brother back in, "Yaad"(Jamaica). But he always gave me the vibe that deep down inside, he was just like the guy that used to follow my mother everywhere; "The Door Man".

One time while Ralph was coming around, Randy was sick with flu like symptoms. He had been this way for a couple days. Ralph had stopped by to do his usual; sip his beer, count his money and smoke his ganja. When he realized that Randy was sick. He stopped what he was doing and became really attentive to Randy's condition. So he told my mother that he could heal him. My mother was very skeptical about it at first. But Stoney told her to chill out and let Ralph help him. So, she did. Ralph began to chant some Jamaican words out loud and sipped from a liquor bottle. He took my brother to the bathroom and ran water in the tub. He picked my brother up and dunked him in the cold water a few times, all the while still chanting. He grabbed a towel and wrapped Randy up tight and then placed a shower cap on his head. Ralph took Randy back to my mothers room and laid him down in the center of the bed and continued to chant. He picked up his joint and lit it up. When he took a drag from the joint he then put his face close to Randy's and began to blow the smoke directly into Randy's face. Ralph turned on the music and turned it up loud and got even louder with his chants as if he was trying to be louder than the music. After about 10 minutes of this, Randy got up in the middle of the bed and began dancing in the middle of the bed as if he never was sick in the first place. Ralph made Randy some tea and even poured a little of whatever he was drinking from the bottle and told him to sip it until it was gone. Believe it or not, Randy never caught another cold for the rest of his childhood. It was a moment to remember.

Ralph and his boy didn't stay around that long. One late night after not seeing Ralph in months, there was a frantic knock on the door. My mother went to the door and opened it. It was him. I knew something was wrong because he came in the door in a quiet panic, but crying and sobbing. My mother just guided him to the living room. She asked him over and over again what happened. He finally belted out, "They killed him, They killed him," melting to the floor, crying out loud. Come to find out, Ralph had just got to one of his trap houses. The Boston Police ran in behind him to raid the place when he walked in. So he ran up the stairs. By the time he got to the top of the stairs, his boy had committed to a standoff with the police. When they heard Ralph running down the back steps, he knew they would run around the back to try and catch him. Right then, he knew it was over and did what he had to do. Ralphs boy fired off a shot, killing a cop. The Boston Police then opened fire, leaving Ralph's boy dead with 27 bullet holes in him. After that night, we never saw Ralph again. Rest in Peace, Stoney.

With all the different energies coming in and out of our house, it was bound to get worse. Somehow my mother reconnected with her old cuban boss man. This time he didn't look so well and looked like he might have started using his own product as well. But he was very much so still the boss. But this time around, he didn't have as many guys with him.

In the middle of the night I was awaken by the voice of a woman talking loud in the living room. She was very cocky and aggressive in her conversation. Usually, my mother is running everything. She was big on respecting her house and not being so loud because my brother and I were there. But this lady had no regard for my mother and her rules. I used to wonder why my mother didn't put her in her place like she'd do everybody else.

The next day on the way out to school, I went to peek in the living room, and there were 2 women in there. A big fat light skinned lady was sitting up in the single sofa chair with her head laid back sleeping and a short little lady on the love seat sleeping as well. This was the first time I had ever seen the two ladies. Later that day, when we got home from school, we heard the music bumping coming up the stairs. When we got in the door, I looked down the hall toward the living room and seen that big fat lady in the living room dancing her ass off. We smiled and laughed, and she kept right on going. My mother was in the kitchen frying chicken and doing something that she never really did. She was sipping on a bottle of Hennessy. I don't know what happened while we were at school, but mom was in a good mood this day. All the windows and shades were open, and the house smelled like she'd been cleaning. My mother told the big lady to turn down the music a little and come into the kitchen. My mother said to us, "Let me introduce you to my friend.....", and before she could say her name, the big woman cut in and said, "Let me guess, You must be Shannyn and your Randy". She was tall for a woman as well. We looked up at her with an immediate love for her as her personality was as big as she was. She was super confident, funny, and hip to everything. She stuck her hand out and shook both of our hands like little men and told us her name was Andrea. From that first touch, I knew she had a heart of gold which was as big as her 350-pound body. Andrea had become my mother's new partner in crime.

We didn't see the other short lady for about a week or so. But when she did show up again, she was with the boss man. After hearing her voice, it hit me; that the voice I heard in the middle of the night was hers. That's also when it became clear that she was the boss man's girlfriend. My first interaction with her was when she came to the house and knocked on the door. I answered it, saying hello and cracking the door open. She said, "Wheres Tara?" But she was in motion to barge in the door as if I wasn't even there. I put my foot behind the door as a wedge to abruptly stop her hand from pushing the door and I said again that she wasn't home. She said, "What are you doing kid? Open the door; I will wait for her inside". I told her she had to come back or wait in the hallway until my mother got back. We weren't allowed to let anyone in if my mother wasn't home. She started to say something else, which I'm sure would be something to try to con her way in. But, I slammed the door in her face. I always had respect for my elders, but not in this case. This little lady was ruthless in every way. She was always telling a story about how she was in some type of altercation with someone and how vicious or badass she was. She was a thief and had no respect for anybody. She was cold-hearted and didn't care about anything. A Very selfish mad at the world type. I knew that her relationship with my mother wouldn't last that long. She would always do something to test my mother. Like I remember my mother telling her not to lean on the bell so late at night because it was loud, and you could hear it throughout the walls of the whole house. She would do it every night when she came and then laughed about it coming in the door, underestimating my mother's gangsta but knowing she didn't like that. Another time, She was high, and for some strange reason, she stood up on the window ledge shouting out random off-the-wall chants. I kept hearing my mother saying, "Paula, I don't know where the f*ck you think you at, but get yo ass down from there". Something about the tone of my mother's voice let me know that she was over this broad.

A couple of days after this, Paula was back at the house. Me and my brother were coming in from the park. We heard some hardcore arguing going on. Mom was about to throw down. Before we could get to our third-floor landing, my mother had started beating this woman so viciously that we knew not to even try to break it up. The woman reaches out and grabs Randy and yanks him in front of her to use him as a shield from the beating she was getting. I don't know where it came from, but my mother slightly paused as she recognized what the woman was doing. My mother's eyes stretched wide, and she got so tensed, representing an official mental snap. From behind the door comes a steak knife in my mother's hand, and over Randy was big strikes of downward thrust into the top of Paula's head, shoulders, and back, stabbing her repeatedly. Blood was everywhere. If it wasn't for Mrs. Delgado hearing all the commotion and running up the stairs, jumping in between it all; and grabbing my mother's arm pulling it back, chances are my mother could have gone to prison for murder.

I was expecting a retaliation from her boyfriend/Boss man. But nothing ever came of it, and Paula disappeared.

We had a jack of all trade street hustling cousin Trenton, but we called Mook. He was from Orchard Park projects. We use to love to see him coming. He was full of energy, well respected in the hood, he dressed very well, always had a lot of money, and didn't like new people. He had this very loud voice that you could hear coming for blocks. Mook was the kind of person that when sh*t hits the fan; you're glad he's on your side. It was like the more he knew about a person, the more he had to have a conscience about what might be coming to them. Especially if they had something he wanted. But if you were someone he loved, you could get anything you wanted from him. Just ask him, and he would. But you didn't want to tell Mook everything. Like if you had a problem with someone, but you know them pretty well, and you knew the problem was most likely minor and going to blow over. Don't tell Mook. He had a way of making little problems, big problems.

But even Mook ended up coming to live with us for about a year.

Even though my mother and him would argue and cuss each other out all the time. Me and my brother loved that he was there. But he wasn't alone. He had his 5-month pregnant girlfriend, Trina, with him. This was going to be Mook's first child. I remember him being so excited about it. This made him even more of a beast in the street. Every night we would try to stay up and wait for him to come in. We were excited to hear about all he did in a day of his life. Even though we were young boys, Mook never talked to us like little kids. To be honest, I don't think he knew better than to talk any other way to us. He was extremely blunt and detailed.

Mook always came home with the goods, though. Big stacks of money and all kinds of tv's, radio's, new clothes, Video games, CD's and of course food for the refrigerator. Or, what we really liked, a Steak & Cheese sub from "Ugi's" down in Dudley.

But more so than me, Mook was connected to Randy. They shared the same video games interest and would have these silent conversations while playing. Me, on the other hand, would be in the living room practicing my dance moves, and also, this is the place where I wrote my first song. Music was always my getaway. Randy was a little more logical than I was, even though I was the oldest. I know now that I was more free-spirited.

Even though we benefit from my cousin's lifestyle, I felt everything and wanted it to stop. Randy saw everything and wanted in, early. Mook secretly started to teach my brother little ways to make money with him. He began to take Randy out with him to different places in his daily journey of hustling. Every night it got later and later until they came back. Because my brother was so into video games, Mook would take him to a Video arcade downtown Boston right outside the hood. The Arcade had a pizza shop next door, and Randy loved pizza. So in Mook's mind, this was the perfect situation and location to set up shop. He would give my brother the drugs he was selling to hold as a decoy. Mook knew that if something happened and the police came, they couldn't search a kid without a parent being present. Even if Mook for some reason got arrested, Randy would know his way back home, and the drugs would be there with him for Mook to get back to it. I remember my mother cussing my cousin out for having my brother out until the early mornings. Mook used to laugh it off but assured her that nothing would happen to him and would do the same thing the next night. Randy loved every minute of it.

Around that time, my mother had met a man that she was highly fond of. He had been coming to the house and spending a lot of time with her. He was a little older than my mother and had a very calm yet stern way about him. Come to find out, he was a U.S. Marine vet in his younger day. That would explain to me his stealth-like ways. Real smooth like. You never hear him coming, and you never heard him leave. We never even heard him raise his voice once. His name, Smitty. One night I was home alone while Randy was out with Mook. My mom was out all day herself. It was a school night. Then about 11:30 pm, my mother finally came in. She came to my room door and peeked in. She looked like she had been up to something but you never knew what it could be with her at times. She asked me where my brother was, and I told her he was out with Mook. She walks away from the doorway but then returns in 5 minutes to ask me how long they have been gone. I told her that they left about 4 hours ago, and she then began to get angry. I went on to finish watching The late-night show with David Letterman. He had Eddie Murphy on that night. I was a big fan of his. Then

Approximately at 1am, the bell rang, and it was Smitty. He comes into the apartment, and him and my mom go into the living room. They chatted for a bit, and then they began to come down the hall toward the bedrooms. Smitty stopped and peaked his head in my room. By then, the lights were out, and he couldn't tell if I was asleep or not. But noticed Randy wasn't there. When they got into my mom's room Smitty immediately, asked "Where's Randy"? My mother didn't answer right away. So Smitty said, "Did you hear me?" Then with a slow reply, she answered with a tone of guilt and said, "Out with Mook". He asked her, "Where?" She replied with an answer that Smitty absolutely didn't like. She told him, "Wesson Ave". All I heard next was Smitty repeat what she said; "WESSON AVE"?, with anger and a tone of disappointment. Then, the sound of a thunderously loud smack across the face instantly followed. I heard her lose balance and fall, and then back to his calm voice Smitty told her, "Go get him". She then got up and pulled herself together, and without saying another word, she walked out the door.

It may sound crazy, but I found a respect for Smitty after that night. He showed a deep concern for me and my brother's well-being and because I knew he was the only man besides my dad who had what it took to bring the kind of order to the house that we needed. After that night, Mook was out of a sidekick. Smitty put a stop to it, and besides; once Mook's girlfriend had the baby, they moved out. It was a long time before we saw big cuz again. But still, more people came after him.

— Another Knock At The Door —

My dad was never really too far from us. No matter what, he knew where we were at all times, and we knew where he was, most of the time. In this case, he lived around the corner from us, just off the back of the Park. He lived in a men's rooming house, and every now and then, he would come to our house to stay the night for a weekend. Although my parents didn't get along very well, they had what I like to call a "Bipolar Love Affair". I always thought they would have been powerful if they'd gotten off the drugs and worked it all out. But quickly, I would snap out of that idea. I knew that some of the laughing, loving, dancing in the living room, to the stays for dinner as a family was a disguise for the hell they were forever getting ready to raise. Just give it a few hours.

From my memory, the good times were always temporary. One Saturday morning, we woke up, and my father was there. He had already been there for about a week. Me and my brother watched way more re-runs of Star Trek and All In The Family than we ever wanted to. I think we were even starting to look like Vulcans.

The doorbell rang and I heard my mother yell out, "Don't answer the door" from the other room. So we didn't. The door downstairs must have been unlocked because we heard some people coming up the stairs. Some of them even stopped on the second floor at the Delgado's and talked to them. In my mind, I thought it's some of my mother's friends. But at the same time, I thought that this might be the turning point of a good week. Because my mother didn't have company at all when my dad was there. It's like they all knew when he was there and nobody would come to the door. Suddenly, a light knocking strikes the door. Without saying hello first, my mother says out loud, "I'm not interested". Then there was some mumbling outside the door. And again, another knock. This time my dad yells out, "I'm busy". Then whoever it was, through the door said, "Hi, we were in your neighborhood today and would like to share some information with you". My dad says it again, "I'm busy". Then a man's voice cuts in and starts his spill about what they needed to talk about. My mother comes out of the room and say's from behind the closed door, "Maybe another time". Then, they knocked again for the last time, and my dad had enough. He comes out of the room agitated, walking down the hall toward the door fast in just his underwear and a hard-on. He snatches open the door wide and tells the people, "How many times I got to tell you, I'm busy". The people ran down the stairs so fast, and my brother and mom and me started laughing our asses off. We went to the window to see who the people were. It was even more funny when we realized Jehovah's Witnesses were walking fast back to their cars.

But, with everything good comes something bad.

Later on that same morning, there was another knock on the door. My dad opens the door, and it was the last person on earth that neither of us wanted to see. It was the Boss Man. The good times, are now officially over. The Boss Man was just as hot tempered as my dad, but he was very snappy and always agitated because of his position. He felt the right to ask my dad where my mother was for some reason. That wasn't good. My dad quickly replied by telling him that she wasn't available and he's going to have to come back some other time. The Boss Man says, "Look, I don't have time for this shit," my dad cuts him off and says, "I don't give a f*ck about your time or what it's for". This turns into a quick battle of words between them. Meanwhile, me and my brother go into my mother's room while this is taking place at the door. We were in complete silence as we watched my mother quickly and desperately throw her clothes on. Then we heard The Boss Man walking down the stairs. He arrogantly turns back and yells at my dad, telling him to tell my mother to come on now and don't make him wait. My father say's, "You'll be waiting then motherf*cker". My dad then slammed the door closed. As he turned from the door, my mother was standing there fully dressed. She told him she'd be right back and then attempted to leave out.

My dad immediately says, "Naw, You ain goin no damn' where". She tried again to passively tell my dad that she'd be right back, and the same doorway where my mom once snapped on Paula, my dad did the same. Feeling disrespected, the look in his eyes accepted whatever his fate was going to be and began beating my mother up. They must have fought for about 2mins straight. Their fights were always a war of mass destruction. But my mother was determined to get out the door. As they came unhinged from each other, my dad made a break for the room, and my mother pulled herself together real fast and made her break to the door. By the time my mother got out the door and down the first flight of stairs, my dad stormed back out of the room. But when he came out, I knew it was over. He had a machete in his hand. I didn't even know we had one in the house. What happened next relayed in my mind for years after. As my mom was going down the next flight of stairs down to the second floor, my dad rushed out the door and swung the machete so hard toward her head that he almost fell over the bannister. But luckily for us all, if it wasn't for her tilting her head, the machete would have chopped her in the top of her head. Instead, the blade caught the bottom of the staircase, and she ran. The machete was so deeply embedded that it chopped a chunk of the frame from the wooden steps out, and he had to go and yank it out with a few tough pulls with two hands.

By then, she was gone. Randy and I didn't cry much, but this was a day when the tears seemed to be never-ending. As wild as that may seem, with all of this going on; in the hood, calling the police is not a first response. But just in case, my dad came and gave me and my brother hugs and kisses like he always did, told us that he loved us, and left the house as well. All of this happened before noon that day.

Hours went by, and it's just my brother and me. He stayed in our room and numbed out on a Nintendo video game, and I was in the living room numbed out on old vinyl records that we still had from when my dad was a DJ. We were in total silence all day and on opposite ends of the apartment from each other. Maybe we were traumatized, and this is how we dealt with it. The day just seemed like it didn't want to quit. Every 15 minutes felt like an hour. About 4:30, there was a knock on the door, and it was Andrea. We're usually not allowed to let anyone in when my mother is not home, but we didn't care at this point. She came in with her bubbly personality, a bottle of Hennessy, and her bags as she seems to always be coming from Clothes shopping. As she came in, we just hugged her and walked off. She goes to my mother's room and finds she's not there. Then she walks down the hall to the living room while bopping her head to her own tune like she always does and she noticed she wasn't there either. She got quiet and must have felt the vibe of the house as she started to assess the condition of the place. Then, out of sincere concern, she says, "Hey, where's y'all mother at, and why is this place a mess like this?" We told her that she was fighting with my father and left. Andrea grabbed her bottle of Hennessy, took a few shots, told me to turn the music up, and began cleaning the whole house. About 2 hours later my mother finally came. When she came in the door, she apologized to us and joined Andrea with cleaning and reorganizing the house. All the while saying she is done with the life she is living, and this all got to stop. Maybe she was trying to convince herself.

But to me, it felt more like one of those moments when you know you're about to get in trouble for something, so all of a sudden, you want to get your act together. Besides, me and my brother were used to that kind of talk from her from time to time. She finally cooked and fed my brother and me after all day of not eating at all. It wasn't like we had an appetite anyway.

My mother had started to sip on some Hennessy with Andrea. She seemed relaxed and not as uptight as she was first coming in the door. They began talking and laughing, having a good time. They were way past the conversation about what had happened earlier that day.

So finally, about 10:30pm, my mother told me and my brother to get ready for bed. We told her that the WWF Saturday Night Main Event was coming on, and we wanted to watch it. She then told us to take a bath and when we get out go in our room and watch it in the bed.

So that's what we did. Everything felt normal again. Me and Randy started jumping from bed to bed rough housing in excitement about wrestling coming on.

Then it happens, the unthinkable. The day went from being like a bad dream, that turned into a nightmare.

There were three bangs on the front door. They were heavy and very aggressive. Me and my brother jumped up so quickly and cracked our room door open just enough to see who it might be. Even then, I thought it might be the police doing another raid. We can see down the hall that my mother and Andrea both were shook and startled. A few more seconds pass, and then Andrea says, "Who is it?" The next thing you hear is my dad's voice say, "It's me. Open the f*ckin door," and then the sound of a rifle cocking back. Right then, Andrea eyes stretched wide and belted out a sound of fear. I thought back to my dad's face and just knew from how mad he was when he left earlier that day that he was here to finish my mother off.

In the next moment, I remember my mother taking a deep breath and surrendering to what was happening. Almost like she just accepted that this is it for her. The next thing she did was snatch the door open wide while shouting, "The Kids….". Before she could get the rest of her words out, I saw the barrel of the rifle forcefully come through the door and straight into her chest. Simultaneously I heard three trigger pulls and what sounded like marbles in a class bottle. My mother fell to the ground and instantly grabbed the barrel of the gun, wrapping her legs around it with a death lock grip. My dad tried his best to get it loose from her. He grabbed the butt of the rifle and dragged her body down two flights of stairs, ripping her shirt off in the process causing deep skin bruising and wood rash all over her body. He stopped right in front of the Delgado's door. He began striking her to get her to turn loose the weapon, but nothing could get her to let go. She started sounding like a broken record on repeat, saying, "The boys are in the house, The boys are in the house," as if she was trying to get him to come out of a demon-possessed trance.

Then all you heard was police sirens coming from every direction. Because this situation tilted the needle on the "should I, or should I not call the cops" meter. Somebody did. Because of the sirens getting closer, my dad ran off without the rifle, leaving it behind. The Boston Police found my mom in the hallway on the second floor, still holding on to the rifle. Even they had to pry it out of her hand. When the officer finally got the rifle out of my mother's hand, he faced the barrel downward. When he did, Three combusted bullet heads fell out of the barrel of the gun on to the floor.

While we were waiting for the ambulance to come up, the officer turned to somebody in the Delgado's apartment and says, "Did you guys hear gun shots?" The Delgado's said, "We don't speak no english," and closed their door. The officer then turns to another officer and says, "Somebody must be praying for this lady".

After the Ambulance took my mother away to the hospital, me and my brother shut down. Andrea was a complete wreck. From that night, the last thing I remember was my Aunt Linda and her husband Ben outside, both drunk. She was screaming at the police, asking them what had happened to her niece. Also, there seemed to be 50 Police cars, fire trucks and ambulances all with their lights spinning lighting up the night in the neighborhood. Hulk Hogan had nothing on the Main Event that took place at 56 Moreland Street that night.

Months go by after this and once again, its like nothing ever happened. Unfortunately, everything is back to normal. I guess mom retuned the favor and dropped the charges on dad. Because as crazy as that night sounds, my dad never served time for the situation. But he did disappear again for a while. You would think that after this my mom would've really pulled herself together. But no, she wasn't the type to give up. She picked right back up where she left off. Maybe she wants to be Valedictorian.

— Left Behind —

My mom's addiction got even worse, and the dysfunction in our lives had become the baseline. My mom had and missed so many wake-up calls. Yet, she snoozed. Leading to me and my brother missing so many days of school.

For the most part, we woke up when we wanted to, eat what we can find, and play all day. But mostly in our walk-in closet. Where we had dirty clothes piled up to the door knob that hasn't been washed in months.

It got to a point where after we'd take a bath, We would flip our underwear inside out to get a second or third wear out of them. And sometimes for dinner; The Delgado's used to send us up some rice and beans if they had any leftover.

A woman comes to the house one morning, and she tells my mother that her time is up. We had met this lady for the first time six months before that day. She was an African lady, and she wore Sally Jessie Raphael glasses. We didn't like her from the beginning because she brought a weird vibe with her. Like she was a school teacher or something that was taking her job way too seriously by showing up at your house. But I couldn't really put a finger on it. My mother excused us from the room and began to talk to the woman. Me and Randy, of course, was eavesdropping. I heard my mother saying things like, "Yes, I feed them, look how chubby my baby is getting". The woman then says, "Well, what about Shannyn? He is completely thin"? My mother told her that I was an athletic kid and danced all day around the house. As the woman kept pressing my mom, she began to lose her composure. Before I knew it, my mother was hardcore cussing the lady out. All the way out the door. But a few days later, the woman comes back. But this time the woman brought the Boston Police with her as an escort. Once again catching my mom completely off guard. As usual, the house was a mess and completely dark when she came in; and it was daytime. My mother just woke up but had been sleeping for the past 24hrs. After privately talking with the lady again and what sounded like emotional pleading for another chance. My mom told my brother and me to come in the room, and she started to cry. She told us to pack some clothes for the weekend. So we did. While we were packing, I heard my mother ask the woman where she was taking us. The woman told my mother that she was taking us to a family that wanted us out in Cape Cod. The way she said it, for some reason, I thought that the woman was just saying that to poke at her. I didn't know it then, but my brother and I were placed in the Newspaper ads/Boston Globe as 2 Orphaned black brothers, looking for a home. But what the lady replied to mother must have worked. Because my mother lost it. She then ran downstairs to use The Delgado's phone and started calling everybody in the family. This was a day her pride was totally removed. She ended up calling the last person in the world she wanted to know was going on. Ma. We heard her crying from downstairs. In the meantime, The Child Services worker was rushing us to get our stuff together. Asking us if we are ok and if we had seen our dad. Her demeanor was foreign to us. Then whenever she called us her kids. We really disconnected. All conversation dropped. My mother finally came back up the stairs and said, You can take them to my sisters. She will take them right now. My grandmother came to the rescue once again all the way from Florida. Before we left out, we gave my mother one last great big hug and kiss. She was crying, but I could tell she was holding back a lot. Me and Randy, we didn't shed one tear. Because in the back of my mind, I was thinking, this was about to be one big adventure.

I remember leaving out with our big burgundy suitcases and bags. We put our belongings in the trunk and front seat. Out of all the times me and my brother would fight over the front seat of anybody's car, neither of us felt that urge at this moment. Before we pulled off, I looked back across the street up at our room window. It was closed and fogged. But my mother was standing there in the window, watching us pull off. Her face had a look of defeat.

It took us 12 minutes to get to my Auntie Breena's apartment. In which is the same apartment that we just left three years before in Upham's Corner. My grandmother left it to my Aunt and her new husband.

This ended up being the longest weekend we have ever spent, anywhere.

CHAPTER 6

Middle School

— The Cards You Were Dealt —

It was inevitable that we ended up at my Aunt Breena's. After all, she was one of the only people that frequently checked up on me and my brother. She would come to pick us up when she could. She'd pull up in front of the park and tell us to get in, taking us back to her apartment to bathe and feed us. Sometimes we stayed the whole weekend. On school nights, she would drop us back off home. But most of the time, my mother never even knew we were gone anyway. We loved going to the blockbuster to pick out Karate movies with Aunt Breena's husband, Keith. He was a fanatic. They were a young couple and did most of the stuff we liked. For the most part, we liked it over there.

Even though my aunt was just starting out in life with her three little girls and Husband; they took us in and made room. We had good times and bad for those almost four years that we were with them. I ended up having a serious nervous breakdown and had to be hospitalized for a night or two. I remember while in the hospital, my mother showed up. But my aunt had a few words for her, and, of course, they got irate. The doctor had to come in and tell them both to leave the room. The doctor told them that I was a kid with the stress level of a 35yr old man, and it had completely beat down the walls of my immune system. They told my mother she had to leave because by then, she had lost total custody of me and my brother by court order. By then, Aunt Breena and Uncle Keith had become our lawful guardians.

I can say the good definitely outweighed the bad while we was with Aunt Breena. But with what me and my brother was going through psychologically, I began to feel like we was making things bad for them.

At school, me and Randy had begun getting harassed. But not by other kids. Every week, it seemed like there was some type of investigator from the Boston Police Department or DSS coming to question us about either my mom or dad. We used to give them a hard time, though. They would ask us questions like, "What's your mother's real name" we would say, "mommy". Then they would ask, "What does your mother's friends call her?" Again, we would say, "Mommy". Questions and answers like this would last the whole session when they came. We could tell they used to get so mad at us. So much that when they realized they weren't going to get us to cooperate as easy as they thought, they would start throwing mental jabs like; "You know your dad is a dangerous man, right"? Or, "Your mom doesn't really love you," "don't trust your dad. If he hurt your mom, he will hurt you too". I guess that struck a nerve with me because I remember getting mad about it. So I told that lady right then. With a straight forward mean mug face, "He might hurt you, but he won't hurt me". From there, they ended up signing my brother and me off as some totally brainwashed kids and realized they weren't going to get anything out of us. So they stopped coming. But weeks later, they tried to put us in counseling. They gave us some young U-Mass student. A white girl from the suburbs of Rhode Island somewhere who was trying to get her degree in Social Service or something. I guess they were hoping that they could get us to open up about our trauma. She would come and get me out of class on Thursdays and take me to a private room in the school to talk. She was always trying to prove that she was trustworthy. So one time, I asked her, "Why every time we talk, you have to write down what I say?" Her answer was simple, "Because what you say is important". I began to think she was cool. Plus, she had all the board games I liked, from Trouble to Connect Four, Candy-land to Hungry-Hippo. But it wasn't until after a few months of playing all the games that I was stumped. We had a meeting with Our Social Worker; Malina. She repeated something back to me that I had mentioned to the counselor at school. It then came to me that they were all together. My trust instantly declined, and I stopped speaking up. Even the board games were no longer fun. It wasn't long before the counselor stopped coming. But that was the day that I learned a valuable lesson about trust. Trust is a game of gain for some people, and they will use it against you for their own victory. So, "Anything you say can and will be used against you"; is a piece of law that I hold in the back of my mind from that day on. Still to this day, I have no desire to play any over-the-table board games.

Just as we started to get used to living with my Aunt back at my grandmother's old apartment, they dropped the bomb on Randy and me. We came home one day, and they were packing. I knew we were moving. But where, I didn't know.

Come to find out. We were moving to Braintree.

Neither me nor my brother liked that idea at all. Braintree is a suburban town on the outskirts of Boston. The South Shore. The only thing we knew about Braintree was that there was a mall there that was just about to be renovated, and it was way too far from where I was most comfortable. We had no other choice but to go with the flow. But at least we didn't have to change schools. But I dreaded getting up every morning to take that cramped up ride back to Dorchester. Just think, 7 people in a 1988 4-door Hyundai Excel, and a car seat for the babygirl. This went on for about a whole school year until my aunt and uncle finally got a new car.

But overall, Braintree wasn't that bad at all. I just felt like I wasn't supposed to be there. Especially that long. There were plenty of nights that I cried with anger. I just couldn't figure out why my mother wouldn't finish the program that she was court-ordered to do by the judge. It was simple to me. Finish the program; Get your kids back. I started to think that maybe she loved crack more than us.

She would call every now and then and make promises about how it wouldn't be too long before we were back with her. She also used to make us promise her that we wouldn't give up on her. But, It really felt like she gave up on us. Because there were times that we didn't hear from her for a long time. Then on top of that, Aunt Breena and Uncle Keith stopped her from calling the house all together.

I remember overhearing our case worker telling them that she will never get herself together if they keep letting her call and talk to us when she wanted. That made me angry. Because I had accepted the fact that my mom wasn't going to get help and that meant to my young mind that me and my brother would never see her again. The idea of that swelled my anxiety even more. It kind of felt like emotional torture.

I entered 5th grade at the Paul A. Dever Elementary School the next year. I had found out that my mother had got a new apartment. She was back in Dorchester, off of Hancock Street. It was another drug-infested neighborhood. The Cape Verdeans had it on lock. So needless to say; my mother wasn't doing any better than she was when she first lost custody of us. But I had enough. I had it in my mind that I was going to force my mom, in some way, somehow to take care of my brother and me. I was so frustrated with living with my Aunts family. I would do anything to get out of there.

I didn't care what the conditions were at my mother's new place. I was ready to go. Then for some reason, out of nowhere, my aunt allowed me and my brother to go stay the night with my mom at her new place. That only confirmed to my anxious mind that maybe they wanted us to leave or needed a break too. Or, maybe they wanted us to see for ourselves that she hasn't improved. The first night we get to my mother's new place. She goes out. It felt normal again. But this night ended up being a special night for me. On this night, she wasn't out as late as I had known her to be. She comes in early, about 11 pm. We were still up.

When she came in, she had 2 guys with her. One was a drug dealer from Academy Homes and hoped to be a manager in the music industry. The other was a popular DJ from Roxbury who just came off a worldwide tour with a superstar of that time. I guess somewhere in their conversation I was brought up by my mom that I can sing and dance. My mom called me out of the room and introduced me. The first question they asked was, "Who is your favorite singer". I said, "Bobby Brown". Of course, because he was where I was from, and I had family members that knew him personally. The DJ's eyes lit up like I said something right. They went on to say, "Well, if you ever want to be as big of a star as him, then show me your dance moves." So I went back to the bedroom, got my dual tape deck boom box, and brought it to the kitchen. That year, three members from the New Edition went out on their own calling themselves BBD and they had a hot dance song called, "Poison". I turned the song on and with no shame in my game, gave it my all. I can still remember Randys face in the process. He had a smirk on his face like he ain believe these guys was the real deal. Or, like Maybe I was doing this for nothing. Turns out, this was an audition. I was so excited about it. I was a little man with big dreams and big hopes.

The weekend is over, and we go back to Braintree. But with everything good comes something bad. When we get back, we go right into a different vibe. Before we left for the weekend, I was asked to do something, and I guess I didn't get it done. I was sitting on the floor watching tv. Uncle Keith was on the couch across from my aunt. She was braiding one of my little cousins' hair. At the same time, she was scolding me about whatever it was I didn't do. That somehow turned into some back and forth of words. Cause I admit, I sometimes could be a little bit of a sarcastic and mouthy kid. But it didn't last long. Just as soon as it started, it was over between us. She made her point. A couple of minutes passed, and then a commercial came on between the sitcom we were all watching. So I went to get up to go into the other room but came right back to finish the program that I was watching on the tv.

But my Uncle Keith, from the other couch, reading the newspaper, yells, "Sit down". It took me by surprise because he didn't say anything the whole time my aunt was setting me straight. So I said while standing there, "I'm going to get a piece of paper". He then throws the newspaper down and stands up fully agitated, saying, "You telling me you ain gonna sit down?" This was the moment I told myself that whatever got to happen, so be it. So I told him, "NO, I ain sitting down". He came over to me and grabbed me, and threw me to the floor. I think he thought that once he threw me down, I would stay there submissively to his size and authority. It must have taken him by surprise that I got back up again. That made him even more mad and now he is slinging me around the living room. I was mad and in rage. Because I knew I couldn't beat him up, and I was tired of feeling like I was being controlled in that house. I was the oldest kid in the house, and it felt like my responsibility was way too much for me to handle. The problem didn't go any further; that night. But everything happens for a reason. Even though I wasn't Extremely bruised and battered, I immediately thought this was probably a way out of this living situation. While all this was going on, my aunt did nothing. I just wanted out.

The next day was Monday, and all day while I was in school, I kept going back in forth in my mind about what had happened the night before and if I was going to go back to Braintree that night. Even the thought of the social worker telling me that if I ever ran away and went back to my mother's house, they would send the police to get me and then send me out to Cape Cod crossed my mind. But by the time I got out of school that day, I didn't care what that lady had to say. I went right back to my mother's house.

Later that day, just like I knew; my aunt pulled up at my mother's house and I was outside sitting on the back of a car. It was like I was waiting for her. She told me to go get my stuff. I told her, I'm not, and I'm not going back. She yelled at me some. But she eventually pulled off.

The next day, Randy came. At that time, Randy wasn't staying anywhere I wasn't. We ended up going to school every day that week. But of course, here comes our social worker with her annoying ass. She sat me down and told me straightforwardly. "You know you boys cannot stay here". I asked her why and she replied, "Because your mother is unfit to take care of you, and the courts have not said it was ok yet". No matter what she said, my mind was made up that I was not going back.

In my young life, I have already learned from my environment that mostly everybody I knew that ever wanted something out of their reach had to lie, cheat, and steal. Naturally, I never believed in any of that. But since they all had tactics to get whatever information they wanted from me, I adapted quickly and joined their tactical ways of gain. In the conversation, the caseworker goes on to say, "It's not safe here, and besides, your dad may come back just like he did before". It was like a bell went off in my head when she said that. I asked her, "If you took us from my mother because it wasn't safe, then why would you put us at my aunts house; It's no different?" Her demeanor changed, and then she got concerned in that direction. She, of course, asked me what I meant by that.

Now, Every relationship or marriage have problems. Some big and some small. So, My aunt and uncle would fight every now and then. But nothing to the magnitude of how my mom and dad did. So telling the caseworker about their little fights, I knew it wouldn't get me what I wanted. So I went on to tell the caseworker that, "With everything you know about my mom and dad, you don't have anything on record about them beating us, only about them beating each other. Well, my uncle beats me up, and he always finds reasons to beat us, all the time". I had come to realize that the whole sending us to "Cape Cod" was a bluff. So I even threw in, "If you gotta send us to the Cape, then I'd rather that than to go back to Braintree". But her comeback answer put me in my place quick. She said, "Well, the only thing about that is the situation in the Cape has changed, and we would have to split you and your brother up to do that". Just to hear her say that I started to cry. The caseworker started gathering her things and said, "Shannyn, I'm going to give you a responsibility".

She wrote down her personal number and gave it to me. She told me that if anything happens here while she tries to work this all out with the court and our lawyer, to please give her a call. I told her that I would. She hugged me and left.

Right then, It was confirmation to me that even if it was just for a moment, the liars, cheaters and thieves get what they want.

Years later, I found out that uncle Keith was upset about something else that day. He was under a lot of pressure. He had lost yet another job due to my brother having another fight at school. He was in the newspaper looking for another job that day.

He was hurt behind the accusations and it took years for him to forgive me. Because at the end of the day, Uncle Keith loved Randy and me as his own and has; since long before he had his own kids with aunt Breena.

Overall while we lived with them, he enjoyed having two boys he could pour into. He even had us in Tae-Kwon-Do classes to follow in his footsteps with his best friend and Master Sensei Rob Stevenson.

Not only did I apologize about it. I also thanked him for stepping in and doing his best with my brother and me. The lessons never seem to stop though. Because now I know that hurt people; hurt people.

My 5th-grade year is over, and it was a long time before we ever heard anything from our social worker, Malina. In fact, so long that we had no doubt that we'd ever hear from her again.

The summer has just begun, and we settled in and got quickly adjusted to the new neighborhood. I can still remember every car riding by that had a booming system playing NWA's N*ggaz4Life album. As that was the sound of the season.

This is where me and Randy started learning and becoming our own individual identities.

Along with his video games, Randy got interested in the neighborhood happenings. With his quick run with my older cousin Mook, a seed was planted. Randy was attracted to the life of hustlers. It was a must that he found out and knew who all the number 1 dealers were in the neighborhood. So he did. Randy was a smart kid. A real forward thinker. He used to take electronics and appliances apart piece by piece to see how it works and then put them back together for fun. But Randy knew when to speak, and most importantly, he knew when to be quiet.

But he didn't miss anything. One way or another, he was determined to be, Down. He noticed that all the dealers would scroll through the neighborhoods on bikes. When they got flat tires, he would tell them he would fix the flat for a fee. At the time, he didn't even know how to fix a flat tire. Before we knew it, our back porch was full of mountain bikes and parts. Among other stuff, they would get him to hide for them in the house. Because of his very laid-back demeanor and proof of loyalty and hustle, the Cape Verdeans gave him the nickname Chubbs. They looked out for him and had his back to the fullest. One time on a Sunday, he was out riding his baby blue Mongoose Mountain bike that he loved. He asked me to go with him to the next neighborhood over. He wanted to pick up a video game from a friend and didn't want to go alone. So I got on the back and went. When we got over there, it was like a ghost town. Nobody was out, which was unusual. As we were riding in the street, we saw some older guys we had never seen before on a bike just like we were coming in our direction. We didn't think anything of it. But as they got closer, I felt there might be some trouble. When they finally passed us, for a few seconds, I felt like we were clear of any drama. But, I was wrong. The guy on the back hopped off and ran behind us. He told us to get off the bike, and we told him no. He grabbed the handlebar and yanked it. We didn't care how big he was, we were ready to fight for the bike. But when he pulled out a pocket knife, flicked it open, and showed us that he was ready to use it, we backed off. The guy hopped on the blue mongoose bike and took off catching up to the other guy he was with. Just think, two young boys getting robbed at knifepoint. Randy was heartbroken, and so was I. I knew how much work he put into it. The bike made him feel like he was one of the big boys. We walked back over to our block, and when we got there, Randy told one of the guys that were out there what had happened with tears in his eyes. This was when I realized that my little brother was connected a little deeper than I thought. The guy he was talking to started to ask Randy all kinds of questions. As he was answering, everybody else got involved quickly. There was one guy out there that everybody respected the most, Fraydo. For some reason, he got the most upset about it. He started screaming and getting hype over the situation. Before we knew it, it was about 15 dudes out there learning about our problem. Fraydo says, "This lil'n*gga ain even bussin'nuts yet and n*ggas is pullin out shanks?" Fraydo then told everybody on the block to start walking, and that's what they did. He told Randy and me to show him where we were and point them out when we saw them. He said, "I want to catch these n*ggas myself". As we all was walking, the small posse expanded to about 25 guys. We finally caught up to the guys, but they ran. But unfortunately for them, everybody knew who they were. Maybe it wasn't for us to know what happened to those guys from that point on. But the next day, somebody rang our first-floor bell and left two new mountain bikes in front of our door. When I think back on this, I realize that the thought of calling the police never crossed me or my brother's mind. Some people accept that you just have to take a loss in some cases. Well, my brother wasn't those people. He revealed to me that day what street justice and protection looks like.

— My First Time —

I finally got called back by "The DJ" and his partner. I was super excited about it. They told my mother that they wanted to start a boy band and make me the center of the project. But first, they wanted to get me some experience. Also, to make sure I was serious and really wanted to do this before they started investing their time and money. So they put me in a situation with another management team that was already rolling and had a group of their own. A girl band. They wanted me to do a feature on a song with them. They wanted me to rap and dance. I was all in. But we had one problem. I couldn't write raps. So they pulled in another kid that was about 14 at the time. He was a good MC, Scott. But we called him Scoe. We both had musical skills but had our weaknesses. So he began to teach me how to rap, and I taught him some dance moves. Through this, we became good friends. Later, we ended up becoming the original members of a group. Later on, adding two more guys. But me and Scoe, we recorded our verses at somebody's home that had a studio set up. It wasn't the best situation, but I looked at the glass as always half full even then. So I gave it my all. Scoe laid a reference for me, and then I went behind him to replace what he did. The producer ended up liking the way it sounded with us both on the track, so he mixed us both together, and that was the first time I had ever heard my voice on a song. We didn't even know the girls that were singing on the song.

The session was over, and I remember getting a copy of the music on a cassette tape. I listened to that song every day until the next weekend that we were all scheduled to meet and have our first rehearsal for a big show coming up. Until then, I would keep rewinding and playing my part of the song over and over again. To hear my own voice over a beat quickly developed the urge to do another song.

It felt like forever for that week to pass.

We finally meet the girls. There were 4 of them, and they all could sing very good. Once we started practicing it became a never-ending thing. We practiced and practiced some more. Like every other day, I was getting picked up and dropped off at somebody's house for another rehearsal. This is how I spent my whole summer that year. I never got tired of it. I was committed to the idea that I would be somebody big out of this. But I was beginning to wonder what had happened to this big show we were supposed to do. Because for a while, all the adults stopped talking about it. It was like we were just going over what we knew already. Then one day, while we were all taking a break from practice. The girls' manager came in and told us all something that was both good and bad news for me. He told us that he was proud of us for working so hard. But now, it's time to put it all to the ultimate test. He said that he just got the date for our next show and it would be a month from now. One of the girls says, "Where daddy?" He replies, "Apollo, in Harlem, New York". Everybody jumps up, screams and hugs out of excitement.

But right then at that moment, secretly, is where I learned that I had a slight case of stage fright. Some people fear what they don't know, but in this case. I most definitely feared what I knew. I used to sit up on Saturday nights until 3 or 4 in the morning just to watch the Apollo on tv every weekend. So I knew that if the crowd didn't like you, they were in their rights to rudely boo you until you either left the stage or a dancing clown would come out and sweep you off. The images in my mind of that made me practice even harder. As the summer was coming to an end and the weather was getting cooler. The time is fast approaching for the show. Weeks before, the managers of the girls rented a charter bus and told us all to get as many people as we could to go to New York to support what we were doing. I told my mother, and she told everybody she could. But nobody was interested. But I did get two people that I could always count on to go, and that always supported my dreams, my two older God-Sisters, Pam & Venus. Between them, my mother and brother, that's all the support I needed.

The night before we got on the bus for New York, my mother fried some chicken and made sandwiches to take for the ride. But that night, I couldn't sleep. I was up late thinking about all kinds of possibilities that could happen. Some thoughts were positive, and others that were worse case. I remember the butterfly feeling that wouldn't go away all night. Then I remembered something that I heard an entertainer say on tv about being nervous before a show. "Nerves before a show is normal. Even the best entertainers in the world get butterflies before performances". This was something that I thought about most of the ride over to New York. But I was ready in the back of my mind, and I knew this was what I wanted. There was a moment on the bus when I turned to my mother and said, "Now that I'm going to be famous, when is somebody going to ask me for my autograph?"

Going to the Apollo was a big deal for me when I was a kid. Until then, I didn't know anyone who had ever made it to that stage from where I was from. So I thought that was the beginning of celebrity status. Because after all, the show did come on tv.

Although my mother had a big problem with her addiction. She never deliberately allowed me to think that my dreams weren't possible. She said, "They will come, but don't worry about that right now. You just get on that stage and show off tonight". I told her I was going to "rock it". Then I fell asleep.

We get to New York City, and this is my first time. I loved it. To me, it was just like Boston, But way bigger and way more people. With all the skyscrapers, New York Cities skyline was breathtaking. I immediately understood why they call it the city that never sleeps. How could they? Every nook and cranny of the city was alive. Not only was it busy, but it was also very fast-paced, a hustler's playground. Like Roxbury on steroids. But I loved the energy.

We get to the Theater for soundcheck. I was in total awe. I had what they called an "old soul" and couldn't help but think that I will be performing on the same stage as Michael Jackson, The Temptations, James Brown, The O'Jays, and countless others that my dad had in his collection I listened too. There were some other kids there that would perform too that night. One act, in particular, stood out because they were twin brothers, and they Tap Danced. They were really good.

After soundcheck, we had a little time to hang out before showtime. So my mother took my brother and me out to walk the city. We were all over Harlem. Pam & Venus disappeared on us. But that's not out of the usual for them. They could always handle their own no matter where they go. You know, some real "Rose from the concrete" type chicks. We stopped at a pizza shop and got a few slices of New York Pizza to eat. The biggest slices I've ever seen. While we were there, my mother said she had a surprise for us when we got back to the theater. We couldn't figure out what it might've been. We tried to get her to tell us, but she wouldn't. In the meantime, we ended up shopping along 125th street in Harlem. In New York, everybody had a hustle. With everything that I have been through and seen in my life so far up to that point. I saw something there that I have never seen back home. Back home, crack was a drug addiction held by the grown-ups. But never have I seen a kid the same age as me walking the street with a crack pipe in his hand looking for his next hit. To see that was a lesson in itself.

No matter how bad you think your life is, there is always somebody doing much worse.

Until this day I hated that at seen that kid. Because for a long time I wondered how his story would end.

It's getting closer to showtime. So my mom started to get me back to the theater. When we got back, Pam & Venus were high as hell. They were ready for the show and were hyping me up, wishing me well, and to do a great job. They asked if I was scared and I told them I just didn't want to get boo'd. They reassured me that nobody was going to boo us because they were there and would make the crowd scream for us even more. I believed them. As I'm talking to them, my mother taps me on the shoulder and tells me to turn around. When I did, it was my mom's real dad, my grandfather. He still lived just through the tunnel over in Newark, NJ. At that time, my mother and him still didn't have the greatest of relationship, so I was surprised to see him. Having that kind of support was important. It gave me more confidence to do what I came to do. But now that I had seen my grandfather and he wished me well, I was really ready now. I leave them to go backstage to get with the rest of the crew to start a mini rehearsal. I realized that the same nerves and butterflies that I had started to shine through on everybody else.

It was like the more I seen their nerves revealing the more mine went away. But Scoe, as always, was calm, cool, and collected. His personality always made me wonder if he was like that because his dad raised him.

I was a curious kid that watched everything and everybody. I started to notice that the closer we got to show time, backstage started to come alive more and more. All the other acts began to get dressed and rehearse. A lot of "Momagers" cussing out their kids and jacking them up. Even one kid from down south dropped out of the show altogether because her stage fright and anxiety were through the roof. The people who worked there were hardcore and very straightforward with everybody. Every rule they gave you led to a disqualification if you broke them. But what I didn't like the most, waiting. And don't even ask how long before you go on because nobody ever seems to know. In a setting like this, the worse thing you could do is watch the monitor of the live show happening while you wait. Because that same competitor that you were just talking to seems to have all the confidence in the world and their act well-rehearsed; still just might get Boo'd off the stage. As you can already hear the dancing clown music from a failed performance. To actually see it would definitely wreck your nerves. You have to remember that this is New York and the Apollo is just something else for the townies to do for the night. Booing people just cause is a normal thing to do for them. This is why they say, "If you can make it in New York, You can make it anywhere in the world".

One of the stage managers of the show came down to the dressing room and yelled out, "10 minutes to show time," and then the timer on the wall starts counting down from 10 minutes to the show start. Everybody got excited all over again and started moving around. You can also see on the monitor that the house was already packed.

The choreographer of the girl band I was with told us to run through the routine a couple more times. As we started to gather ourselves, there was a scream from up the stairs and then a big commotion. Not a violent commotion, but the type that said somebody important was up there. For some reason, the person that came to my mind was LL Cool J. Maybe because he was my favorite rapper at that time, and I knew he was from New York, wishful thinking. So all of a sudden, the ruckus started to come downstairs where we were in the dressing room. First through the door was an oversized guy whose head almost touched the ceiling. He overlooked the room with a mean mug as if he was looking for somebody in particular. Then some beautiful girls stepped in. Everybody in the dressing room stopped what they were doing and began to turn their attention toward the door. The voice coming down the stairwell became familiar, but I couldn't figure out who it was. I don't think anyone else did either. Then through the door was the new big-time actor on the scene who just came out with one of the biggest movies of that year. It was none other than Wesley Snipes. He played the main character in the movie "New Jack City". Everybody in the dressing room started a frenzy. But what comes out of his mouth next totally tripped me all the way out. He says, "Wheres Shannyn at? I need to see him"? Out my mouth come, "Oh Snap, It's Nino". Because to be honest, He played that role so well that I didn't even know his real name at the time. He walks over to me and gives me a firm handshake. I was a star-struck kid. This was the first movie star I have ever seen in person. My first question I asked him was, "How did he know my name". He squatted down to my height and told me, "Everybody is out there waiting for you to perform, so I had to come to meet who this kid was". Really I didn't believe it, but I accepted that as the truth. My very next question was, "Can I get your autograph?" With all the cameras flashing he says, "Not until you give me your autograph first, lil'man". And just like that, not only is he the first movie star I have ever seen in person, but the first person to ever ask me for my autograph. Out of the blue comes a little notepad and a pen, and I signed my name on it. Then in return, he did the same. Before he walked off and went back up, he gave me some well wishes for my future. This was a moment that I have never forgotten and one reason I started to take my craft so serious at a young age.

Finally it's our turn to hit the stage. It got real when I saw the Lucky Rubbing Tree block. They must keep it locked away because it wasn't on the stage at soundcheck. The girls went out first and started the routine off, and they did just what we rehearsed. But at first, they were getting a mediocre response from the crowd. But at least they weren't getting boo'd. Then in the middle of the song, it was time for me and Scoe to go out from stage left & stage right. When we stepped out onto the stage with our raps the audience erupted in a way that I was not expecting at all. Nothing but cheers and chants. The energy was amazing. Nothing that I have ever felt before. A new love. Trapped in the idea that I will be a star one day. At the end of the night, we came in 2nd place. The Tap Dancing twin brother won it all that night.

The manager of the girls was upset about where we placed in the competition. But overall, I was pleased. On the way back home, I couldn't even sleep because I couldn't stop replaying my experience on the stage.

Years later, I was told the story about how "Nino Brown" knew my name. Thanks, mom!

The new school year began, and I entered the 6th grade at the Grover Cleveland Middle School in Fields Corner. I knew a few familiar faces but didn't have many friends at all. Maybe it was good that I didn't because this school was considered a school where many bad kids attended. But at that time in the city, most of the Boston Public Schools were. This school year was the year that I was changing. Literally. I started growing hair on my body in places I never had before. New physical changes and the feeling of concern about how I looked and appeared to my friends and; girls. I was coming through the stages of puberty. My attraction to girls got intense, but I had an issue that most boys I knew didn't have. I didn't have any game on talking to a girl I liked. Because although I wanted to be a star. I was more shy than people actually knew. So I would love to get around my older cousins and friends. I was always trying to learn the lingo and their methods to attract the ladies. I learned quickly that everybody had their own unique way. But I think the best advice that I got when it comes to girls that I still carry with me today came from another one of my uncles. Uncle Luke. He was a heavy drinker but that didn't stop the lesson. I told him that I had a crush on a girl and that she might have been a little out of my league. He told me straightforwardly, "Go get her". I told him that I didn't know what to say to her and I don't think she likes me. He said, "Then how you gon'know if you don't talk to her". He took another sip from his Gin bottle and said, "Boy, the worse thang a woman could ever say is no, and that's it. It won't kill you. But at least then you'd know". I thought about that for a while. I let his words become the foundation to say something to her the next time I saw her. When I did, I already kind of knew it wasn't going to go well. Because her resting face said, "Eew" all over it from the time I approached her and started talking. Then me with my anxiousness and nervous stumble of words told her flat out, that I liked her. She didn't say anything. She just stared at me. So I asked her, "Do you like me back?" Her answer chewed my frail little confidence up. Without any hesitation she said, "No". Uncle Luke was right, a "no" is the worse. So to play it off and ease that long dry swallow of rejection. I just vocally assumed, "Oh' cause you got a boyfriend already". She says, "No, because you're a bum, and why you wear a trench coat. You're the only kid that where's a trench coat". She walked away, leaving me standing there while laughing at me. Paralyzing my drive to hunt for what I like and want. This led me to believe that I should only date who pursues me. Leaving the little confidence that I had handicapped. It was easy to do. I was already a traumatized kid. It was just something else to throw in my bucket.

— Designer Bagged —

My mother and Andrea are now tighter than ever. Andrea even moved in with us. They got into a routine of going out a lot. They would leave early in the morning and come back late at night. But when they came, they had money. Not the kind of money that my mother used to get when she was dealing drugs. But enough for them to shop, get high and now give me and my brother some cash to get lost. Or as my mother would say, "Find something to do". Every time they went out, They would come back with all kinds of Shopping bags. Andrea was a big woman, but she dressed very upscale. But she only wore dresses. When my mother would go out with her, she would get dressed the same. My mother told us to get up one Sunday and get dressed to go out with her and Andrea. So we did. Because we knew their routine, we also knew that it would just be another boring Sunday sitting around the house all day. Usually, they would leave on the bus. But on this day they had somebody's car. I don't know whose car it was. But without a license, my mother was driving. We stopped to get something to eat, and then we got on the highway out to the Natick Mall. We get in the mall, and my mother sends us to one of the toy stores, and that's where we stayed most of the time. Every now and then, My mother or Andrea would come to the store to check up on us. But every time they did, they'd have more shopping bags than they had from the previous check-in. This is how I remembered them coming home on the days they would go out. So right before we left the mall, Andrea said she wanted to go to one more store. So we all went. When we got to the store's threshold, all the detectors went off. Of course, all the eyes and attention came towards the store's front entrance at us all walking in. Andrea held her hand up and said out loud, "Don't worry, It's me, this happens all the time". All in the same motion, she is walking towards a lady working there dressing up a mannequin. When she got up on the woman, Andrea opens up her big pocketbook, shows the woman what's inside it, and says, "This is always embarrassing". She explains to the woman how she had knee surgery a few years back, and she has Metal pins in her legs, and if she'd like, she would show the woman her doctor's documents as proof. The store lady said, "Don't worry sweetie, you don't have to explain". The lady told the security that it was a false alarm, and they walked off. Andrea went on to pick up a few shirts and other clothing and went into the dressing room to try them on.

We must have been in the store for about 10 to 12 minutes before she said they didn't have anything that fit her and she was ready to leave. So we all started walking back towards the door. As we were walking, she got the store workers attention and raised up her hand one last time saying, "Hey, I just want to let you all know that I'm leaving. Sorry about making your detectors go off, Have a good day," and we were gone. We got back to the car and right onto the highway. In the front seat, smooth ass Andrea pulls up her dress and pulls 6 thousand dollars worth of brand named clothes from under it. Me and Randy looked at each other with our eyes stretched and mouths wide. We all started laughing, but it quickly got quiet. It stayed that way all the way back home. We were riding with the real Thelma and Louise.

I was far from a naive kid, so I knew they didn't have that much money considering the bougie-expensive department and boutique stores they were shopping in. But because I knew of a lot of people doing credit card scams at that time, that's as far as I thought was going on. But at Sidewalk University, the courses were advanced. That was the day I found out what Andrea's hustle was.

Another slick-talking, quick walking, booster. A Robin Hood for the fashionista's of the street, she had clientele and everything. I remember all the dope boys and prostitutes used to wait for her on Hancock Street to get off the bus with all her bags. She would tell them all to wait while she came in the house and set up her vendor-type display. She would leave the price tags on everything just so they'd know the real price of the items and would understand her charges.

Me and Randy had soaked up the sticky finger skill. But this wasn't for me at all. Years before this, there was a moment when I went with a few boys into a corner store to steal some chips and candy. We all grabbed a couple of bags and ran out. I was expecting the store man to come chasing behind us. But he didn't. Something came over me while we were running. I stopped and let the boys I was with run on. I turned around, went back into the store, and placed the chips back on the rack. The Spanish man said, "I should call the police on you". I just stood there and stared at him like a deer in headlights. I wanted to ask him, "Are you?" But nothing came out of my mouth. He leaned over the counter and told me, "A thief is the worse kind of criminal. People work hard for what they want, and here comes you to steal it. Be anything, but don't be a thief". He then told me that they were mine since I already took the chips. "Take the bag, but don't come back until you have money". I grabbed the bag and took off. I carry what that man said to me until this day. Not all hood lessons are bad. But after I knew what those day trips were about, I always stayed home. But Randy had been going out with my mom and Andrea quite often. Quickly, he became a pro.

He would come home with all kinds of name-brand clothes. In fact, he kept both of us fly for a whole school year. I can't say that he was easily influenced by anything. But he had a lot of heart for the schemes. Sometimes you can just tell what a kid might turn out to be in life. And Randy always made me feel like he would be some type of Kingpin. Maybe.

Andrea went missing, but this isn't unusual. She does that from time to time. When she was missing, Randy and my mother had begun going on "day trips" alone, with or without Andrea. Survival meant, by any means necessary.

A man comes to the door one day with a little boy. He asks if my mother is home. I told him to hold on and went to get her. When she got to the door, she seemed to know him as if he was familiar but not that good. She asked him what he wanted, and he told her that he wanted to ask her something. He came off a little shook and nervous. He was a square for sure. She told him to come in. When he did, she directed him to the living room. I had never seen the guy before, so I wanted to know what was up for myself. So I started eavesdropping from the other room. He tells her that he hopes he is not offending her by what he wants to ask her. She told him to say what he had to say because he is here now. With the streets always watching, the man makes his spill and says, "I understand that you and the big lady know how to get clothes and sell them". She told him, "Yeah, so what's up?" He told her that he had a significant amount of money to pay if she could get some name-brand clothes for his kids. He then pulled out a wad of cash and asked her if she could do it today. By the end of the conversation, she agreed. The man goes back outside with his son, sits in the car, and waits. She then started to get herself ready. While she was throwing on her clothes she told us that she was about to go to the malls. Randy immediately began to throw on his clothes too. He turns to me and asked if I wanted to go. My first thought was to say no but on this day, I jumped up at the last minute and threw on my shoes and jacket. I went too. We get in the car with the guy and his little boy, and we pull off. Once we got to the mall, the guy took his son and went in his own direction. We began picking up and moving. It was smooth sailing. We had no care in the world for a while as to what we was doing. Up and down the escalators, from store to store and end to end of the mall, we were getting it in. Then after about 2hrs of drilling, a suspicious vibe came over me. Kind of like that feeling that I had at that corner store. I didn't necessarily want to put the stuff that I stole back, but more so, the feeling that there was no way nobody can see how careless we are moving in and out of the stores. My mother had even separated from us and went her own way. My brother had gotten into a mode that I've never seen and teaching me the ropes. But I was totally over it and ready to go. After I grabbed my last item, I bought a pair of Guess jeans that I just broke the security tag off of. I rolled it up and stuffed it in the sleeve of my jacket. I looked at the clock on the wall of the store, and it was time to meet back up with my mother.

I then told my brother, let's go and began to walk toward the doorway of Macy's. Randy must have caught something that I didn't and told me not to go the way I was heading and follow him. I did. He led us toward the doorway with an escalator right outside the door. As we got on the escalator, two white guys were coming up the escalator in the wrong direction towards us. When we met in the middle of the moving stairs, we tried to pass them. They barricaded us. When I looked up at their excited faces, I knew they were some type of cops. We were busted. When we got down to the bottom of the escalator, the cop asked us where's the lady we were with. Our answer, "What lady?" They brought us to the back of one of the stores where they had a security office set up. Little did we know, we were shoplifting right in front of it. One of the officers was really hardcore and racist. He would ask us questions, and right when we would give some type of answer, he would cut us off with his answer. Too bad he was right about most. He asked, "Where you guys from?" Right when we were about to say something, he would jump right in and say something like, "Let me guess, Roxbury, Dorchester, Mattapan, I'm so sick of all you crackheads and poor gang members coming out here, keep that sh*t in your own dirty neighborhood". Then, "Wheres your dad?" Once again, before we could answer, he said, "Let me guess, some-where locked up, don't care about you or just left you; Just like your mother is doing right now, look". He then pointed at the monitor where my mother was on camera leaving the mall. But me and Randy knew better than that. I told the mall cop, "She wouldn't leave us," and from there, we stopped talking. The more we didn't talk, the angrier they got and started calling us all kinds of racist slurs. But we were used to this type of energy. 5 or 10 minutes went by before we saw my mother reappear on the monitors coming back into the mall looking for us. By then, the Burlington Police got there. When my mother came into the back where we were, the first thing she did was look at us and apologize to us.

The mall cop asked her if she was responsible for us, and she said she was. Then the

Burlington Police Officer pulled out his handcuffs to place her under arrest. She turned to the Officer and asked him to wait until we left out. She didn't want us to see her get cuffed and placed under arrest. Luckily, the officer was understanding and said OK.

As me and my brother was walking out, we turned and gave my mother a hug and kiss. The mall cop escorted us out along with the guy and his son back to the car. He then drove us back to the house without saying a word to us. When we got out, he gave us $40 and pulled off. We had never seen him again.

This was the first time I ever intentionally went on a "day trip" and it was my last. I thought I was the bad luck piece that made that day end the way it did for a long time. Still, I don't know if I was. But later, my mother told us that the man we went out to the mall with was part of the downfall. Because he gave my mother half of the money upfront, he was scared she would run off with it. So he followed her around the mall with his son. I even remember the little boy being very hyper and loud. While she was doing what she was doing, the little boy saw her. When they were walking out of one of the stores, the little boy screamed out, "ooooooh papa, your friend is stealing". Somebody in the store overheard that, and of course, blew a whistle.

I hate to say it, but the social worker and the family were right. My mother wasn't exactly ready to regain custody of us. In fact, she never did. We were just as hardheaded as she was and followed suit by not following the court orders either.

— Tough Days —

In school, I wasn't doing so well. I was failing 60% of my classes. Except, Mr. Stevenson's classes. He was a Brooklyn, NY native who had overcome some life struggles. He always had some type of testimony to tell. He taught social studies and math. I was really into social studies, though. He had a way of teaching it that made me understand. That class sparked my interest to want to see the world. Along with gym and theater, that was all that my mind could take in at the time. I knew I was a smart kid, but I had so many mental blocks that would sidetrack my attention. It didn't help that I was a daydreamer on top of that. There were a few kids in my homeroom class that were cool. But I still was kind of shy and pretty much stayed to myself. Just when I thought I was a nobody, here comes a girl who had seen me sitting in the cafeteria at a table by myself. She was a pretty 7th grader. She boldly walks over to me and asks me my name. She then told me her name. She sat down next to me and started to talk to me as if we had known each other for a long time. She was up on everything and knew just about everybody in the school. From the beginning, she was nice to me and never changed. I couldn't tell what it was exactly that was going on with her in her personal life. But I connected with her in a way that I knew her home life was no better than mine. But she covered it up very well. So did I. I felt like she could detect my broken spirit just like I did with her. But we were just kids and didn't know how to bring it up. Some things that maybe should be said sometimes speak the loudest when you stay silent. I used to look for her at lunchtime every day. But towards the end of the school year, she just stopped coming altogether. Even though it crossed my mind, It wasn't easy to believe that she had dropped out. She was too full of life. But on campus, you never know what people are going through. It was a long time before I saw Leah again.

The Grover Cleveland Middle School was just one of the four middle schools I went to, and here is where I learned that being a loner can sometimes attract wolves. Because I was always by myself, I was picked out as being weak. So I had been getting bullied by a local crew. Some of the members also went to school there. One day after school we were dismissed. I came out of the building with a class-mate, and we were walking toward the train station across the street from the school. Out of nowhere, there was a big commotion coming from a crowd in the middle of the street. Then I noticed the crowd was moving in my direction. As I'm looking for where the crowd is going and what seems to be a fight, the commotion stops, and all of a sudden, the attention is on me. A dude pops out of the crowd that I had never seen before, and he was in rage. I was in shock. He wasn't even a student at the school. I asked him what the situation was all about, but he never gave me an answer. Even then, there was a creed I lived by. If you touch me, we fight, but if you can't tell me why, I would try to avoid the scuffle. Before I knew it, this kid obviously had a hyper-growth spurt. He was an 8th grader and a gentle giant. He always dressed fly for a big kid, and you never saw him without his headphones on blasting his music. Everybody knew and respected him. I used to see him in the neighborhood on Hancock Street all the time. But we never spoke. Big Malik, out of nowhere, steps in between me and the other dude. He pushed him back and told him to stop starting trouble. The dude made a few more attempts to make this fight happen but eventually walked off with all kinds of threats and promises. Everything happened so fast. But the kid that was walking with me never left my side. He was ready to fight along with me if it came down to it. All the kids that were out there instigating the fight became disappointed that they didn't get to see any action. They began following me and throwing things at me, all the way into the Fields Corner Bus and Train Station. Once I got on the #17 bus, they started throwing objects at it until the bus pulled off. After this day, I was marked as the kid to pick on even more. It was bad enough that my home life was full of emotional and mental drama, and now this. I started hating going to school. It got to a point where I would do something in the school day to make the teachers give me detention just to avoid the busy dismissal bell.

Because of the mindset of my older cousins, I knew I could have made that problem go away. But I knew that this would just make it an ongoing issue. Until this day I never knew what that beef was all about. But over the years I would see that guy from time to time around the city; and every time he had that same energy.

Overall, my mom and I thought it would be best that I got pulled out of that school. That's what I was hoping for. So that's what happened. They transferred me to a school out in Charlestown, The Edwards Middle School. I wasn't there that long. Because the school year was ending soon. I didn't know anybody there, and there were a lot of white kids. To me, the school seemed to be more stiff. Like a military school. It was quiet all the time. No distractions that concerned me, no kids running in the halls during class time, and I didn't see any fights. The coast is clear. So now I have a new problem. I couldn't stay awake. I was literally going to school to go to sleep. I found the peace that I was looking for. But now, I can't academically relate to the advanced education curriculum. That school made me feel like I was stupid or had a learning disability. I admit it was at a better school. But, now I feel out of place; and not one teacher that I could relate to like a Mr. Stevenson.

I learned that I should have been more careful of what I asked for. Because you just might get it. But there will always be an obstacle to overcome or something you have to give up to keep it. From that moment on I knew that uncomfortable times meant it was either time to fight or move on.

As the summer was coming around again, we got word that my grandmother was moving back to Boston. The whole family was happy about that. Before she did, uncle Bryce had moved back two years before. I don't know what happened to him while in Florida, but he came back a different person. He had got in trouble with the law. That quickly became normal for him. My grandmother, in just a blink of an eye, went from living in Florida's paradise to right back into the pits of family drama. Uncle Bryce eventually got himself caught up in a robbery case and was sentenced to 4 years in prison. That broke my grandmother's heart but of course, she never left his side.

Ma ended up staying with my aunt Nellie in Hyde Park. My aunt Nellie's place became the family's new meet-up place for almost every occasion especially because that's where Ma was. When my brother and I would stay the night over there. My grandmother and Frank use to take us with them to visit my uncle in jail. I remember the first time we went. We would ride far out somewhere in the countryside of Massachusetts. To me, it was like a campsite. They even had a pond. They had a check-in desk and all kinds of shady-looking guards. My grandmother's boyfriend, Frank never went in. He would always sit in the car in the parking lot and patiently wait while listening to his down home blues and smoking his cigars. Every time we'd go visit my uncle Bryce, my grandmother would bring him groceries and those guards would ravage through those bags like it was a gift from Santa. I remember being pat-down and the guards giving us the rules of the visiting ground. From standing inside of the check-in house we could see uncle Bryce standing behind the boundary line, waiting. When we got the release to go out the door, Randy and I would run over to him and show him big love. I'm sure he appreciated it, but his demeanor always seemed emotionless. He always had a sad vibe. He had changed a lot while he was locked down. I always thought it was because my Aunt Carmen divorced him while he was locked up and had moved on. Sometimes when we would visit him, I thought he didn't want us to come. For the most part, because I felt like he didn't want us to see him in that way. And maybe even a little ashamed of himself.

But what he didn't know is that I already knew why he was locked up. I overheard my grandmother telling someone over the phone about the situation. Two white girls from South Boston that my uncle had known claimed that he robbed them. But in actuality, they had sold him their jewelry and went and bought dope with the money. One of the girls was married to a Boston Police Officer. When her husband asked her where is the jewelry he bought her, she brought the attention on my uncle as a stickup man. My uncle was then arrested for strong arm robbery. All because the woman didn't want her cop husband to know she had an addiction. Out of all the things my uncle got away with over the years, he is sent to prison for something that he didn't do. He was a real one, though. He took that time on the chin and never blamed anyone or looked for anybody outside my grandmother to help him. I learned 2 things from my uncle in this time. One: Karma will always catch up with you one way or another. You can't outrun it and its never on your time. Some people acknowledge that Karma is very real, and others disregard it. But the science of life never lies. For every action, there is an equal and opposite reaction. Two: If you can't do the time, then don't do the crime.

Just when I was getting use to living off Hancock Street. Damn, It was time to move, Again. The landlord told my mother that he had sold the house, and even his family who lived in the building had to move.

So my mother began the process of searching for a new place. Since we liked that neighborhood. We were hoping that we could move somewhere close to it. We didn't want to lose contact with the people we came to get so familiar with. The whole neighborhood was a vibe. You had your hard-working 9-5 people. Nobody ever messed with them. We even had a cable guy that lived in the basement that used to run us free cable. We had all the channels, from HBO & BET to Showtime & Playboy. You had your drug dealers, but most of them were well-spoken and looked out for everybody. One night a man tried to rob my mom in front of our door and told her that he would kill her, me and my brother if she didn't give him her money. She recognized the man and told the neighborhood guys. The next day; they caught him and brought him back to our front door. When my mother confirmed it was the same guy. They beat that guy down and stomped him to sleep with their Timbaland boots on. We never saw that guy again. In our neighborhood, there were also Pimps and Hoes. One pimp lived in an apartment with his hoes. Even his sister worked for him. The Sub shop seemed like it never closed. Which served the best chicken parmigiana sub. Three streets of friends that were down for whatever every Saturday morning. But what I was going to miss the most was the non-stop action that the neighborhood couldn't seem to cease.

Something was always going on, and everybody had each other's back.

About two weeks before we moved, I was walking home. As I got closer to the neighborhood, I saw a few guys I knew on the corner. About four blocks from my street. I stopped and kicked it with them for a bit. One of the guys was a dealer. He must have been about 16 years old and very flashy with his gains. I usually just say what's up and keep going, but not on this night. I had only been standing out there for about 20 minutes, just joking and laughing with them before I noticed a car circling the block. Even as a kid, I always watched my surroundings. I hipped the guys to the car, and that was that. Before you know it, that same car pulls up to the curb smoothly. A man steps out of the car with a big triple fat goose coat on with an oversized hood with fur on the edges. Nobody made a move. It wasn't like the guy was frantic when he got out. He kind of came off like he knew somebody, and he was going to play a prank. But this was no prank. The guy pulls out a Glock and says, "If anybody run, I'm poppin you". Then he goes on to say, "Who got it? I know y'all n*ggaz got it out here," and started tapping everybody's pockets. The hooded robber then gets frustrated with one of the guys for not having any cash, so he slapped the boy in his throat. He ended up gasping for air on his knees alongside the fence. Meanwhile, I tried to fade into a slow starting power walk, and he yells, "Where you goin?" I just put my hands up and told him I was going home. The man then pointed the gun at me and asked, "They got you holding for them out here or something?" I had no reply, and he turned his attention to somebody else. I then ran off, and I ran all the way home. By the time I got home, my mind was changed. All of a sudden, moving didn't sound like such a bad idea.

— Windows Of Life & Death —

And the cycle gains momentum. Back to Roxbury we go, less than 5 miles away. We were close to our old neighborhood, yet so far away. We moved into a seven story building called the Haynes House. We moved on up just like the Jeffersons. But there was nothing deluxe about the life we continued to live there. We lived on the 7th floor—apartment 708. There were so many people who lived in that building.

Over 200 apartments that were altogether. But there was something about that place that I really loved; the windows. It was the best feature of the apartment. We lived at the back of the building. So our windows faced Downtown Boston. The windows soaked up the whole wall from left to right. The view was beautiful to me. I would sit in that window every chance I got—especially when the sun was going down. As the sun would fade into the background of the skyline of the city, the lights of all the buildings would get brighter until they became a night glow. The famous landmark "Citgo" sign would light the whole Fenway park area. That was always a sign that a Boston Red Sox game was going on. Sometimes The Prudential Building would have the lights turned on, orchestrating a shape or seasons greeting. I used to wonder how they did that. The John Hancock building is made of all glass, so the reflections and shadows of the other buildings around it were a sight to see. If I looked to the left out of the window, the Longwood Medical area was in view right past the Ruggles Orange line station. You could also see the Madison Park High School Football team practicing in the school season. I had an old soul. So I would light incense and turn on WRBB/88.9 at 7 pm and listen to them host and mix the best Reggae radio show of all time. Reggae music always took me to another place. I would even start gyrating and grinding my skinny body as the groove would catch me. Yea'mon! I would dream so big from that window. Letting my mind sink into it. Way beyond what I even thought was possible for a stressed-out poor kid from Roxbury.

As usual, my mother was either not home or locked up in her room with a few of her new crack addict friends that she quickly got acquainted with in the building. At this point, me and my brother are pretty much officially raising ourselves. While he was in our room playing a never-ending game of Nintendo, I was in the living room moving the furniture around to create Boston Garden's 7 point stage. My audience? The whole world that was outside of my window.

Since my dad left behind all of his Vinyl records, I would dig in the crates and pull out some oldies but goodies and play them on our old Panasonic record player. I had a whole concert sequence. But every night was a different singer or group I would imitate. I would start off with the old slower songs first. I would talk to my audience and imagine I'm getting all of the crowd's participation and interaction. It was either a candle or a remote control that I used as my microphone.

I would jump from the couch to the floor, left to right and back on top of the arms of the couch and end tables as if I was on top of a speaker entertaining. I was loud, and so was the music. And I didn't care. Totally disconnected from the matrix that was going on around me, I wasn't even there. Just lost in the zone. In my mind, I was somewhere in another city or country doing what I felt was right to me. I would do this until 1 or 2 o'clock in the morning. At least 3 times a week. As my mother and her guest came in and out of the front door all night, she never once told me to stop what I was doing. Nor did the neighbors ever complain about the live sold-out concerts going on over their heads.

All I ever wanted to be was a kid. A kid that lived a normal life and had a chance to be whatever I wanted to be.

I guess with all the practicing and dreaming, I put that energy out into the universe. Because I haven't heard from DJ Splyf and "the Manager" Ethan in a long time, since the Apollo show to be exact. They popped back up again. They both came over one night and said they wanted to talk to my mom and me. They told me that they saw me as a solo artist and booked some studio time on Newbury Street at Synchro Sound. They wanted me to do my own songs. Not only that, but they had just booked K-Solo and a new Rapper on the scene by the name of Redman. The Manager Ethan asked, "Do you think you could be ready in time to open the show?"

I told them I was more than ready. A few weeks later, I'm in the studio. Not just any studio, but a real Gold and Platinum hanging records on the wall studio. An SSL board, Thousands of buttons and lights, a 4 thousand dollar Microphone, and a soundproof recording booth with a window looking into the control room where everybody could sit and watch me. Reminding me of the view from my living room window. There was other artists there that day that I looked up to and took notes from. They were under the same umbrella that DJ Splyff and Ethan had. I was the youngest of the bunch.

That night I remember how anxious I was to do my song. I was a sponge that night, soaking it all up. About 10 pm, they called my name and said I'm up next. Everybody was hyping me up and just as excited as me. I go into the booth and get set to do what I've been rehearsing. Not one drop of doubt in my mind that I was about to have my first hit song. Then it happened. I went to say my first line of the song, and out of nowhere, puberty came through my vocal cords into the mic and played back through the headphones and into my ears. At first, I thought I was just nervous. But it was a moment that I had to come to grips with. By quickly understanding that I'm not little Shannyn anymore. I just didn't sound like me. My voice was cracking and projecting awkward and untimely horse sounds. I had developed that lump in my throat like I was about to cry. But I sucked it up. Thanks to DJ Splyff, he coached me through it.

Because he knew that LL Cool J was one of my favorite rappers, He told me to rap like I was covering, "Mama Said Knock You Out". I did my best. The name of the song I recorded that day was called: "I Had Enough". Overall, the song came out ok. I loved it anyway. Especially after it was mixed and touched up with some digital studio magic. It came to life.

I would put that song in the tape deck of our home stereo, and back to the window, I would go. Perfecting my craft. But as the show was getting closer. I started getting more ideas for my upcoming performance. So I told Ethan I think I needed dancers to help my show. His first response was, "No". He thought that would complicate my first solo performance by overwhelming me. I didn't argue or even put up a fight. Because my mind was already made up about it. I was determined to make it happen. So behind his back, I pulled together my female cousins to help me. At first, they didn't take me seriously. But my cousin Dionne reeled them in. They started coming over, and we began to put together the steps to back me up for the show. Everyone in the building started getting curious about what was going on in our apartment. Even the Muslim family across the street from the building I lived in let their daughter be a part of what I had going on.

Not only did it come together, but it came out to be a very professional-looking act. Just weeks before, I was imitating Jodeci, Perfect Gentlemen, and Another Bad Creation, in the middle of that living room all by myself. And now, I have my own song and my very own Fly Girls.

Finally, the day of the show is here. I was ready. My girls were ready. Me and my cousin Dionne even gave them a name. The show starts, and they introduce me with my new stage name, Shizzy B. & UA (Undivided Attention). The show was a success. We did very well. But, nothing ever came of it.

Even though there were a few good memories while living in that brown brick building. Those memories didn't hold a torch to the life that was really going on inside of the apartment. But whatever didn't kill me made me stronger. I had to adapt. The building we lived in was on a street between 2 Projects, Ruggles Street Projects, and the infamous Orchard Park Projects. Not forgetting that Lenox Street Projects was at the beginning of our 2-mile long street.

Every other apartment in our new building lived someone that was an addict of some type of substance. I remember feeling like I was living in some type of laboratory experiment. Like, what would happen to humans if you put them all in one big apartment building; Give them all access to crack and heroin and then wait to see what the results would be.

There was one lady that we'd see all the time in the neighborhood, usually in Dudley Square sitting on a bench or something. I used to think she lived on the street. She was about 45 years old and always wore a Scully cap and a long black jacket. I remember she had very long black Pocahontas-like hair. But later, I learned she also lived in our building. She was always drunk, and you could find her crying and talking to herself. Sometimes I would see her and her clothes would be wet from her urinating on herself. But when you looked at her in the face, you could tell that she was most likely a very attractive woman back in her younger years, and I couldn't help but think, what was her life like back then. What caused her to choose Sidewalk University. She had a daughter and a grandchild that would come once in a while to visit her. You could tell that her daughter loved her very much, and because she did, she wouldn't give up hope that her mom would get better from whatever had happened to her in her life. You could also tell that the woman's living conditions and depleted state of mind were breaking the woman's daughter's heart. She was always emotional, like she hated to see her mom in the condition she was in. But no matter how the daughter found her mom, she wasn't ashamed of her and would allow her mom to love on her and she would do the same. One day, I got on the elevator to check the mailbox for my mother's welfare check. The elevator stopped on the 3rd floor where the woman lived.

She got on. I said hi, but she didn't say anything back. It was early in the day, and she had a different look than her usual, being drunk. She just had a blank stare into the elevator floor buttons. It was like she wasn't even there. Her eyes were red and you could tell she was deteriorating fast; emotionally, mentally, physically, and spiritually. With everybody in the building being so busy and doing nothing simultaneously, I felt like somebody should have noticed this lady's condition. But they didn't. For some reason, I did. About 2 weeks later, all of us kids was out in the hallways of the building playing and chasing. We would go from one end of the building to the next. Down one back stairwell, and up another, from floor to floor of the building. Every time we would get to the 4th floor, we would smell a tremendous and intensely foul stench. To the point where even in our chase game we all agreed that the end of the hall on the 4th floor was off-limits. Every day for 3 days, the smell got worse. The evening of the third day, I was back in the elevator going down to the laundry room. All I was hoping was that the elevator didn't stop on the 4th floor. Because by this time, the smell had the whole floor engulfed, suffocating you because you didn't want to breathe whatever it was. As the elevator floor display counted down, it passed the 4th floor. But, to my surprise, it slowed down and stopped on the 3rd floor. The doors opened up, and standing there were 2 coroners with a dead body wrapped up in a body bag trying to get on the elevator with me. The smell on the 4th floor was nothing like the even more powerful scent that I experienced on the 3rd floor. I almost threw up from the smell. But, I stepped out of the elevator anyway. I didn't want to ride the elevator with a dead body. Come to find out, the woman had committed suicide in her apartment.

After that day, I don't remember anybody being sad. Nobody went to the woman's funeral—no moment of silence. Nobody sent condolences or even had a concern about the woman's daughter that everyone would see visit her. Just like those live testing vessels they use in laboratories. Failing the test could result in death, and nobody would care. Only the strong survive.

— Overheating —

Because of the new district we lived in, the Boston Public School system allowed another transfer of schools for me. This is the third middle school I went to, The Taft. Considering I was a grade ahead of Randy. We both reconnected and attended the school together. Taft Middle School was located in Brighton, just one town over from the birthplace of John F. Kennedy. A town that was an extension of the hood, but mostly caucasian townies. But it was a good school. If you missed the school bus, just hop on the #66 bus from Dudley Station in the hood, and it would drop you off in front of the school. The teachers were somewhat bougie, but you can tell most of them had adapted to the inner city kids that was bussed in that they had to teach. I learned a few things about myself that year at the Taft Middle School. One being that 7th-grade Algebra was a subject that told me I wasn't that smart. Not my strongest subject by a long shot. My god-sister Pam even gave up on tutoring me. I couldn't blame her. Another being that I wasn't accepted into the popular circle of the kids. Maybe because being a follower just wasn't my thing, and kissing ass just to fit in was out of the question. The 3rd was that I had an emotional and mental PSI. Meaning I would let everything that bothered me pile up. I would hold it until I'd explode. Overloaded from stress and life pressures. Situations that I couldn't change or even grasp the understanding of. A young broken pride that is screaming out as loud as I can for somebody to hear me. Yet, nobody does. An overwhelmed mind, and every day, it got more heavy. Spiritually being pulled in every direction, yet none proving to me that either way is the path to where I would know lack is dead. Just a kid with no sign of hope that everything would be ok. Not yet mature enough to even have the slightest thought that God just might have a plan. Constant and continuous disappointment has now turned into aggression. I'm now strong enough to punch complete holes in the sheetrock walls of the apartment and building. All it took was a "No" about something

138

I wanted, an unfulfilled promise or a bad grade on a test. In which a "C," on any graded school work was me doing my very best. Or, go outside and be outnumbered by the neighborhood future menaces lined up to test how tough I was by an unnecessary instigated fight. Outright trapped in a life that I didn't think I deserved. I really just wanted to be a good kid and entertain the world.

One day I went to school, and I was totally in my head. Thinking about way too much at one time. Tired of everything. Especially what had just happened at home in the past couple of days.

I go to my 2nd period class and I didn't even talk to my only friend in the school that year, Jamaican Alton. When I got to my seat, the teacher told the class to get ready for the test that she had been teaching a lesson on for a week now. There were 5 rows of 5 desks from the front to the back of the class. The teacher walked by and placed 5 copied sheets of the test on the first desk of each row. As usual the first person in the row would keep a copy and then pass the rest back until everyone in the row receives one. About 5 minutes go by and the teacher is ready to start the test. As I came out of a daydream, the teacher specifically asked if I was ready for the test because she didn't see a copy of the test in front of me. But then she quickly realized along with me that nobody on my row had a copy except for the kid in the first seat, Dez. Dez wasn't necessarily a bad kid, but was a product of his own environment. He also grew up in a gang-infested neighborhood in the South End and always portrayed as a gangster. But he was a follower. Smart too. But some days, he was cool, and other days depending on who he was around, he would switch up on you. He just thought he was a real badass.

It was his duty to have a problem with somebody every day. On this day, I asked him to pass the papers back, and he said, "Wait n*gga!" With already being agitated, I told him to hurry up. But it seemed like my demand provoked his childish ways. Dez began to purposely take his time until the teacher said, "Dez, you're holding up the class; pass the papers back so we can get started". Dez stood up and yelled at the teacher, "Damn, didn't you hear me say wait". I don't know what Dez was going through this day, but he then grabbed the papers and flings them in my face. This is the exact moment that I learned that pressure bursts pipes. I stood to my feet and viciously attacked him. The whole classroom started screaming and chanting. Most of them provoked me to go even harder because they didn't like him. I was hitting him with so much built-up rage, frustration, and force that I even began to think that the punishment didn't fit the crime. Especially after I realized that he was no match. Still, I dragged him from one side to the other of the classroom. Desks flipped over, papers everywhere, clothes ripped up, exhibits knocked over, just a total release and slaughter. It got so bad that teachers from the other classrooms had to come in and peel me off of him. I didn't want it to stop; beating the brakes off this boy.

They get us to the assistant principle's office, and Dez is bruised, swollen, and crying. Me, on the other hand, had a total feeling of relief. Unbothered by any of the expected consequences from his boys or the policy for fighting in school. The assistant principal Ms. Bolt was a black woman who you could tell was also from the hood but made a good life for herself. She was aware of the difference in characteristics and personalities of Dez and me. She asked us what happened, and I remember her chuckle as Dez was trying to explain. There was a look in her eye that I knew she was content with me getting the best of him. Because her and the rest of the faculty knew Dez to be a bit of a trouble maker and had a reputation of disrespecting the teachers. After we told her the breakdown of what led up to the fight, she split us up and placed us in two separate rooms with thin walls. She went on to call his mother first to let her know what had occurred. Since Dez was always in trouble, Ms. Bolt was more familiar with his mother. I remember hearing her tell Dez that she hated to call and disturb his mom where she worked in a city courthouse. I was shocked to learn that. Because he had a mom that would get up every day and work hard to provide for him, and he wanted to be something obviously he wasn't. Then she called my neighbor Ms. Jaunita's phone, who lived directly across the hall from us. We didn't have a house phone. So Ms. Jaunita had to go knock on our door. My mother gets to the phone, and Ms. Bolt tells her that I had just been in a fight. My mother immediately replies, "Oh'god, Is the other kid ok?" Ms. Bolt's face expression morphed, puzzled. She then asked my mother if she knew that I would be in a fight that day? My mother paused for a few seconds before she answered. Then she straightforwardly told her, "No, ...Not today. My mother went on to tell Ms. Bolt that I was a good kid, but I was under a lot of stress". Ms. Bolt asked her why and my mother flat out said, "Because of me". Ms. Bolt caught on really quickly as to the state of lifestyle I lived at home. She asked my mother if she wanted to speak to me, and she said, no. She went on to tell Ms. Bolt that whatever consequences you have set for fighting in school will be fine. She reassured Ms. Bolt that she wouldn't be having any more problems out of me. She never did. But honestly, after that, I sometimes wondered what life would have been like for Dez and me if we could have traded moms and lifestyles.

I didn't know this then, but I know now that my mother probably knew what was wrong with me that day. A week prior, my mother didn't come home for almost 2 days. In that time me and my brother had got hungry. Besides making sandwiches, hot dogs, and cold cereal; I had never tried to cook. Fortunately, we did have food in the house this time, but it had to be cooked. I got to a place in my mind where I was ready for the challenge. So ready that I knew exactly what I wanted to cook. But, there was one thing in the way. The Kitchen was so dirty and nasty that cooking was a mission impossible. So I just rolled up my sleeves and took it upon myself to clean it all up before I made my first attempt to cook a full meal. The floors was sticky and greasy from careless spills of drinks and food over time. The trash had piled up in the corner to the top of the doorway. The smell had become horrific. But as my first song said, "I had enough". Even though I was so angry about the condition of our new apartment, and what seemed like the least of anyone's concern. I just turned on the stereo and let the music blast to numb me out from the task at hand, and I got to it.

I began grabbing anything that didn't belong in the kitchen. Careless of the item's importance and throwing it all in trash bags. Because to me, if it was in that kitchen for as long as it has been condemned, it must haven't been that important. I started taking the trash down the hall on our floor to the incinerator to create space. When I got to the bottom of the mess, on the floor were maggots squirming. I grabbed the biggest pot we had and filled it with water. I cleared the stove of any debris and turned on the pot of water until it came to a boil. I then went to the closet and got all the cleaning supplies and products. I poured in some bleach and PinSol. Then I took the hot pot and poured it all over the floor. Believe it or not, that moment had motivated me to keep going. Because that immediately killed the smell, and somehow, seeing the gunk and stickiness bubbling and dissolving let me know that I wanted more out of life. So I scrubbed and cleaned for the next 4 hours, none stop. Randy even came into the kitchen a few times to see what I was doing. I remember him asking me, "Why you doing this; She supposed to do this, not you". I never gave him an answer. But I had one and just didn't say it. When I think about it now I realize that I just didn't know how to put it into words then. All I knew is I didn't want to sit in my own funk and become whatever life has thrown at me.

It's now 1 o'clock in the morning, and still, no sign of my mom. I have finally started and finished cooking. I have to say, I did a good job, and we ate until we were full. Just in case you're wondering what It was, I had imitated the cooking styles of the women in my family. So I had rinsed and singed an eight pack of Chicken wings. Seasoned them with the famous Lawry's and black pepper. Got a plastic shopping bag from under the kitchen sink and filled it with flour. Dumped the chicken wings in the bag and shook them up. Put some crisco in a pan and turn the fire on to medium until the grease was hot. Before I could even put a piece in, my adrenaline was pumping. I was scared of the grease popping on me. But I dropped a piece of chicken in the grease, and the sizzle began. I then quickly put the rest in. I put a lid over it and then began my instant mash potatoes and a little pot of peas.

Because I wanted my mother to see the work or good deed I did, I stayed up as long as I could. But after the day I had, I just turned off the lights and fell asleep on the living room couch.

My mother finally walked in the door about 4 am. Because it was dark, I couldn't tell who it was, but I knew she had someone. She made a quick scurry to her bedroom with her company. When I heard her door close, I just fell back to sleep. Later that morning, about 8am, I guess she realized the big difference in the house. She woke me up to questions about who I let in the house. I told her that nobody had come in, but a few people came looking for her. She went on to ask me, "Then who came and cleaned the house". I told her that it was me. She stared at me for a few seconds but never said anything. She just walked away. At that moment, I don't know if I was expecting a "Thank You," a pat on the head or a "Job well done". But from there, the feeling of caring less began to grow inside of me. That very night, my mom had even more guests over. She was so gone into her addiction that she didn't even realize that she hadn't had a conversation with us for almost 3 days, and we lived inside of a 950 square foot 2 bedroom apartment. But needless to say, the party continued.

The next day I went into the kitchen, and I saw used dishes back on the counter and in the sink, unclean. Something about that had broken me down inside. I suppressed it and became silent with no way to release my anger. Nobody even knew how loud I was screaming inside.

Thank God, I had my dads old record collection. That night I began to organize all 1500 of the vinyl records and put them into Alphabetical order. I had nothing to say to anyone for a few days straight. But Dez, he didn't know that.

— Last Chance —

There was one moment we lived in that building when I was really proud of my mom. It was me and Randy's birthday week. She didn't have any money. I don't know how she did it, but she figured out a way to give us a Birthday party. It wasn't an all-out extravagant party, but we had all party essentials music, food, some friends and dancing. Coming from her at that time, it was a glimmer of light for me.

Where usually I didn't invite friends from school to my house. One Friday after school I did. It was Alton. We had plans to meet with some girls who lived in my neighborhood from school. But I first wanted to drop off my school bag. When we got there, I told Alton to wait in the living room for me. He said, "Cool'mon". I knew my mom was home. But of course, she was in her room and had company. I wasn't in my room long at all. But when I went back to the living room, I noticed Alton was sitting on the couch right in front of a homemade crack pipe. It was one of the most embarrassing moments of my life. But my friend Alton never said anything.

You know how they say, "What you fear is what you bring the most energy to?" Well, this was one of the biggest reasons I never asked my friends to come visit. I just told him, let's go. I picked up the crack pipe and called for my mom to come out of her room. As my friend and I walked out of the door, I introduced her to him while simultaneously passing her the homemade pipe. From that point on, I was done being a victim.

Almost 3 months later, we got an unexpected early morning knock on the door. It was a bitter sweet day. While I was in love with my view from my window and more new friends in the building, I hated all the traffic coming in and out of our apartment along with the conditions we lived in.

The knocks became loud and rapid tight-fisted bangs on the door. It was urgent. I walked toward the door and said, "Hello ?" The voice on the other side was a man who said he was looking for my mother. It wasn't just any voice, but you know it's serious when it's a white man's voice at that time of morning. At first, I said that she wasn't there. Because that's what she told us to tell anyone that came to the door before she went to sleep. But the man became overly persistent. When he got tired of me giving him the run around he told me through the door, "It don't matter if your mother was there or not, I have a key, and if you don't open the door, I'm going to come in and complete my job". That threw me all the way off. I panicked and got frustrated trying to figure out what he meant by that. So I had no other choice but to run to my mother's room and wake her up. I told her that somebody was at the door and they needed to talk to her. Of course, she was upset with me in the moment. But she got up. I was thinking, who ever it was, they were about to get cussed out. She gets to the front door and snatches it open, and a crew of 6 men was standing out in the hallway. It was the Boston Housing Authority police and inspector. The BHA Representative held up a big yellow sign and told us that we are officially being physically evicted. My mother was stunned. But accepted it as No Surprise. She asked him if she could get them the money later that day, but the man told her she was 5 months too late and that wouldn't be possible at the time. The man wouldn't even let her close the door. The men walked in and, without wasting any time, started snatching up everything that wasn't bolted to the floor. I was once again totally devastated. I immediately suppressed what I was feeling in the moment and started helping the men bag up and move clothes and furniture. I remember making a trip down to the truck to put a load on. When I came out of the building, all my friends were outside. A girl that I had a crush on and even a couple of the boys who used to pick fights with me all the time. None of them said anything. I could tell by the look in their eyes that whatever beef we had was now squashed. I knew they all understood what was going on. I was crushed and embarrassed. Today I know that in that moment was one of the days I lost a big chunk of confidence in myself. Even though none of this was my fault, I felt beat down and defeated. That was the first day I ever had the slightest feeling of giving up on my mother. Like, the disappointment wasn't worth it. I didn't want to become like that girl whose love repeatedly got shattered by someone who couldn't love themselves. Even if its your own mother.

We had some decent furniture too, but the movers was tossing and throwing everything we owned like it was all trash. When I saw one of the movers aggressively put one of the speakers down, I told him, "Can you please not put that down so hard? I don't want it to break". He laughed and told me, "It don't matter cause if ya' moms don't have nowhere to put this sh*t, we taking it to the dumpster anyway". Quickly, I got back upstairs to my mother and asked her, "Where are we taking our stuff?" Out of shock about what was going on around her, she just told me that she didn't know. I was mad, but it wouldn't have made any difference to show it. So I became desperate and started shouting out all the places in my head where I thought we could take our stuff. Then one place that I said set off a light in her mind. My mother was a friend of a businessman who owned a few historical buildings and businesses in the Roxbury part of Boston. She met him one time while she was in Rehab. He owned the liquor store in Dudley, the same one my father used to work in when we were younger. On the first floor of the building was a Jamaican clothing store, A Chinese restaurant, The liquor store, and The neighborhood's favorite Spinelli's Sub shop. But upstairs over the storefronts was all abandoned and unused space. Since we couldn't afford storage. This was the place, all of our furniture, Record collection, pics, and memories were laid to rest. We never seen that stuff again.

CHAPTER 7

The Community Center

— Combustion —

Here we go again! My grandmother just moved out of the basement of my Aunt Nellie's house and into her own studio apartment in Mattapan. She's only been there for a couple of months now, and here we come with our sad sacks and bags. This is when I believe my grandmother had begun to give up on my mother and was more broken-hearted by her failing choice of life. Without any hesitation, my grandmother took us in. But the struggle was real. We weren't quite old enough to go out and get jobs to help out either. So thank God for Frank, my grandmother's longtime boyfriend. He really loved my grandmother and looked out for us all. Even though he didn't live there. The only furniture my grandmother had was her bed and a sofa. Everything else was neatly stacked to the side along the wall or in the corner, in boxes and bins. Even though we had a roof over our heads, we all kind of lived out of bags. Me and my brother would take turns sleeping on the sofa. The other would have to sleep on the floor. That's unless one of us lost a bet, and then it was a week on the floor for the loser.

We lived that way for about another six months. Once my grandmother realized that my mother wasn't immediately going to check herself in at Dimock Street rehab to get clean, and also knowing my dad's condition and situation, she made up in her mind that she was just going to raise us herself.

My grandmother only had a 6th grade education, and she still somehow landed a job at Tuft University Laboratory downtown Boston; In the Chinatown section. It was a good job. She loved it and they loved her there. There was a "No kids allowed" policy, but she got an exception for us through the head Dr/Scientist there that took a sincere understanding to the life and responsibility she had at home with us. They kept our names on a VIP-type list. Just in case we ever needed to go there in an emergency.

Me and my brother saw all kind of stuff up there. It was the first time I had seen a two-headed chicken. Or, a chicken being incubated outside of its shell. I would burn the doctor's ears off asking so many questions whenever an opportunity allowed it. I was always excited to go to Ma's job, but the worse part was getting to school every day. Not because I didn't like school. But because now we have to get up and commute from one end of the city back to Roxbury. Rain, sleet, shine, or snow; A dreadful 4:30 am alarm clock would torture us every morning. I hated that.

The first scheduled public transportation bus of the day. We was on it. Every day we got more familiar with the faces on our 28 bus route until they all got familiar with us and began to look out for me and Randy. Most of the time we would sit next to each other. That way, we could keep an eye on one another and everybody else too. We were very overprotective of each other. The buses were usually jam-packed from the front to the back. Everybody mixed in, from the local junkies and weirdo's to the hard working professionals of the city. I remember hearing 2 ladies talking about us. One of the ladies asked the other, saying, "Why are these 2 little boys on this bus so early in the morning?" Then the other would say, "I can only imagine...Mmm-Mmm- Mm...". There was also another lady who would wake us up whenever we caught the same bus from time to time. When we would get to Dudley station, and we were sleeping too hard, she would tap us and say, "Hey gentlemen, we're here. Have a good day"! I always thought she was like a school teacher or professional office worker, but I never knew her name.

Luckily for us, when we got back to the former building we lived in, The front desk African security lady would let us in the building against the eviction policy. She actually lived next door to us in the building too. We gave her, and her disabled daughter our living room set when we got kicked out.

We would go back to our old floor, and Ms. Jaunita would let us wait there at her apartment until it was time for us to get to the school bus stop. One morning I remember sitting there watching her smoke a cigarette while connected to an oxygen tank. As I'm staring at the tank with caution signs that say things like flammable and keep away from fire. I couldn't help but think, how many other people in this building were either dying slow or in a rush to end it quickly? Also, thinking that we could all blow up in this apartment at any time now. Those were long days. Another morning I couldn't help but notice the eviction notice that was still on our old apartment door, #708. I just stood there and stared at it. I was thinking; why every time we move from one place to another, it's always abrupt and unclear what's going to happen next?

Why is life giving me so many hurtful curveballs and disappointment? I made a decision that day. If I ever had kids, I would never let them live through anything like this. I will never give them an opportunity to feel pain and cry over anything that would disappoint them. I never cried over anything else that my parents were doing from that day forward. I fully accepted who my parents were and stopped expecting a change from them.

The following school year, we were transferred for the last time to the Woodrow Wilson Middle School in Dorchester. This was my last year of middle school. It was closer to where we lived. My grandmother had enough of us getting up that early and worrying all day about us being ok. At this point in our lives, underneath the mask; me and my brother were some stressed-out kids. Everything that we've been through had now started to show in our personalities. Even toward each other at times. Not forgetting to mention a spurt in our testosterone levels too. Knowing that there's nobody around us that we can take our frustrations out on, we had finally displayed traits of our upbringing and environment. We had turned our anger on each other.

As young brothers do, we would fight and argue about and over anything. But usually, That would be at home behind closed doors. This particular week, tensions were high. One day before school me and Randy got into a fight. Any other time, all of our frustration would be exhausted by the time we left out the door, and whatever the issue was, nobody remembered or even cared. Just went on with the day. But on this day, the anger lingered on to school. We had a 7th-period class schedule, and one of our classes was together. Even in school, everybody knew how close me and Randy was, including the teachers. Well, on this day, we ended up continuing our family feud in that class. One sarcastic smart-mouth remark led to a reply with the same energy that would cause the issue to escalate. Before we knew it, we were locked up in an all-out brawl. We were fighting each other like we saw our parents do. With raging force and malice. We gave that classroom a whole new seating arrangement. While doing so, the teacher is screaming at us to stop. Our friends were confused and didn't know whose side to take, and I remember one girl crying and saying, "But they're brothers". But we didn't care. We had to get it out.

Years of held back tears and unacknowledged fears. Built up anxiety and pressure that seem to never have a decompressing button when we needed it. But still we wasn't trouble makers. Up until that day, people had never seen us have that type of energy toward each other. In fact, the impression that we had on other kids and some adults that didn't really know us; was that we had a pretty normal and balanced life.

— Beginner Classes —

I have a very big family. But out of everyone, I didn't want to hang out with no other than my favorite cousins, Ski & Wiz. Every chance I got, I was at their house up to something. I even had sex for the first time there.

Ski was a little older than us, but he never minded us hanging out with him from time to time. When we did, It was a must that we figure out a way to get in trouble. Anything from weed to girls to random fights with other kids from their neighborhood and more. It was always something.

Ski seemed to know everybody, and even though he was a side street hustler, he always kept a job. Wiz, on the other hand, was my age. We were different in some ways but had some things in common. Wiz was the cousin that reflected back to me what I wasn't. But most importantly, who I was. We were respectfully competitive against each other. Like iron sharpens iron. But I have to admit, even with all my talents. Wiz had confidence that I didn't develop just yet. I didn't know that then. But overall, both Ski & Wiz always looked out for Randy and me.

One Saturday morning, while I was doing my chores. The house phone rang and my grandmother answered. It sounded like it was for her. But about 30 seconds later, she called my name and told me to pick up the phone. When I did, It was Ski. He had a part time job at a community center in Dorchester. They were having a party that night, and he asked me if I wanted to come. I told him I did, and that same night, I went. I had known about this community center since I was younger and only had been there once or twice going to the talent shows that my mother would take me to there. The party was in the auditorium and turned out to be a very good time. There were a lot of kids my age there, and nobody seemed to be shy at all. The music was loud, and everybody was dancing; and dancing really well. At first, I didn't dance at all. I was a little stunned at the fact that the last time I was in that building, I had seen a dance group perform called the Funk-A-Fects. A group of choreographed Pop-lockers and Breakdancers that combined a light show. That was back in the 80's.

Ski had been telling me about some boys that he wanted me to battle in the past few weeks. They were there too. When he came into the auditorium to check on me, Ski told me that he wanted to introduce me to somebody when the party was over. I told him, "Cool," and that was the last thing I remembered him saying before he walked off. Because the whole time I was talking to him, I watched the dance floor. The DJ had been playing Hip-Hop the whole time so far. But then, after 9 pm, he switched it up. He started to play Reggae, and the party went to another level of energy.

I wanted to dance, but the fear of rejection was in control. But luckily for me, 2 girls approached me. One of them said, "Hi, Whats your name?" I told her what my name was and she laughed and said,

"Shannyn?", That's a girls name", My only reply was, "Sometimes". But she goes on to ask if I had a girlfriend. I said no. Then she says, "Well, good, cause my girl has been checking you out since you got here". I was so shy, and I don't know why I began to get nervous. That combination isn't good for anything but a big goofy grin. So I said, "Where is she?" The girl smirked and looked at me like she couldn't believe I didn't catch on. She says, "She right here". The same girl she walked up with. She goes on to introduce us. I quickly noticed that the girl was super quiet and shy. Right then, in the back of my mind, I was hoping that it was the girl talking that was interested in me. She was more of the speed I was attracted to. But, It's true; you are what you attract. The girl who introduced us faded into the party and left us standing there together. Both of us; shy, young, and clueless. So there was only one thing left to do. We went to the dance floor. I don't know what was going on in her mind, but all I was hoping was that this girl could at least dance. To my surprise, she was a quiet storm. She pulled me in close and started grinding to the music. That's all it took for me to get loose.

Without ever speaking, we both knew there was some kind of chemistry. We were so into the heat of the moment that we had a crowd around us before we knew it. Everybody started screaming, shouting and chanting us on. For the rest of the night, we were paired. Even when the DJ mixed in some R&B, We danced until the party was over.

As the music equipment was being broken down and everybody was leaving. Me and Ski rejoined in the lobby of the Community Center.

He told me not to leave just yet because he was going to get the person he's been trying to introduce me to. After a few minutes passed, he came back with this guy. He didn't look like much, but he had an air about him as if he was somebody important. As they approached, the man looked very familiar to me. I was sure that I had met him before.

But I didn't know his name. My cousin Ski tried to introduce us and before he could say a word; out of the man's mouth, he says, "I know this kid already, that's Tara Jenkins Son". Then Ski said, "Cuz, this is who I wanted you to meet; he be putting on all the shows here". The man asked me what school I went to and how old I was. After I told him, he asked me to return to the Community Center the following week.

I asked him why and he said, "I want to audition you for my group". My eyes stretched and I said, "What group?" Ski jumped right in and told me it was those same boys that he wanted me to battle. They were a popular inner-city dancing boy band. Their name, "Tuff Assignment". I told the man that I would come. And I did.

The audition turned out to be exactly what Ski had said. A dance battle. I battled every member of the crew that day. It was tough, but I made the cut. The whole group began teaching me the counts to their show routines that same day.

From that day, The Community Center was home away from home.

It didn't take me long to get to know everybody. Being confirmed as one of the group members, quickly made me somewhat a part of the in-crowd. I liked being at the Community Center. Even Randy, got comfortable there. That environment was right on time and just what we needed. A belonging; with newfound friendships and unity.

Going to the Community Center became a new daily routine for us right after school. I couldn't wait to get there. I had fallen in love with the auditorium. It had a professional-sized stage that I would practice on for hours without anyone saying anything. Nobody knew that I used to sit in my window and dream of being on a stage just like that.

When I look back now and think about it. The Universe had to be listening.

Weeks went by with me rehearsing with the group. I had made enough progress that they started telling the manager that I was ready for the next show coming up. We were all pumped and excited. I couldn't wait to be introduced. The night before the show, I went to the manager's house. All the group members were meeting up there. We had to try on our new performance wardrobe. But when I got there, I learned that the manager also was a clothing designer and was making our costumes himself. I was totally impressed by his talents. Come to find out, he was the same guy that put together all of those choreographed pop-locking, Breakdancing, big stage production light shows. His name, Trevar Michaels.

I was super excited to make my debut with the group the next day. That whole day up until show time I was practicing my part and couldn't wait to perform. Finally it's time. We get in the community center van and began our trip to the venue. I don't know what came over me, but all of a sudden, I ended up with the biggest case of butterflies I had ever experienced. For some reason, much worse than the time I performed at the Apollo. We got to the place, and I made a break for the restroom. When I got in there, I realized that I literally was scared sh**less. A spirit of low self-esteem and lack of confidence took over me. Right there in that stall, I started thinking of so many ways and excuses to stop the performance moment from happening. I hated what I felt. Because unfortunately, I made up my mind that I wasn't going to perform. In my heart, I just didn't feel as ready as I thought.

When I came out of the restroom, I told one of the members where my head was. He didn't believe me at first. But after a while, they realized that I had folded. When the host of the show announce our name and brought us to the stage. I wasn't in formation. Needless to say, Trevar was pissed. While the rest of the members performed, I sat there in a seat by myself, watching them. The whole time beating myself up on the inside because I let fear win. But still, I was taking mental notes of their stage dynamics.

While sitting there, I began to let all of the negative thoughts take over in the back of my mind. Like, "I'm not good enough," and "they're better without me" or what I really didn't want to happen; Trevar kicking me out of the group. The guys came off the stage leaving behind a great performance. I couldn't help but notice the response they got. It was loud and alive.

When we got back in the van, nobody said anything to me until the next practice.

I just knew these guys were going to be mad about my actions. They were, but instead, these guys ragged on me, choking so bad as they recapped that night. One of the guys even said he noticed I was in the restroom for a long time and knew I would chicken out. We all laughed and joked about it for a while before we began practice. An hour into it, Trevar came into the auditorium with a Newport hanging from between his lips. He stopped the music, walked over to us and put us in a new formation. I didn't know what was going on. He told us not to move and shut up. Then he began to pace the stage. He walks in and out and in between all of us. Like he was sizing us up for something. He then walks right up to me in my face and said, "You better not back out of another f*cking show". He put on a new song, and for the first time, I was learning a professional choreographed routine from a Legendary Boston Choreographer.

The Community Center had become that place of molding for me. Strengthening my personal independence as well as responsibility. It was the place I also got my first job. A city-funded grant that paid the inner city kids to clean up the neighborhood for eight weeks of the summer. The Red Shirt Program. I hated it! But when I received my first check, I knew that I would be right back there on Monday morning. Complaints and all. I gave it my all as long as I could. But the hot sun beaming on my Red Shirt got old fast. But that experience made me realize even more that I had to figure out quickly who I was, a field worker or a leader. So somehow, I got in good with the community centers administrator. She had heard that I didn't like my position outside. At first, she tries to talk me into sticking with it for the last four weeks, since all of the other summer camp counselor positions were already filled. But a few days later, she created a position for me in the building. The woman knew how passionate I was about dancing and performing. Surprisingly, she assigned me to the auditorium. It was still labor work, but instead, cleaning the auditorium and organizing the props and lights. But that didn't make any difference to me. I was in the one place I wanted to be all the time anyway. And now, I'm making money to be there. $8.90 an hour for the rest of the summer it is.

The lesson for me was this; life will put you in situations and circumstances that you must speak up and fight to get out of. If not, you become programmed to think that you are like everybody else.

A year quickly went by, and my popularity with the group became a little stronger. Especially once we started writing and performing our own original songs. Our performance schedule increased to almost 3 shows every weekend. We seemed to be continuously practicing, Monday through Friday for at least 2 to 3 hours.

One day in rehearsal, we started to make up a new routine without Trevar. I began to create an original combination that came pretty easy to me out of nowhere. The rest of the group didn't even question it. They just went along with it but added on their ideas here and there, and I would incorporate them. I realized then that I had something that could work for me. But I recall one time I was getting a bit of a big head. Full of myself and thought that everything I did was the best thing since sliced bread. I had just finished a routine, and I was so proud of it too. I asked Trevar to come to check out what we had worked on. He did. When he came in the auditorium, he sat in the first row, center seat. I couldn't wait to impress him.

The music starts and we go at it full out as if we was in a showcase competition. Shouting and chanting like how we usually do when we feel like we know the routine well enough and got it in our muscle memory. Once we were done, we gave each other high fives and confirmations of excellence and esteem building. As we sat on the edge of the stage. I asked Trevar confidently, "How was that?" He uncrossed his legs and sat forward to the edge of his seat, and his reply, "That f*ckin sucked". Once again, the rest of the members began to laugh at me. Trevar then got up from his seat and walked over to the stage, broke my whole routine down, and told me all the ways and reasons he didn't approve. Without saying a word and totally humbled I couldn't do anything but take his direct and brutal advice. What I didn't do in this moment was allow my mind to go into that wave of negative thinking. I never once got the idea that I wanted to quit on this. At the end of the day, his words and directions were the best thing that ever happened to me moving forward. Even though his words crushed my little newfound confidence, I took notes and studied them until they became a part of my own style. A style that connected the old school to the new school of hip-hop Choreography.

I went on to becoming one of Boston's hottest choreographers. Just 14yrs of age and already making money under the table around the city. Outside of being our manager and/or mentor of our popular group Tuff Assignment. Trevar Michaels was a devoted community worker. With all of the single-parent homes and young mothers puzzled about what to do with their sons; He had an idea to start a new after-school program, BTM (Boys To Men Academy). After Trevar told me what the plan was, I was the first in line to follow his lead. I was all for a program dedicated to keeping young black boys off the hardcore streets of Boston and doing something more productive and out of harm's way. Mostly out of his own pockets and some light financial assistance from the community center to cover the welfare of the boys, we got to it and made it happen. We only had a few activities for them to do in the beginning. But luckily Dancing was the highlight and attraction for most of them. But before any of that; we would first tutor and help them with their homework directly after school. That was highly important to both Trevar and myself. Of course, the mothers were highly in favor of that too. Almost immediately, we saw improvement in the boys. In their school grades, as a group and individually. The program morphed into real true friendships and the beginning of a brotherhood that would last them a lifetime. Sort of like a sorority for young boys with discipline through dance and army-like drills.

A lot went on in the years that I was at the Community Center. Mostly good things, but of course, I have memories that stand out that aren't so good. One day like normal after school, I stopped at Sun's Pizza on the corner of Blue Hill Ave and Harvard St to get something to eat. I get the order togo to make it to the Center in time for the first kid to arrive to the BTM Program. So I hurry up and eat, and as usual, the kids start walking in one by one and two by two's. One kid came in and had a look on his face like he wanted to talk to me. But it wasn't urgent at all. As he was setting up to do his homework I walked around and checked up on each one of the others to see how their day at school was. It was my daily routine with them. When I finally got over to this particular kid, he says, "I just saw your dad". I thought nothing of it and just replied with "Cool; How much homework you got"? So he pulled it from his bag. But right after, he said,

"Why does your father collect cans on the street?" The question took me by surprise. An automatic emotional and mental stir. Usually, I would have a quick reply; in this case, I was slow to the draw. Because in the back of my mind, I knew why. But all I could think of to say was "Because he likes money". The kid looked a little puzzled by my answer as if he knew what I told him was a lie. So now there's an awkward silence, and he is now looking at me from head to toe. Like he's Sizing me up in a way that says something doesn't add up for him in his young mind. Being a witness of who he believes me to be; a good dude that has it together and had a great life. But now fading into recognition that I was embarrassed and angry at the same time from his question. The kid seemed like he had a lot more to say or ask but fell back from pressing. Somehow it was like he understood that there was more to me than just dancing. He was one of the only kids in the program that had his dad at home. I realize now that it was just as shocking to him to know that "Shannyn's dad" is collecting cans a block away from the community center as it was for me.

In the state of mind and lifestyle that my dad was in, it would have been worthless for me to say anything to him about it. A week later, my dad came to the community center. But not to support what I was doing exactly, but asking me for $20. It was payday too. At that moment, I had two emotions going on that totally conflicted within me. One; I was still mad about what my student saw and asked me about him. Then, Two; I always wanted to be the kid that honored his parents and was happy that I could even help him with the $20 spot. Even though I felt like I knew what he most likely was going to do with it.

But if it wasn't one thing, it was always another. With the popularity that I have gained with dancing. It brought on all types of energies. I became that guy that either you liked me a lot, or you extremely didn't. Another one of my students pulls me to the side privately. I knew it was something serious because I noticed that he had a tear in his eye. He too had a question and asked me, "Why don't the Floyd Street Boys like you?" I told him that I didn't know and asked him why is he asking me that? Come to find out, he lived in that neighborhood, and the "FSB" knew that he was a student in my program. I never found out who it was, but whoever it was sent a message to my student for me. It was just a common and typical threat of "Watch ya Back". Of course, I took a mental note of it, but my first concern was to calm this kid down and assure him that nothing would happen to me. Because unfortunately in the hood kids see, hear, and experience their environment early in life. There's almost no way to get around it. So this kid took what they said to him to heart for the sake of knowing better.

It's known in Boston, If somebody threatens you, it's usually a promise. Nothing to take lightly. But because I refuse to be the type that would add gas to the flame. I had no message to return, and better yet. I didn't let my family know of this. I knew that if I did, they'd want to fight fire with fire. In other words, they "Bout that life".

— Fallen Heroes —

It was my last year at the Woodrow Wilson Middle School. Looks like mom finally got it together and was ready to do things the right way.

She met with us and told us that she had some good news. When she told us what it was, we were excited. We were very forgiving.

She had somehow got herself into a "Shattered Homes" program for women who regained custody of their kids. It was a shelter. A week later, we moved in, and everything seemed to be going smooth. Me and Randy, for the first time, had our own rooms.

The neighborhood was familiar so we quickly made friends with the other kids on our street and in the building. But better yet, now we live within walking distance to where Ski & Wiz live. So now every chance we got, we were making our way. Because even though we had friends, our first choice was to always be around family.

Life took another turn for us in our time on Holiday Street. Mom was doing her very best to be that mom that we never had. It was our first time since before her drug-dealing days on Seaver Street of her at her best and doing good. There was laughter and good vibes in the Shelter apartment. Almost every night, she'd watch me practice my new dance routines or watch me and Randy clown around until she'd laugh herself to sleep. She was up early cooking every day. At least breakfast and diner. Washing our clothes and even staying on us about homework and school. Amongst our friends, she became the cool mom that everybody liked. She was even once again courting with her old fling, Smitty. It was almost like she was convincing herself that this was who she was. Might I add; it looked great on her.

I finally graduate, and the summer is back in blaze. I am now a summer camp counselor, and on top of that, Tuff Assignments performance schedule just went up a notch.

One day after practice, I went home to shower and change clothes because me and a group of friends planned to go to a party that night. When I got home, I realized that my mother wasn't there. So I go straight into the kitchen and grab a cold piece of fried chicken out of the refrigerator that my mom had cooked the night before. As I'm eating, I go into my bedroom and turn on my usual music. Some kids would say I was weird, but It was always old-school music. I'm talking really old school music, Like; Blue Magic, Chic, Delfonics, and even Hall & Oates. I even decorated my room walls with some of the old vinyl records we had leftover from the eviction. I loved music. As the tunes were playing, I checked my closet to see what outfit I could put together for the party. Once I decided on that, I was ready to take a shower. So I took off my gold necklace, rings, and bracelet and placed them on top of my dresser. I grabbed my towel and underwear and went to the bathroom. As soon as I turned on the water, the bell rang. I had no clue of who it could've been, but maybe it's my brother. So I went to the door and to my surprise, it was my uncle Bryce. He had been home from prison for a year now. Something was off about him on this day but I wasn't too concerned about it. He was dressed up like he had either went to court or had a job interview. He asked me where my mother was, and I told him that I didn't know. He asked me where I was going, and I told him that I was going to a party. The music was loud, so something told me to go to my room and turn the volume down. When I turned around, he was standing in my doorway. So I asked him where he was coming from and he said that he just left from Ski & Wiz's house, but nobody was home. But his eyes wandered a few times as he was talking. He then walked over to my dresser, picked up one of my rings, and put it on his finger. He asked me, "Whose is this?" I told him it was mine. It was obvious. I had all of the initials to my name on my rings. Then what comes out of his mouth next kind of took me back a little. He says, "Let me borrow one". I will never forget the look on his face as he asked me that. It was like he knew what he was going to do but hated it at the same time. So I laughed and asked him, "What do you need it for?" In that moment, his answer told me something about him that nobody had ever told me up until that point. He said, "Because I have a date tonight". He turned his face from me, disconnecting any eye contact. It was like he knew that I knew he would try to jerk me over and he couldn't help it. Neither could I. He puts the ring back down on the dresser. Then I started to make my way back to the bathroom where my water was waiting. I told him I had to go soon, so I had to get in the shower. I closed the bathroom door and at last stepped in.

About 2 minutes later, I heard the front door close. That ended up being the Longest shower I ever took. Because I didn't want to, but knew better to expect the worse. I didn't want to believe, that who I looked at as a protector would be someone I'd have to protect myself from. I wrapped the towel around my waist and opened the door to the playing of the song by the Delfonics "Trying to Make a Fool of Me". I made a slow walk back into my room and looked over at a bare dresser top. Still in the back of my mind saying, "He's just borrowing it". That day I faced a hard truth. My "Super Hero" uncle was a dope fein.

It was years before I ever made mention of this.

What a summer it has been, even though the community center has proven to be an overall good place to be. Home began to be that place where drama would find me. Just when you think your past is dead, a situation will arise that can and will resuscitate it. One night, Smitty out of the blue had come by to visit my mom. She was cooking so she invited his company into the kitchen. My room was off from the kitchen, so I heard them talking and laughing for a couple of hours. Randy was in his room playing video games. When the food was done, she told us to come eat. So like usual, we grab our plates and go back to our rooms. Smitty goes into the room with my mom and as he ate they were still talking. I can hear them through the thin wall. This lasted for bout another hour or so. Then, what sounded like a good conversation and good company turned ugly. I don't know what happened, but her room door busted open, and my mother was cursing him out. I opened my room door to see the problem, and my mother was walking back toward the kitchen. Smitty seemed to be upset as well, walking behind her. But he kind of digressed when he saw me looking outside of my room door. But still, they were fired up about something. I told them to cut the sh*t but didn't really feel a need to get between them.

Then mom said something that pissed Smitty off, and he started to take a step toward her. Smitty is a big guy and not known to take any mess from anybody. So my mother, in her well-known defensive reflex, grabbed the knife that was still on the counter she was cooking with. Just like old times. She then yelled out, "Don't walk up on me mutha'f*cka". But Smitty was also known to be hard-headed. Smitty continued in his approach to "jack her up". But before you knew it, without even a shout or scream, Smitty walked right into the point of the knife and was stabbed. Blood immediately started to flow down the front of his stone-washed blue jeans. The only thing Smitty said was, "B*tch, you cut me?" My mother told him that he shouldn't have walked up on her. Then she said something that I wasn't expecting at all.

"Now get the f*ck out cause you're bleeding on my floors, and I just mopped". Smitty was pissed, but he backed his way down the hall to the front door. All I could do was get him a couple of towels to apply pressure to his wounds. He took them and began to walk down the stairs to his car. Meanwhile, my mother called 911 herself. Quite calm if you ask me. To be honest, Randy and I were just as calm as if this is a normal lifestyle. Totally submitted and used to it. Five minutes later, it was like you could hear every police siren in the area at one time. The Boston Police arrived. The whole neighborhood was in their windows, on their front porches, and outside. Everybody got their eyes on 22 Holiday Street. One of the officers came in the apartment to get a report. One officer asked me what happened, and all I told him was that he had to ask her. So they did. They sat her down in the kitchen and questioned her. She didn't give them any kind of attitude or anything. When they got all the information they needed, I remember one of the cops looking down at the knife used and sarcastically saying,"Yeah, we got us another OJ Simpson on our hands tonight guys". All of the cops started to laugh. But so did she. She smirked at the cop and said, "Funny". But me, I didn't crack a smile. They then told my mother to stand up, and they began to read her rights as they placed handcuffs on her. As they walked her down the hall and out the door I had already grabbed the mop and bucket. I never seen Smitty leave in the ambulance, and I never seen her be put into the back of the police car. All I knew, was the next day, I had a show at the community center for the summer camp kids and that's all I knew to put my cares into at that time.

What a crazy year 1994 had been, we didn't even live at 22 Holiday Street for a full year. The summer was in full blaze and my biggest mission was to save as much money from my summer job checks as I could. Because I wanted to do my own back-to-school shopping. Getting told I couldn't have something because it was too expensive got old. I didn't really complain about it then, either. I just knew now that it was my responsibility to provide myself with what I wanted. All I wanted was 2 pairs of Jordans, a pair each of Grant Hills, Ken Griffeys, 2 pairs of Adidas (Classic shell toe & Top Tens), and whatever my money could buy at Marshalls and J.City. Because the coming school year would be my freshman year in high school. I wanted to look my best and feel like I was part of the in-crowd. I remember being so excited about it, yet nervous at the same time. Either way, nothing was going to stop me from being the flyest freshman at either of my top 2 picks for high school. West Roxbury High School (Westie) or Madison Park High School.

I picked those schools not just because some of my older family members attended them but because that's where I felt most of the popular kids in the city went. But still, I had 2 more months of the summer to get through.

Despite what went down between my mom and Smitty, I could say that things were ok for most of our time living there. But, with everything good comes something bad.

Mom did her best but she started to unravel. B+ for effort. As the summer weeks rolled by, I noticed that she was coming in later and later each night. Already scarred by our past experiences, my mother's behaviors began to seep through. Like as if "DeJaVu" began to set in on us.

One night, me and my brother got home from the Community Center, and as usual, we came in and began to raid and eat anything that we can find in the refrigerator and pantry. Long days at the community center had a way of working up a good appetite. When we first got in we noticed that my mom's bedroom door was closed, and she wasn't home. Lately, this had become the story with her. But something about her not being home and her room door being closed was new and didn't sit right with me. Before you knew it, it's about 10 pm now, and my brother and I are well into our nightly routine. He would be in his room playing his video games, and I was in my room listening to my old school tunes while on the phone with a girl. As far as living with my mother; this was the first time we had a house phone since Seaver Street.

All of a sudden, my brother comes into my room and tells me to come to look at something. I thought nothing of it, because he showed no emotions that told if it was a big deal or not. But by the look on his face, I knew that I had to go with him at that moment. I then told the girl to hold on, and I followed him. I just knew that all he wanted was for me to see what new level he's beat on a new video game, as he would want to share this with me from time to time. But this time, My brother walks right past his bedroom and into my mother's room. I stopped just right past the threshold of her room door as he continued to walk around the bed. He stops, points, and looks on the floor. His face became quickly disappointed. Right then, before I even took a step forward around the bed, I knew what it was. When I got to the other side, There was a homemade Crack pipe made out of a plastic Pepsi bottle. Even though my brother and I never spoke on what we thought was going on with her; it became evident that we both were thinking the same thing lately. It just so happened that my brother took it a step further and went snooping.

Both with tears in our eyes without ever letting one fall, we momentarily snapped right back into a mindset that comforted us best. Unworthy and defeated. Sucking up disappointment yet again by telling ourselves that this was to be expected so we can't be affected at all by this. Like a wall around our true feelings. Just to protect ourselves from facing and accepting that feeling of being played.

Today, I could say that this was a time that hurt me the most. Perhaps even the first time I experienced having a broken heart. Because underneath it all, I wanted what we had going on to last until I was grown enough to move out on my own. In that apartment, I had that feeling that most young boys in the hood get when it comes to making it in life. That burning priority and motivation to take care of their mother by giving her whatever she wanted because she sacrificed something to be a great mom.

I was ready to make all of her non-believers eat their words about her. I was ready to honor her.

That same night, not long after, we discovered that my mother had relapsed, yet again. We knew that we couldn't stay there. We knew it wouldn't be long before she'd spiral back down into a world that we were old enough to know wasn't going to work for us. So, we decided to pack our bags. Because a promise was broken.

Randy got on the phone and called no other than my grandmother. He told her what had happened and said that he didn't want to live there anymore. It was like he wasn't even asking her if we could come there to live. It was more like he was just letting her know that we were coming. All I can remember hearing her say was, "I guess, Come on". As he hung up the phone, a vibe fell over me. Anger mixed with embarrassment, mixed with backtracking mixed with frustration and mostly feeling like I was about to return to that feeling of being a burden on my grandmother again. Feeling like she didn't deserve raising two teenagers after raising all 4 of her own kids on her own. So I went out on the front porch and sat on the banister. Thinking of what I was going to do next. Dreading going back to my grandmother's old fashioned lifestyle. Taking nothing from the caring woman that she was. As my brother gathered his things, I sat out there until the taxi cab pulled up in front of the house and blowed the horn. I can still hear him saying, "You ready? The cab is here". I looked at Randy and told him I wasn't going. He looked at me and asked where was I going. I didn't know at that moment, but I did tell him I wasn't staying there. I went on to help him grab his trash bags full of his belongings and video games and put him into the cab and told him I would call him the next day. By the time I got back to the second floor, I looked off the front porch and could see the cab take a left at the top of our one-way street.

I go back into the silent house and finish gathering my things. At first, I thought about waiting for her to get in so I could say something about her relapse. But that idea quickly faded because I was so angry and done with her that I didn't want to hear the excuse that I knew she'd try to come up with. I was already drained by this point. Right when I got that thought in my mind to give up on who I thought would help me. Surrendering to making that call to my grandmother to let her know I was on my way too. It hit me. Trevar Michaels. I called him and told him what had happened, and he wasn't sure at first. But after 10 minutes of talking, he gave in and told me I could come and stay for a little while, or at least until this all blew over. 25 minutes later, my cab was blowing the horn. This was the last time I ever lived with either of my parents.

— Help Me To Help You —

Living with Trevar was completely smooth. I liked it there. Not only was he the manager of our boy band, but Trevar camouflaged as a big brother, a dad, and overall mentor. I really looked up to him and respected his views on life. I learned a lot from him. A lot of young people from around the city of Boston did too. You could say that Trevar was quite the flamboyant type of man. Some would even say a gay man. Considering his artsy lifestyle that most men wouldn't find interest in, especially in the hood. But to me, none of that even mattered. I don't even know why those types of things never bother me about a person. I was never the judgmental type and was always comfortable with people who could be themselves. Trevar was always himself. He didn't live far from the Community Center, so some nights after practice, we would walk. As soon as we got in, Trevar would check his voice mail and begin to cook. He was a great cook. It was still summer, so I would turn around and go back out the door to kick it with my friends in front of the house while he did. I learned quickly that Trevar was a gin sipper. The more he drank, the more the real him came out. He would usually be on the phone, and he'd be cussing whoever it was on the phone out. Every 15 minutes, while still on the phone, he would come to the front door of his house and cuss out whoever was there. He was loud, dramatic, and funny as hell. A gin-drinking cusser with a heart of gold that everybody loved for being himself.

It's almost time to go back to school with just three weeks left. I just about got my money up and ready for back-to-school shopping. This was going to be my freshman year. I was ready.

The summer job program was over, and I was just waiting on my last check that was due. I finally got paid on a Thursday and quickly cashed it. I remember I couldn't wait to add it to the rest of my stash and count it all up. When I finally did, I had saved up $1345. It may not sound like much, but I was proud of myself. I "nickeled and dimed" the whole summer.

Later that night, while I was in my room listening to music, I heard Trevar call my name. He told me I had a phone call. So I went downstairs to take the call in the kitchen. When I picked up the phone, it was my grandmother. I wasn't surprised by her call. But for her to call me when she did instantly alerted me that something was up. She always starts any phone call with small talk. Even if she has some important news or gossip. She never gets right to it. So I go through the motions by quickly answering her footnoted questions like, "How are you," "did you practice today," or "what did you eat today"? Something like that. She then says, "I just got a call". I asked her who she got a call from. She said, "Yo mama". I asked her what she wanted. She tells me that my mother had been arrested for a petty crime and that she was going to be in court the next morning. I asked her whether she was going. She said, "I don't want to, but I guess I am. Somebody got to see what's going on with her". I really didn't have an answer for that. Suddenly, I got angry for my grandmother calling me to tell me this news. Because my mind was made up at that moment and all I knew was that the next day, I was going shopping. We abruptly hung up due to her having another incoming phone call on the other line. Trevar cooked, and I didn't even eat. I just went back upstairs and went to bed. The next day I wake up and I'm feeling much better than I did when I went to bed. But, unfortunately, I couldn't help feeling some type of way about my mother being in jail. The whole morning became a drag. I kept telling myself that what she was going through was not my problem. So I turn on my music, take a shower and get dressed. Before I knew it, the clock said 10:50 am. That just told me that all the stores I wanted to go to shop are all about to open. I had the timing all calculated in my mind. If I left in the next 10 minutes, I could be walking in the footlocker door by 12:15 pm. Just a quick ride on the #22 route bus to Ashmont Station and then hop on the Redline train to Downtown Crossing. Yes, Let the shopping begin.

I finally leave out and began my walk to the bus stop. Usually, the buses would be coming down Talbot ave rapidly. But on this day, for whatever reason; this is not the case. Gaining more and more frustrated with every passing minute. I must have waited for almost 30 minutes. That lead me to start walking. By the time I got to Codman Square, my mother's problem dropped on me pretty heavily. I suddenly turned around and looked back down Talbot Avenue, and out of nowhere, I finally saw the bus. I hurried to the next bus stop in effort to catch it and get on. When the bus finally pulled up, and the doors opened, I fell back from the 3 or 4 other people that had been standing there waiting. I watched each of them get on, but something wouldn't let me move forward. The bus driver closed the bus door and pulled off without any hesitation. Now I was even more frustrated. But now I'm putting one foot in front of the other heading towards the Dorchester courthouse. It was a few blocks away. I get to the courthouse, and outside is my cousin Ski with a few other guys cleaning around the courthouse. He was doing his court-ordered community service that day. I go up the stairs and into the court. I go through the metal detectors, and immediately I saw 2 or 3 more people I knew. But on this day, I didn't have time to talk to anyone. So I kept it moving to find out what courtroom my mom would be seeing the judge in. When I got the information, I proceeded where she would be. When I walked into the courtroom, the first person I saw was my grandmother. She was already there sitting in an aisle seat. Although there was quite the crowd that day, I remember there was an open spot right next to my grandmother on her row. I walked over, and she looked up, and I could tell she was as surprised to see me there as I was. I sat down, and for an hour and an half, we listened to other people's heartbreaking cases. I couldn't help but notice all of the cases were similar. Marijuana possession, Disorderly conduct, Domestic violence, and Shop Lifting. Crying "Baby'Mothers" that has been abused by the same person they're begging the judge to let go. About 15 young black men with no real understanding of their marijuana charge and many public defenders have been defeated in their efforts to enlighten the ignorant. Probation violators being placed under arrest before they can even plead their case while their families cry. A young girl with a gun charge because her boyfriend didn't show up to court to claim that the gun the police found in her car was his. The whole time, case after case, my grandmother is shaking her head in disbelief of the chaos. At this point, I don't even know why I'm there. Meanwhile, I'm numb to all of it and got eager to see what my mom's case was about. I couldn't tell if I was there to support my grandmother or if I was there because, for some reason, I felt responsible for my mother's actions. Finally, the judge told the bailiff to bring in the next set of prisoners from holding. Without a doubt, we knew my mother was in this group. Because we heard her loud mouth coming from the back with not a care in the world. Me and my grandmother looked at each other and shook our heads. She just had that gift to gab and seemed to know everybody in Boston, including the bailiff. She came through the door chained to a few other women, and she had all of them laughing. They go through a couple of cases and finally got to my mother's. They called her name, and she stood up. When she did, that's when we made eye contact. From the look on her face, I could tell she didn't expect me to be there that day either.

After learning what she was arrested for, I realized that it wasn't that serious. In my mind, I was thinking that they were going to let her go and just put her on probation or something. At least that's what it looked like. But that didn't happen. The judge dropped the bomb and said, "I'm seeing that there was a warrant for her arrest". She never showed up to court for a previous case that she had. The judge turned to her and gave her an ultimatum. Either she pays the fines and court fees today or goes to jail for the next 45 days. The judge specifically asked her if anyone was there that could help her with that. That's when she looked over at my grandmother and me, and on that day, I knew my grandmother couldn't cover the damages. At the moment, I just didn't know why I felt so compelled to do something. So my arm flenched as if to raise my hand, and my grandmother quickly grabbed my wrist, turned to me, and said, "I know that's your mama, but you don't have to do this if you don't want to". Still, I raised my hand and gave a gesture that I would take care of it. The bailiff immediately released her from the chain gang she was linked to and made her sit on the other side of the prisoner wall. When I looked at my grandmother again, She looked angry but had a tear streaming down her face. The bailiff then walks over to me, bends down, hands me a piece of paper, and whispers, "The court clerk's counter is downstairs. Make your payment and bring the receipt back".

I got to the counter, gave the lady the paper. She types the case number into her computer. A few seconds pass, and then she says, "That'll be $536.13". I almost passed out. Still, I paid it with anger in my heart and accepted that my school shopping would be limited. I was so mad at myself for speaking up. Cursing my own self out on the inside. I go back to the courtroom and gave the bailiff the receipt, and soon after, they gave my mother the signal that she could leave. We got out into the hallway, I had nothing to say, but I hugged her and kissed her, then I just left. By the time I made it to the first store, I wasn't even in the spirit to shop. But I did get my first pair of Jordans and a pair of Ken Griffeys; and just a few mix and match outfits from J.City Clothing store. A week later, my mom was arrested again.

CHAPTER 8

Soul Ties

— A Planted Seed —

One day after an early show I was approached by a young lady. Not quite my age, but older than me. She was the mother of a little girl whose act was on the same showcase that my group Tuff Assignment was performing. I have seen her around the city before, but I never actually met her; until this day. When she walked over to me, she told me that I did a good job and noticed that I have a lot of fun when I perform. I told her thank you and that I do. She had the typical "Momager" personality, a subtle dominance and a way of critiquing by way of complimenting. Even though I could tell she was older, she carried herself with a younger girl swag. She was up on everything that was happening. As the conversation carried on, she ended up telling me a few things about myself that I wouldn't even think she'd know. I mean, after all, we have only seen each other a few times around the city at different events. We didn't even know any of the same people or hung amongst the same crowds. But somehow, when we were in the same vicinity, we were always within an eyeshot of each other. I can't say that I was flirting or even truly attracted to her, but I noticed her for whatever reason. She did had some game though. So it sparked an interest in my mind as to how she even knew that I was already sipping Hennessy at 15yrs old. She also informed me that she knew after shows, I rarely went to the after-parties or hung out with my group members. But what really got me was that she knew I no longer lived with Trevar and now living back at my grandmother's house. If I knew then what I know now, I would've known that she had done some research on me. As street smart as I thought I was, I yet wasn't aware of the mindset of older women. They have a way of getting what they want. Around this time, I noticed that more older women have been attracted to me rather than girls my own age. I never knew why.

We stood there and talked for about 15 minutes. She said, "You're much cooler than I thought you'd be". I asked her, "What did you think I'd be like?" She said, "Just like them" and pointed over to a couple of my group members being loud, wild and hype with some girls. But really just acting their age. She then asked, "What are you doing tonight," and before I could answer, she slightly giggled and said, "Let me guess, going home to watch a movie and sip your little Hennessy bottle?" We both laughed, and I told her she was correct. She made a suggestion and said, "Maybe instead of going home tonight, maybe you can come by and hang out with me for a little bit". Now in the back of my shy mind, I thought, " Why would this woman want me to come to her house?" My first answer shot down her suggestion, and I told her maybe tomorrow since it would be Saturday. She said that's cool and went into her pocketbook and pulled out a pen and piece of paper, and wrote down her phone number. She said, "Call me when you get settled in tonight". I said. "aight". I had a beeper then. So I gave her my beeper number in return. We closed our conversation with a hug, and we walked away. Later that night, I finally got home, but it was still only about 9 pm. I took a shower, and even though my grandmother cooked, I still made a sandwich. I went back into my room, threw on a movie, and, of course, crack open my little bottle of Hennessy.

I began to sip and start allowing myself to relax from the day. About 30mins later, I get a beep. Right away, I knew the number. It was no other than Evelyn. There was no doubt that I was going to call her back. It was like I already knew what the conversation would lead up to. It was something about her vibe from earlier in the night. So I twisted my bottle cap and turned my bottle up for a little more courage and then made the life-changing call.

She answered, and we both beat around the bush a bit initially; but then right back to where we left off. She asked me if I was feeling my drink yet. I told her, "I'm good,". It was only a half-pint. Not too long after that, she asked me if I was going back out tonight since it's Friday. I told her that I wasn't, but I did plan to help my grandmother as I usually did with Saturday morning chores and helping her to the laundry mat. She laughed and made a joke saying, "What a good boy". After that, the conversation jumped from being cool and chill to insisting on me coming back out to hang out with her. For my every excuse as to why I couldn't go, she had an even better reason why I should. She asked me what my favorite meal was. Then, what's my favorite dessert? Her questions went on and on. The questions didn't feel like they were coming from a place of trying to get to know someone. They felt more like a checklist. Finally, after an hour of chatting and going back and forth. She said, "I'm having such a good time on the phone with you; I ain'got nothing to do, so I'm gonna come chill with you". I told her that wouldn't be cool because my grandmother is here, and we wouldn't have any type of privacy. She laughed and said, "I'm not trying to come in anyway, just come outside, and we can kick it in the car. I just want to talk in person". So I agreed. By this time, I was feeling my buzz. So I gave her my address. I asked her how long she'd be before arriving, and she told me about 10 to 15 minutes. We hung up the phone, and I began to throw some clothes on. By the time I went to the bathroom and got dressed, just like she said, she was there within 15mins. It was a chilly and damp night. The air had that scent of rain or snow.

We sat in the car and we continued on rambling about even more stuff. The energy remained the same. But once again, she began to further provoke me to come back to her place. She kept telling me that I wouldn't be disappointed if I did. I thought about it for a few seconds and was about to tell her once again that I'd pass. I really couldn't tell you why I was so withdrawn from the idea.

But, right before I could get the words out. She told me that she'd bring me back home that same night, no matter what time it was. I looked at her with my shaking head and a smirk on my face and said, "You just don't take no for an answer do you?" She turned to me and quickly replied, "That's not my style". So I told her that I'd be right back. I went upstairs, turned off my TV, and grabbed my pager, hat, and pocket knife. My grandmother was already in bed, so I didn't even bother to let her know I was leaving out.

I get back in the car, and it was no time getting to her place. She lived in a brick home but not the projects. But Franklin Field projects was on the next street over. She had 3 Bedrooms, 2 bathrooms, all new furniture, and she had the place pretty tight for a single mom.

I took a seat in the living room, and she turned on the tv for me. As I sat there, she began to go back and forth from the kitchen as we never stopped our conversation. I had only been there for 10 minutes, and I quickly noticed she had a new vibe about her. For one, her confidence went up another notch, but yet, she was more calm and chill. All of a sudden, an aroma from the kitchen got intense. It was a familiar scent, and it smelled delicious. She stood in the doorway of the kitchen and asked, "Can I get you something to drink?" I said, "What do you have?" Her answer, "I got everything you like". I said,

"Everything like what?" She walked back into the kitchen and yelled out a couple of beverage names. Then, she said with slight sarcasm, "Oh' and I got you some Hennessy"; she walked back to the doorway and held up a fifth to show me. So, That was my choice. A double shot over the rocks.

She went on to tell me that the food was almost done. I then asked her what it was. With a playful devious smirk on her face, she said, "Don't you like Steak & Potatoes?" I said, "Hell yea, It's one of....." And once again before I could even finish what I was going to say, she cut me off and said, "...One of your favorite meals, right?" Then she said that was her surprise, cooking for me. I don't know what it was, but at that moment, something struck my mind that confirmed to me that she had been asking around about me. I got up and stepped over to the kitchen, and I noticed she had already started preparing to cook before she came to get me. So the food didn't take long. When the food was done, she fixed me a plate, and we ate. It ended up being a late dinner. I could still remember watching Arsenio Hall. I even told her that one day I would be on that show. She laughed and said, "With who, Tuff Assignment?" I didn't think it was funny at all, so I just told her, "You never know". She then grabbed the bottle, opened it, and poured me another drink. I asked her to pour her some as well. But, she said she didn't drink. Once we were finished, we sat on the couch and talked some more. The vibe was good. So much that we totally lost track of time. But after a while, she started to show signs of being tired. After all, it was a long day. So I told her that it might be time for me to go. She asked if I needed her to take me back home. I told her that she seemed tired and that wouldn't be necessary. I grabbed her house phone and called a taxi. Before we knew it, we were back in a full conversation while we waited.

In preparation to go to bed directly after the cab was expected to pick me up, she excused herself and said she would hop in the shower. She told me if the cab came, to just close the front door when I leave out, and she would lock it when she was finished with her shower. I told her "okay," and she went into her bedroom bathroom and closed the door. She was in there for about 15 minutes, and then I heard the water turn off. To see if I was still there, she called my name, "Shannyn?" Yes, I'm still here I replied. The cab was taking much longer than we expected. So I happened to pull the shade to the side and peek out to see if the cab was out outside, maybe looking for the address. But to my surprise, It was snowing heavily. There were already 3 inches of snow on the ground. My reaction was loud, like, "Oh My Gawd". She opened the bathroom door and said, "What?" I told her the conditions outside, but she didn't seem bothered at all by it. She yelled from her room and asked for the last time if I wanted her to take me home. I felt as though the circumstance was too crucial and besides, it was already after 3 am at this point. So I told her no. I don't know what she was doing in the room, but I sat out in the living room for about 10 minutes while awkward silence was over the house. I even called for another cab, and the dispatch told me it was a high volume night, and there were no cabs in the area. I hung up the phone and sat back on the couch. It was then that I finally heard the wind blowing outside.

And then, out of the silence, her voice. "Well, you don't have to sit out there by yourself". She invited me into her bedroom. A jolt of curious excitement overcame me. Yet, I still think I expected her to bring me a pillow and a blanket.

So I took off my coat and left it on the couch. I walked into her room, and she was sitting on the side of the bed, still with her towel wrapped around her. She had a one seat sofa recliner next to her bed. So I took a seat. She could tell that I was a little nervous. So she told me to relax and get comfortable. I did. I took off my sneakers and leaned back in the chair. We didn't talk as much as we did in the living room, but another kind of conversation was going on. This time, she was talking, but with her body language. I began to notice that she was looking at me with an eye of her own curiosity and subtle seduction. I would catch her eye, and she would smirk and make vocal sighs of playful frustration. At this point, I've accepted what I knew was coming. With one last attempt to check my attraction temperature, she goes to her dresser draw and grabs a big t-shirt. She stands at the foot of her bed, and she dropped the towel. That was the moment that all of my gentleman-like ways went out the window. She put the shirt on, and she laid in the bed. She turned and looked at me one last time.

At that moment, the energy in the room changed. Like the tables turned, and she had a little doubtful yet the nervous reality that she was about to allow something to go down that she's never done before. And now, I was ready. Needless to say, my clothes and her shirt joined in a mess on the floor, and we began our journey into soul ties.

The relationship that we had never became a committed one. It was always about lust, sex, and believe it or not; wisdom. But, the funny thing about the wisdom is that it came with a price. In our 2 year connection, I learned a lot about the mindset of women. She would shoot straight from the hip, raw uncut, no games. In some of our conversations, I remember feeling like this was her way of protecting me from something. She would get very passionate about what she was telling me at times. I would just sit there and sponge it all up. To be honest, I didn't even know what to do with that information at the time. But little did I know, she was planting a seed. A seed that would prepare me for a lifestyle that she either saw coming or best fit for me.

Even though we had an understanding set in place that she suggested, sometimes she would break her own barriers. Although I did grow to care for her, it began to show that her feelings were deeper. In my mind, I measured her depth by the things she bought me and did for me. But she always told me that she knew my feelings for her would change for her one day. Considering I was almost half her age. But she wasn't wrong. As my 16th birthday was coming up, her realization of a future for us had presented itself. As quickly as it started, this semester was coming to an end.

Our final night together was life-changing. We had just finished having sex for the last time. Just like any other time, afterwards; we talked. But this night, the seed planted was watered and begun to sprout. She laid in the bed and said she needed to tell me something. I already felt like I knew what it was. So I was ready. She sat up on the side of the bed with the bedsheets wrapped around her. She wasn't crying, but the look in her eyes seemed beat with emotions. "Do you know why I was feeling you when I met you"? I told her, "No, I don't, but to be honest, I thought you were a little crazy at first". As we giggled with a bland energy, she slowly started to shake her head, no. She went on to tell me why she pursued me and her original intentions. Overall, it was about having someone she can rebound with from a very dominating ex-fiance. She wanted to know what it felt like to be a dominate person.

She further tells me some things about myself that I know for sure at the time, I didn't see in myself. She said that my fun-loving and maturity was unique considering my age and the environment we lived in. She told me that I was a natural protector and leader because of how I watched over my brother and how concerned I was with both my mom and dad's recovery. She said that I was here before my time and she's always felt like she was in a room with a man her age. When she began to speak about the sexual part of our connection, that's when a tear fell from her eye. Telling me that she planned to put it on me and make me chase her all over the city of Boston in the daytime with a flashlight. She paused, and with a light laugh, she said, "That sure didn't work out the way I saw it".

She finished up by saying, "Shannyn, When you get older, you are going to be a very special man". She continued on to say, "Women will throw themselves at you, and not many men will like you". This is just a small summary of what she said that day. But what she said and did before I left her house for the last time changed the paradigm of my life path.

She goes over to her tall dresser, and out of the top draw, she grabbed a stack of cash. She walks up to me and says, "What you have is something these little hood rats out here think they can handle. They all play games. But don't let them play with you. Make these little b*tches pay you if they want to lay with you". "As you get older, you'll learn that they will". She then puts one thousand dollars in my hand. I then gave Evelyn her key back and started walking to the Lee School. We saw each other a couple more times around the city after that. But Evelyn and I never reconnected again.

— A Covering —

There was a blizzard coming. Massachusetts had issued a state of emergency and had broadcast that the city would be shut down. When this information came in, I was at the Community Center. Once they announced that the center is closing early and the scheduled van rides home would be canceled for the night. I gathered my bag and brand new coat that I just got myself for Christmas and began my travels home. It was dark out, and the snow had already begun to fall. I had to take a bus to Ashmont station, then get on the trolley rail to Mattapan Square, and then get on another bus to take me up Cummings highway to drop me off at the top of my street. But because of the increasing snowy conditions, the last bus I needed was off schedule. So I thought I would walk to the nearest convenience store to grab a few snacks for the rest of the night because we would be snowed in officially in a few hours. When I came out of the store, I looked to the right and saw my mom. At this point, I hadn't seen her in about a month. She was walking toward the store and because I had a hood on. She didn't notice me at first. But what I noticed about her was that she didn't look so good. I don't know where she was coming from, but I was totally concerned that she didn't have a coat on. Just a green sweat shirt, black dusty jeans, and a pair of white dirty Reeboks. So I said, "Hey, Where you going?" She turned and said she was going in the store while noticing it was me. She gave me a hug and a kiss on the cheek, but I could tell she was disappointed that I caught her in a low moment. We stood there and talked for about 5 minutes. In that time I suggested maybe she should move back to Florida considering her life condition. I knew she didn't have anywhere to go for the night. So for a quick moment in the back of my mind, I thought to tell her to come back to the house with me for the night. But I knew better than to ask that. Because my grandmother had finally put a stop to her coming to the house. She was through with my mom and her choice of lifestyle.

I asked my mom where was her coat and hat? She shamefully looked at me and said that she didn't have one. Right after she replied, I saw the bus I needed slow down and stop at a yellow light that just changed to red. Without thinking and in a sudden adrenaline rush to catch that bus. I took off my coat and threw it on my mom, kissed her, told her to call me, and took off running up a short side street in order to catch the #30 bus. I caught it.

— The Wedding Party —

That very same year, my God-Sister Venus was getting married. Venus was the oldest of 3 children of who my Godparents turned out to be. Elijah and Faye, that is. A southern Geechie couple who also fled from the deep south in search of higher ground from the drowning racism and Jim Crow laws. I don't know exactly what they went through or experienced while they were there in Florence, South Carolina; But thank God they made it to Boston. To me, they were black excellence. The very first power couple I've ever seen in my life. A lot of my friends thought that they were island or Caribbean people because they talked so fast with a type of broken English dialect that only love could understand. They also made me understand that they loved me too. They even took me with them on a family trip as a kid. It was my first time ever leaving Boston, Mass. They took me to their hometown. Back to the farm and property that they grew up on. It was the first time I had ever stayed in a home with no bathroom in it. I remember my God-Sister Pam would have to wash me up in a pale. Right in the middle of the living room in front of everybody while watching a black and white TV. Boy, did I love running around on that farm playing with all the animals. When I got a little older, my God-Parents noticed my attraction to the sound of a piano. So they bought me my first Casio Keyboard for Christmas.

I've been in a couple of weddings before this one. I guess I was too old to be a ring barrier in Venus's wedding. And now, I'm tall enough to be a groomsman. After all, I am a teenager.

At the reception portion of Venus's big wedding day, I have to say; I had a ball. Because one thing my God-Family knew how to do other than work hard; was celebrate and have a good time. Thats just what we did. The love and energy was in the building. The wedding party had been introduced, the food had been served, the cake had been cut, the lights went low, and the Bar was open. The families of both the bride and groom intertwined and made new memories that we all still share today. The men of men gathered together as the women did the same. At one point, I noticed my God-Brother EJ disappeared along with a few of my other cousins. But I found them. They were outside in the back of the parking lot. I could see them from the side entry of the venue. I heard them laughing and carrying on as if they were in a barbershop. But only this time, there were extra Remy and Heineken bottles out the back of EJ's trunk. He saw me in the door-way looking for them. So he raised his hand with his beer bottle to signal me to come over where they were. So I did. I don't know what I walked into, but I know it was a moment that I will never forget.

When I got over to them, I was offered a beer and a shot of Remy. They all thought it was my first shot of Cognac, so they all did a shot as well. In some way, it was like a welcome into manhood. Or, at least that's how I took it. Usually, things like this happen at family celebrations. After the shot, the conversation took a turn. But nothing bad at all. We began talking about women and relationships, just the basics though. Like, the ups and downs that come over time. The very popular loving quote, yet complaint about women and how you can't live with them, but you damn sure can't live without them. I was seriously taking notes that night. I mean, how could I not with being surrounded by so much wisdom. Then it happened. I was starting to feel good, and I remember hearing the music from inside. I could even see inside the doorway where the family was on the dance floor. There was a clear eye path from in between the cars in the parking lot. Then, there was a tap on my shoulder, and it was an offer to take a couple of tokes of a joint. Now, I have smoked a blunt before this moment. But never out in public or in front of the family. So I took a couple of pulls from the well-rolled joint anyway. I didn't want the fellas to think I was a square. After my second inhale, I passed it on. It took but only 2 to 3 minutes before my mind began to zoom in and out. All of a sudden it was like I was there, but not. Kind of like a dream. My God-Brother EJ is known for getting people totally wasted so that he can have a memory of his "well doings". A true cannabis connoisseur and an overall really good guy. He was the one that taught me how to drive and even came with me to get my license.

But Let's just say EJ is "King Iron Lungs".

The guys could see I was high as a ceiling fan, and EJ started asking me random questions about everything at once. My mind scrambled a bit, but I knew what was going on. I was answering all the questions without holding back. But there was no way to stop me from laughing.

As a little boy, I saw him do this to many before me. This was just one moment of the many times that I fell victim to his shenanigans. The music from inside the reception seemed to get louder and louder, and all the questions began to fade out. Everything being said started sounding like a mumble mush of words. It was only about 15 minutes that I was even out there. But that's all I could stand. The music from inside was calling me. In some way, music has always been my savior. My natural instinct kicked in, and I excused myself from the guys and started making my way back to where the grooves were trailing from. Before Beyonce did it, Frankie Beverly and Maze mixed with the well-known electric slide was all I needed to be triggered. Before I walked off, my God Brother hit me off with a couple of sprits of cologne to tone the scent of weed down. I can still remember hearing them laughing at me as I walked away. I was baked.

When I made it back inside, the function hall seemed to be even bigger than it was before I stepped outside. But, I went back in with one mission. I just wanted to dance. Old school, new school, it didn't matter. I danced with any and everybody that stepped up.

Now because I knew there were "no kids allowed" at the reception. I believed that I was the youngest in attendance that night. But boy, was I blessed to be wrong. As I was dancing and surely making a spectacle of myself, I placed my eyes on a young lady that was there that I was sure I had never seen before. It was inevitable that we made eye contact because I couldn't take my eyes off her for some reason. Now normally, light skin girls weren't a chase for me. I usually went for the darker-skinned girls. But in this case, there was an exception. She was sitting at one of the tables that surrounded the dance floor. She was sitting alone right upfront. She stood out. She had on a yellow dress and a T-Boz from TLC hairstyle. Now I have never really been the type to approach a girl because dancing usually sparked most of my connections. Because, let's face it, girls like guys that can dance. Now I'm sure with all the courage in my system at the time, that gave me the necessary leverage to hunt. I was mesmerized and stuck on stupid. There was no way I could pass up on this moment. I had to know just who she was.

I break away from what now has become somewhat of a R&B-Soul mosh pit. I walked over to the table where she was. She could see me coming. I noticed immediately how she all of a sudden tried to unplug our connection by turning her head, cutting off our eye contact. In my underdeveloped security of myself, I took that a couple of ways. For one, I thought maybe she was there with someone else, and two, maybe she's just shy. Yet still, I kept in stride until I was standing in front of her. I reached out my hand, and I asked her, "Do you wanna dance?" I couldn't believe how fast she answered with shaking her head with the quickest no I have ever heard in my life. As I'm standing there while she sat with her legs crossed at the edge of the seat, I took a deeper look into her eyes. While standing there trying to further my intent to get her to the dance floor, I saw that she had beautiful hazel eyes. But also I learned that the "No" wasn't about me, but more so about how shy and pure she was. I thought it was cute. Too bashful to even dance. Then, an abrupt cut in the conversation. "She ain' gonna dance, come on I'll dance wit'chu". It was her mother. She was a longtime co-worker and good friend of my God-Sister, Venus. We got out on the dance floor and 2 stepped for 2 songs straight. As the night ended, I walked her to the door where her father was outside to pick her and her mom up. All I had time left to do was ask her what her name was. She looked at me, blushing and simply said, "Tifani, Bye Shannyn". I watched her get in the car and drive all the way out of the parking lot.

— A Christmas Story —

A couple months after Venus's wedding, winter had come back around. The holiday spirit had begun to take hold over the city in preparation to end the year. So the holiday spirit was in the air. That thanksgiving I was at the Community Center volunteering to give out free turkeys and groceries to the less fortunate. I was always up to doing stuff like that. I felt compelled to do it. Because I knew even then that I came from standing in many hand out lines and hoped that nobody would judge or look down on me. To have those opportunities felt like I knew better than to forget where I came from. So there was never a hesitation to do it.

As the weeks got closer to Christmas, shopping had begun to be an almost daily routine for everybody. My grandmother would get a little tree every year, and we would decorate it. The tree would never be more than 4 feet tall because we lived in a small apartment and always cluttered the living room. But a clean and neat clutter. My grandmother was a very clean and neat woman. She was stern about cleanliness.

There were never a lot of gifts under the tree. Maybe one or two gifts each for me, my grandmother, my brother Randy and Frank. The gifts for me and my brother never said that they were from Frank, but I knew better than to think that the gifts my grandmother got me and my brother were just out of her pockets alone. Frank took good care of my grandmother. Therefore he took care of us. He was a real-life Santa Clause for all of us all year round.

About a week before Christmas Day I got a call from My uncle Bryce's new girlfriend. She had called in place of my uncle to ask me what I wanted for Christmas. Since music was all I cared about, it was a must that I asked for the latest music out at the time. I was definitely my father's son. We went back and forth about how many CDs I could get. Because if it was left up to me, I would want about 5 or 20 albums. I heard my uncle in the background say out loud, "Stop hustlin like ya mother". We all laughed. CD's were expensive back then. We settled on 3 albums. Also in the background he said that he will pick out the 3 of the numerous choices. I said, "Ok, make sure they're good though". He replied with, "Whatever". Before we hung up, he grabbed the phone from his girlfriend and asked me one last question. What did LeRaun need? I told him that I didn't know, but he will be here next week on the 23rd. He said, "Aight" and that he would find out, and we hung up.

6 months before that coming Christmas, my mother had a new baby with a former short-term boyfriend. He had kids all over the city of Boston. But between him and my mom, they had one, Leraun. He was the chubbiest, cutest baby I had ever seen in my life. He looked like a mini sumo wrestler. I was super excited about being an older brother again, but not as excited as Randy. This was his first time being a big brother. It only took 15yrs. But unfortunately, Randy was heartbroken by the experience from day one. The week LeRaun was born, Randy was snatched back into a familiar time. The week my mother had LeRaun; Randy finally went to the hospital to see his new little brother, along with my grandmother. To his surprise, they were met by that same old child care worker that used to work our case when we were younger, Malina. She was there with the Boston Police. They were there to remove our new little brother from my mother's custody. Randy and my Grandmother both were confused, tearful, and, of course, brokenhearted. Because my mom never finished any court-ordered drug rehab programs in order to get Randy and me back into her custody. The document stood for any new coming child that my mother had. To nail it in the coffin. They had detected drugs in my mother's system as well. Randy and my grandmother felt deceived. We all did. Because she was pregnant with the baby boy, we all thought she was clean. By the time I got to the hospital, Randy was gone, and My grandmother was getting ready to leave. She was noticeably broken-hearted by the look she had in her eyes and LeRaun, gone.

My mother was sitting on the side of the hospital bed and her bags ready to go. My grandmother was so hurt that she didn't even want to give my mother a ride home. She silently left. Yet again, attempting to let go of my mother out of disappointment. But I stayed and ended up helping my mother to the hospital's lobby and into a cab with her. On the way to her destination, she told me what happened. We talked all the way there. The last thing she said before we got out of the cab that I know haunted her was what the caseworker said before she left with LeRaun. She said, "I didn't get the first two, but this one will do, and I can retire now". My mother had received her after-grad diploma that day.

Finally, Christmas is a couple of days away. I was ready for the family to gather at one of our family members houses to eat good food, watch the old folks play spades and argue, listen to the same ole Christmas blues songs on repeat, watch sports on tv and wait and see who will be the drunkest before the end of the night. The anticipation was real. Flawed and all, I loved to be around my family. But sad to say, this turned out to be a Christmas nightmare.

As always, I was at the Community Center yet again, this time volunteering to give away wrapped toys for the less fortunate kids in the neighborhood. Someone came to the auditorium and called my name. "Shannyn, you got a phone call". So I left my station and went to the lobby sign-in booth where the phone was. Shockingly surprised, It was my aunt Linda. She has never called me there. When I heard her voice, I could already tell that she had been drinking for the day. She said, "Shannyn, Shannyn". I said with a slight smirk on my face, "Hey, Aunt Linda". I thought she was just drunk dialing and just wanted to tell me her famous "I love you dearly" speech as she would randomly do with all of her family members out the blue. But this was far from a laughing or endearment call. She told me that she thought that I should make my way to her house. Her home was within walking distance from the community center, Just right past Franklin Hill Projects. I asked, "Why aunt Linda, I'm in the middle of something". She said that she knew how busy I was down at that place, but the matter was serious. I said, "Well, how serious?" She said, "It's your uncle Shannyn". I could only think of my grandmother's brothers and think that something had happened to one of them. So I asked her, "Which uncle Aunt Linda?" I heard her lightly sob and out of her mouth came; "Bryce, it's Bryce Shannyn, He's gone". I will never forget that moment. I hung up the phone. I turned and took a look around the whole lobby. Even though people were there it was like the entire building was empty for at least 10 seconds. I immediately couldn't help but to think back to an eerie moment in the summer of that same year. While I sat outside in front of the community center, my cousin Kenny drove by in his Van. As the stop light was turning red; he stopped. I went to wave and there in the passengers seat was my uncle Bryce fully slumped in a nod. I shouted, "Hey!". Uncle Bryce looked up and when he noticed it was me, he swung at Kenny and told him to pull off. I can tell he didn't want me to see him in that way. That was the last time I seen my uncle Bryce alive.

The weather outside was cold, it was sleeting and wet. I walked out the front door and sat down upside the cold brick wall of the community center in disbelief. I remember saying to myself, "She was drunk and didn't know the whole story. This can't be true". My mind started spinning and wondering what the story truly might be. Then, I got up and started running toward my Aunt Linda's house. By the time I got to the corner of Blue Hill & Talbot Ave, I saw my cousin Kenny in his big Blue van and tinted windows. Another one of my hot-headed family members. He was no angel at all.

When he saw me, he pulled over and I got right in. My cousin looked very sad but peculiar in his demeanor. His only words to me were, "Where is your coat, You soaked?" My reply, "At the community center". Aunt Linda was in the van along with my grandmother's other brother, Luke.

We got back to my house where my grandmother was with a couple of other family members who had rushed over to her side. At this point, My grandmother was distraught and did not believe it. You can only imagine the pain of a mother who lost her only son. As family began to flow in with their concerns and condolences, a call came in. It was the Boston City Morgue. They told my grandmother that someone should come to identify John Doe just to be positive that it was him or not. Right there is where I started telling myself, "Maybe it's not even him". Even though nobody has heard from him in a few days. I just didn't want to accept it. I was hoping and wishing. They told my grandmother that it was too late to come that night, and the next shift doctor would be there as early as 7:30 am. When I heard that, I made up in my mind right then that I wanted to go. Because I knew my grandmother wasn't strong enough to go.

I must have been home for about 2 hours before I finally realized that my baby brother LeRaun was there. After all, It was December 23rd, just as scheduled. I finally picked him up and sat on the side of my bed, held him tight and told him "welcome home for Christmas baby boy".

It was a long night. The next morning on Christmas Eve, me, my mom, my aunts (Nellie & Lynn) and also my Uncles best friend Jesse all went to identify what turned out to be positively, my Uncle Bryce. A moment that stained my mind for many years to come after. When they turned on the monitor to reveal his lifeless face, I gasped so deep that I can't even remember how long it was until I exhaled. Everything in my soul froze. I couldn't even cry. Maybe because I was still low-key mad at him for robbing me. What a heavy and sad day it was.

A week later, we laid him to rest in eternity. A snowy, below freezing, and face cracking windy day. Everybody from every old neighborhood and even as far as Florida came. The only person I noticed not there that day, was Kenny. Still to this day, that strikes me as odd. Because they were always together. He was the last person to see my uncle alive.

After they lowered him into the ground, my last words were, "I forgive you". On New Year's Eve, I finally opened the 3 CDs he got me for Christmas. Snoop Dogg/Doggystyle, Keith Murray/Enigma, and Blackstreet/Another Level.

Through that experience, I learned so many lessons.

Here's Three. First; even strong people have weaknesses. Second; don't be afraid to ask for help. Third; forgive as quick as you can.

Rest In Peace, Uncle Bryce.

— The Last Assignment —

Before finishing up my 10th-grade year at Hyde Park High School. I had the privilege, along with four other guys, to go down to Atlanta,Georgia, in pursuit of success in the music industry. I had big hopes and dreams for us. At that time, I think we all did. Atlanta was just starting to heat up; to become one of the hot spots for new up-and-coming black talent. I remember when our Amtrak train first pulled into the station. The first thing that stood out was an Olympic day counter. Counting down the days until the ceremony would begin in the summer of 1996. As we sat in the station waiting on our ride with our baggage and trunks of stage outfits. I think I was expecting our manager to give us that talk that most parents would give to their kids before walking into a store. The very well-known, "Don't ask for nothing, Don't break nothing and be on your best behavior" speech. We were some inner-city kids, and we were all a little rough around the edges. But our manager, Trevar, was in his own zone, but way more chill than usual. Like he was just letting the boys be boys because he knew how excited we were. I don't think I showed much emotion on the outside, but I was full of fireworks on the inside. Even on the train ride down, I kept saying to myself, "Shannyn, this is your chance. Be professional and stand out and don't let your nerves get the best of you, rock every show". I must have said that to myself about 50 times. Because that's what we were there to do. Rock as many shows as we could on a mini one-month tour and hopefully get discovered by a big record label.

We finally get picked up from the train station. The driver already knew where we were going. On the way to our destination, I stared out the window, observing every turn and street name we past. Because I didn't quite know what the living situation would be where ever we'd end up staying. And, just in case something went down, I would at least know how to get back to that Amtrak station. At the time, "You can take the kid out of Roxbury, but you can't take Roxbury out the kid'. So I was always prepared for the worse. A lesson that life never seemed to cease teaching me so far.

The ride seemed to be a little long. But eventually, we ended up in a town called Buckhead. I remember seeing so many fancy mansions and luxury cars. But what grabbed my attention the most was the black faces that the materials belonged too. We finally pulled into an upscale community and then right up to a gate. It was one of those moments that should have been caught on video. Because everybody's eyes got big, and just like pushing stop on a tape deck; everybody shut up. We pulled through the gate, and the first thing you see was a pond with ducks floating and walking around. Then, right behind the pond was a street that led up a steep hill. At the top of the hill was a beautiful mansion. I turned to our manager and asked, "This where we staying?" He nodded his head saying, yes. Once he said that, all kinds of bells and whistles began to sound off in my head. As if my spirit was letting me know I'm on the right track and where I need to be. My professionalism and motivation locked in. Suddenly, I had fewer words to say to anybody and more fire in my bones. We got out of the van, grabbed all of our bags, and got to the front door. We all walked through the double-doored entrance as a team. This was probably the first time I walked on marble floors in someones home. Everything was big, Wide open, and grand. The furniture, appliances, The chandelier and the back yard. There was even a Grand Piano in the living room. I immediately thought of 23 Angel Street. Where my Grandmother on my dad's side of the family lived. She was the only one that I knew who had a piano in her house. Because she played. So this was a moment that I hated that I never learned to play professionally.

It was a beautiful home with multiple bathrooms and bedrooms, three story's of luxury all around. But the best part about the whole house; there was a full professional Recording Studio in the basement. I knew right then that this was the life that I wanted to live. The excitement and anticipation were real.

I was ready for whatever Atlanta's music scene had to offer.

We learned who the house belonged to later that day, but we didn't get to meet him until the next morning. Turns out, the house was owned by the very same man that put me on stage to help curve the energy of an upset crowd from a non-believable Michael Jackson impersonator. Of course, he didn't remember who I was from that time, and I never tried to remind him. I didn't want my group members to think I was trying to get ahead of them in some kind of selfish or privileged way. There will always be some type of tension somewhere between them in every boy band. But there was no denying the chemistry we had on stage.

We must have rehearsed day in and day out. We were on a mission. There was even another boy band that toured with us. They were from the Atlanta area. They were some well-mannered, country church boys and they could really sing. I even learned an old Gospel song from the lead singer of their group that I still sing to myself to this day. They would come over before their rehearsal time and just watch us dance and do our songs. They loved it. They ended up becoming our first fans in Atlanta.

We would perform all over the Atlanta area. Sometimes even 2 to 3 times a day. If it wasn't a talent night at the Fox Theater, then we were at Club 112 or somewhere like that. We were even scheduled to open up for The Notorious B.I.G and Goodie Mobb one of those days. You couldn't tell us nothing. But when we got there, the promoters had to bump our performance due to another famous person that popped up and wanted to do a song or two. We were pissed, so Trevar made a deal with the promoters to allow us to stay and watch the show. Even that was a big deal because we were underage.

The other boy band that we toured with couldn't do some of the shows that we did. Yet, we couldn't do some of their gigs as well. Their genre and image were more spiritual and clean. Not to say that we were totally dirty. But our image was just a little more worldly.

This one show we had must have been the most awkward ever. We ended up performing at a Muslim Mosque. We walked in and the kids in there went crazy. The Muslim leader looked over at us, and you could see he quickly had concerns. He walked over to Trevar and asked him what kind of songs we would sing. Whatever he said to him, it didn't go well. Trevar came back over to the stage and grabbed our mics and mic stands, and said, "Do the damn dance routine, and let's go". We felt the tension, but we had a job to do. As soon as we finished, we walked right outside the door, leaving the kids screaming and expecting more. Needless to say, our songs just didn't match that audience.

In the beginning we opened up the show for the other boys. But that all changed after a show we had at a rolling skating rink. I will never forget that day. It was the first time we ever felt what it was like to be famous as a group. We pulled up in a limousine. It was a long line from the inside all the way out the door and down aside of the building. The other boys got out first. We stayed inside of the limo and watched as they walked past the line while acknowledging their friends and family. We surely thought that because they were from Atlanta, they would have home-court advantage. And, they did. But we had no fret. Because we've been in situations like this before. We just mentally went into the zone we used when performing on the world-famous Apollo Stage in Harlem,NY. One of the most intimidating stages an amateur artist could ever touch.

Trevar came over to the window of the limo and told us while smoking his Newport, "Y'all better tare this muthaf*cka up," and walked away. He had already been inside the venue and felt the energy in the building.

The limo driver came around and opened the door for us and we got out one by one. We were dressed just like a typical boy band. Identical outfits. Everyone in the line got quiet, but they all was looking. We were use to that part. As we moved in unison toward the door, the line started to come alive with rising whispers and giggles. But we didn't come to play games.

Of course, when we got inside, there was loud music and kids skating around already. It reminded me of the Skating rink back in my hood, Chez-Vous. We sat together and waited for the show to start. In that time we began to get even more stares. But we were staring too. How could we not; there were so many girls that I started to think we were the only boys in the whole place. We didn't mind that at all though. While we were waiting, I remember two men came in the front door that looked kind of important. They were looking for someone. They were directed to our manager. They shook hands, talked for a couple minutes and then the two men took a seat.

We must have been there for about 40 minutes before the show started. The DJ finally fades out his last song and points everyones attention to the dance floor. That took no time. The crowd formed and their curiosity began to intensify. It was the first time I looked into the eyes of a consumer that had anxiety about watching me do what I loved. They were ready. While the DJ was warming up the crowd and giving them some updates about the upcoming events at the rink. Trevar was setting up the stage for us. The crowd got even more hype. They weren't even listening to the DJ at this point.

Before every performance, we would say a little prayer. So we did. By the time we finished, we heard the DJ introduce us. "Y'all make some noise for, Tuff Assignment". As we walked out onto the stage. The screams and applause were blaring. I couldn't believe the welcoming response we got.

We use to always start our shows with a quick dance sequence. We would do that to shake out any nerves we had. So we get into our routine positions, and the music finally starts. As soon as we got into step, the crowd lost it. Our high energy, pop-locking, B-boyish, traditional, New Edition, Boston style was electrifying to the Atlanta audience. By the time we got to our original songs, the crowd was already sold. It got to a point that our manager had to walk out and began a barricading walk between the spectators and us. I even recall a moment when I looked over at the family and friends of the other boy band. It was a 50/50 split. Some had a look of defeat, while the others were enjoying it.

We finally wrap up, ending our set. We introduced ourselves one by one. We said, "Thank You for having us". We took our bows, and we walked off the skating floor. By the time we got to the concession stand to get our drinks, the energy in the building had gone to another level. When we turned around the crowd had followed us. Before we could even catch our breath, a girl boldly steps forward with her camera and asks to take a photo. We all agreed. Once we took that photo, another girl asked one of the boys from my band if she could take a picture with just him. When he did, the commotion began. Because now every girl had her pick of who she wanted to take a personal picture with from Tuff Assignment. That's when the aggression got real. I remember Trevar signaling the security of the building to assist what he was witnessing about to happen. They were moving slow. I don't know if it made it worse or not, but when Trevar yelled out, "If you don't want your place f*cked up, you better get 'em out of here". Then, pandemonium. The security had to wrestle through chaotic screaming and wild reaching limbs toward us that were coming from all sides. They finally got to us, built another barricade between us, and guided us to the door. In the moment I remember looking at some of the faces of my band members, and I saw a couple of looks of fear. This was unreal and kind of scary to them. As for me, I loved every second of it. As they got us through the door to quickly get us back into the limo, the crowd followed. Some with skates on, and others with no shoes at all. They began to surround the car and bang on the windows. We were inside with the same energy. Yelling, one high five after another, we were complimenting ourselves as if we were celebrating that we made it. What a feeling it was.

The very next day, at the mansion, we finally got a chance to record with the man of the house; "The Lieutenant". A real documented mogul and producer. He liked us a lot. But for some reason, I felt like he wasn't as excited to move forward with us. To me, it seemed as though Trevar's longtime friendship with "The Lieutenant" was conditional in a way that keeps Trevar, small. So, because Trevar worked for him off and on for so many years behind the scenes and sort of like a sidekick, I realized that Trevar's own ideas and creations had ceilings with "The Lieutenant". Because of my acquaintance with good situations going bad, I was familiar with the vibe that there would be no benefit for us after we left. Our last hope was the two guys who came to the skating rink show. But Trevar broke and told us that they only wanted 3 of us out of the group. He never told us which 3. What a "Tuff" business. A couple of days later, we were back at the Amtrak station with our luggage, nappy heads filled with memories, and a demo with two unfinished songs.

When we got back to Boston. I quickly realized that we weren't even missed. The city immediately casted its reel and began to fish us all back into the reality of our real opportunities. No more than six months later, what I didn't want to see happen, happened. After years of collectively fighting for a dream to be the next big name boy band out of the city, we were done...What a "Tuff Assignment".

— Love & War —

One night there was party at the Carver Den. A popular function hall in the city. Everybody was talking about it weeks before. I wasn't sure if I was going to go, but then my cousin Wiz called me and said he was going and wanted to know if I was. I didn't plan on it, but I played like I did and said I was. I think one of the reasons I agreed was because it was a familiar place that my family knew of pretty well. Wiz's mom was the manager over the building for years. As kids, we use to play in the open space ballrooms running from one to the other going through secret doorways and passages while his mom worked. So we knew the floor plan pretty well.

We got to the party and it was packed. Wiz was dating a girl from the community center at the time and she had brung her sister and all of her girls with her. One of her girls was for me as it was planned. Nevertheless, the hood came out to party that night too. So I mixed and mingled in the crowd for a bit and greeted my friends and some of the new high profiled street legends from the neighborhood.

The Party had been going on for about 2 hours so far and it was a good time. I had on a red Polo shirt, blue jeans and a pair of Jay's. I was feeling good. Especially after a drink or two from the Hennessy bottle that I had snuck in. While me and Wiz was standing along the wall enjoying the booming music and watching the crowd. The ladies that was there for us wanted to dance. Neither of us denied them. Before we knew it we was pushed up against the wall and the girls started moving. It wasn't long before it went to another level. Because the DJ starts mixing in reggae music and they turned the main lights off. We were sweating, dry-humping and grinding like we were all in heat. It was like every song was our favorite song when it came on. But then, as we were dancing me and Wiz at the same time had saw a few guys come in the door. That quickly raised our curiosity because they wasn't from this side of town. They had a rivalry with some guys that we had seen in the party a couple hours ago. So now, I'm on full alert. As I'm sliding side to side on the wall dancing I can't keep my eyes off of the energy of the guys that just came in. They almost seemed to be looking for somebody. About 10 minutes later, one of those guys put a litter in the air and started flicking it. Not like he was trying strike a flame, but instead causing the litter to strike friction to get a spark. He did that repeatedly 3 or 4 times. And then, POP-POP-POP-POP-POP, the whole party ducked low and the panic was a terrifying frenzy for the exit door. The girls that were with us was screaming, confused and scared. So they were also trying to make it toward the front door. But we grabbed them and redirected them back into the party going the other way through one of the back hallways of the building that we knew of. Unfortunately we had to trample over a few people on the floor to get there, But girls that was with us, was safe.

After about 20 minutes and the police had arrived. Wiz's mom finally came in the back where we had taken cover and told us all to go home.

On the way out we had to walk back through the hall and through the ballroom where tables and chairs were all flipped, a few drops of blood on the floor and coats of the people who ran off and left them.

But what sticks in my mind still to this day about that night. As I was walking pass the wall where I was dancing, I saw the red dye smudging of my shirt on the wall. But when I looked up to where my head would have been. There was a bullet hole. Most people knew about that party. Because somebody got shot. But I never told anybody about that part.

I'm well into my Junior Year at Hyde Park High School. I guess you could say the girls are paying attention to me a little more. After all, I was working out quite seriously at the time. Let me not forget to mention that I got my driver's license too. I didn't have a car. But my grandmothers' car will do. My self-esteem finally took hold to a level that I could manage it. Despite my efforts to be an entertainer, A lot of people didn't know how shy I really was. The 11th grade is where I started to get a glimpse of who I was and possibly would become one day. I even remember thinking that maybe one day I would move to another big city.

I remember telling my grandmother that one day I would leave Boston. Maybe I was influenced by Randy already moving to Florida to be with my mom. She finally had enough of Boston and her life as it was. She finally started to clean up her act. Myself and Randy were really proud of her. She worked a job that she loved on a casino cruise ship on Cape Canaveral in Florida. Because of her decision to try and get it right; It was the only reason Randy would agree to go in the first place.

But honestly I think Randy left because he was hurt about him and his girlfriend Carla's break up. He had met her at the Community

Center. I hated to see him torn up about it. Because I knew from day one that my brother was in love with her. But after one school year. He came back to Boston and they worked it out.

I actually loved high school. At Hyde Park High, I had a lot of friends and was considered to be kind of popular, but still, I was the loner type. Yet, I wasn't anti-social or anything like that, I just knew what crowd was or wasn't for me. But I did have the kind of personality that I could flow in any group or crew. Like for instance, one day, I would sit with the Franklin Hill/Franklin Field project kids. The next day I would sit with the white kids, On other days I would sit and talk with the Haitian kids or the geeks and Latinos. I wasn't a trouble maker, but I wasn't a punk either. No matter what table I sat at, I was welcomed. I wasn't a teacher's pet, but most of the faculty liked me. Never considered to be a bad student. But I definitely wasn't the most academically advanced either. I had my favorite subjects, and others that I didn't really care for. Those subjects I almost used no brain functionality to even try to learn. Like, Mr. Etienne's Class, Algebra 2. I hated it! It was like speaking another language to me. In fact, when I saw letters mixed with numbers, it was alien coded to me. My God sister Pam used to try to tutor me in the subject, and again, that wasn't very long-lived at all.

But, what classes I did love were my World Social Studies, Geography, Biology, Typing, and of course, Theater Arts in the school's auditorium. There were only three periods a day that class happened. But that was the class that most of my friends would skip to go to the store, smoke weed, or even leave for the rest of the day altogether. Most of my peers thought it was a cheesy or corny class. And even though I picked up a couple of those bad habits for myself from time to time, I wouldn't miss that class for nothing. Not only did I love the improvisational warm-ups and putting together "on the spot" skits to perform by the end of the class; I had some eye candy that I couldn't take my eyes off of the whole class. She was a Sophomore. Her guidance counselor suggested that she takes the class due to her noticeable high level of shyness. An attempt to break the ice. Come to find out, she was in my brother Randy's class. He used to pick on her because she was so shy. But, what a coincidence. The last time I saw her up until the day she walked into the auditorium, I remember I had walked her to the door at Venus's wedding reception. Tifani; I really thought i'd never see her again. Right away, Everyone could tell that we liked each other. Even the teachers. We would flirt constantly. One of her girlfriends would always instigate us moving forward into dating. I believe she was all for it, even though she would make up an excuse as to why she couldn't. She also didn't want the headache of petty and fast-ass hood girls at her neck every day either. She wasn't the fighter type and I was a popular guy. I attracted all levels of girls. And besides, conveniently enough for me, she was still growing up, and unfortunately, I had a girlfriend by this time already anyway.

My girlfriend at the time was Bajan and went to Dorchester High School. I was introduced to her by a friend from the community center. I thought she was special, but it seemed nobody else around me felt the same. It was like everybody knew that she wasn't fit for me, but me. She had a "witchy" type personality and was somewhat vain. But if I had know then what I know now, her whole personality was dressed in insecurity.

Like any other relationship, we started off nice and sweet. She was the first girl that I openly dated. Meaning, she wasn't a secret. But by the end of our journey, there was a spirit awakened inside of me that I didn't even know I had. Let's just say, some women know how to speak to the king in a man, and others, only know how to speak to the fool inside of him. And that's just what she did.

In a time that I was trying to build my confidence, here I had a girl-friend who preyed on my weakness. Or, at least I thought they were weaknesses. She was more about the flashiness with the way a person dressed and carried themselves. Even though I had a job and had a side hustle, I wasn't flashy about it. I never felt as though designer clothes made me who I was. But that kind of thing always got her attention.

She hated the fact that wherever we'd go, someone would either know me or I'd know them, and they'd always want to talk. One way or another, there was some sort of attention on me. She would say things like, "Why you gotta talk to everybody," or, "you always in people's faces". But I really wasn't. She really just didn't like my spotlight.

One night we were going out. Her cousin was having a gathering at her house. Because it was an event that she invited me too, I wanted to live up to her fly standard. So I popped a tag, threw on some Jay's, and put on some jewelry as well. I couldn't get my grandmothers car that night, so we decided to take the MBTA (public Transportation) (The "T"). We got on the #23 bus at Four Corners in Dorchester, where she lived. The bus wasn't as full when we got on, but it wasn't totally empty either. Just some girls chatting along the ride, an older gentleman that looked like he was just getting off work, a young Spanish couple with a toddler, and a few others sporadically seated throughout the isle.

As we walked to the back of the bus to take a seat I noticed a few guys. All 3 of them are sitting on the very back row of the bus. They all had to be about my age. One guy was even sitting up on the back of the seats. They were a little rowdy, but it's the weekend, and that was normal. But just as quickly as I noticed them, they noticed me as well. Because they did notice me, my instincts told me not to sit down. But I did tell my girlfriend to have a seat. She did. I then stood in the steps of the rear door of the bus. Before we got to a stop at Grove Hall in Roxbury. The guys all of a sudden went from rowdy to whispering to one another. I didn't get scared or nervous, but I knew the energy from the back row was vibrating toward me. As the bus was pulling up to the next stop, I noticed quite a few more people waiting to get on. Those guys saw the people too. By the time the bus stopped, one of the guys was up on me, staring down at me in the rear door steps. The bus driver opened the front door and let the waiting people on. Then one of the guys said out loud, "Rear Door," signaling the driver to open the rear exit. Once the doors opened, one of the guys step down onto the same step I was on. He then said with a conniving tone, "Nice Chain, Homie," and reached his hand toward my shining neck. Because I didn't know him, I slapped his hand away. My first reaction was definitely a reflex. That slap was all they needed to enhance their adrenaline to move forward in their attempt to rob me. The first guy jumped off the bus and grabbed me by the crotch of my pants. He was trying to pull me off the bus. All I was thinking at that point was, don't let them pull me off the bus. So, I grabbed hold of the railing to pull myself back up. All the while, the other two guys are trying to push me off the bus. It became a tug of war. I literally was fighting an uphill battle. It turned into an all-out brawl against what I thought to be just 3 guys. The other passengers panicked with loud screaming and shouting while telling the bus driver to close the back door. "Close the door, they jumpin him, they jumpin him" with real commotion. For some reason, the driver had no urgency to do so. After a full minute of fist flying, head locks, pulling, and pushing. The 3 guys fled without getting one piece of the jewelry they were after, or the beat down I'm sure they would have settled for. Luckily, just a few weeks before this happened, I had got another clamp added to my gold Rolex bracelet. They tried to rip it off my wrist, and it never popped. But, As sure as I was out of breath and thought it was all over. One other guy stood up. He was sitting one seat over, next to my girlfriend on the ride. He was a big guy. I thought he was just going to jump off the bus after it had seemed the commotion was all over. He came off as just a spectating passenger. But he wasn't. He turned to me and also reached for my chain. So the fight started all over again.

But this time, me and the big boy tussled, and I lost my balance. We fell in between two double seats. In his favor, we fell with him having the upper hand. He made a flinch as if he would punch me, and I had nothing left but to cover myself. But he never punched me. He faked me out, quickly snatching my chain, and ran off the bus. It was then that the rear doors closed and the bus finally pulled off. Until this day, I still don't know if that guy was with the other three or just another Sidewalk University undergrad who cheats off of other students' work. When I got up, my first concern was my girlfriend. I couldn't look at her right away because she wasn't sitting where she originally was. All of a sudden, a women's voice yells out, "You's a punk-ass b*tch, some niggas is jumping your man, and you run off?" She was upset at what she observed of her while the mobbing was going on. My girlfriend had run to the front of the bus and pretended as if she didn't even know me. My clothes were all tattered and ripped, and out of nowhere, all the other people started giving me confidence boosters and compliments from what they all just witnessed. One dude gives me dap and says, "You handled them niggas, Dawg". All I was thinking was, how come nobody helped me. The woman yells out, "The bus driver is a stupid MF, and baby, you need to break up with that b*tch". But the one person that stands out to me the most was the older gentleman and what he said. Before he got off at his stop. He comes to the front of the bus and says to me, "Son, You handled yourself like a man. You're very lucky that neither of them had a gun or knife tonight. Unfortunately, you live in a time and place where confidence and good life is frowned upon, good luck and take care of yourself". The salt and pepper-haired man then got off the bus and went on his way. A week later, I watched the news, and those same guys were arrested. They successfully robbed a man at a bus stop for his cell phone and murdered him that same night. The Boston Police caught up to the trio because one of the guys answered the phone when the police called the number to the stolen phone. They went directly to their location.

The love me and my girlfriend shared grew more toxic by the day after this. It was like every weekend, there was some type of confirmation that told me we weren't fit for one another. It was always something. But, believe it or not, she stayed in my life for 3 more years after the bus incident.

From this relationship, I learned early; that what you don't get at home, you'll find elsewhere. I also understood that I'm not the type to give up on anything, so breaking up wasn't even an option for me. I don't know why, but it has always been easier for me to handle the woman breaking up with me than me severing the relationship.

— Risking It All —

Finally, it's my Senior year! One day after school I was approached by an old friend. We didn't go to the same school, but the buses would let the Boston Public School kids in the area all off at Mattapan Station at the same time. She told me that she had started a dance group of all girls. She went on to tell me they had a show coming up as well, and they had started on the choreography. But they weren't as confident about it as they should be. I told her right away that I would help her out. It didn't hurt that I still had a little crush on her. She was the same girl that called me a bum for wearing a trench coat.

I finally got to the first rehearsal with them. I had my work cut out for me, but they all had the heart to get it done. They were all pretty girls, and of course, all of them had boyfriends. That didn't help my reputation being that everyone thought me out to be a lady's man. The boyfriends kept an eye on me, but I never had any problems out of any of them. They were too busy becoming future kingpins and respected what I was doing overall. One of them was even a well-known rapper out of the city. I never knocked their hustle, and they never knocked mine.

Meanwhile, doing what I did best was more fuel added to the fire between me and my girlfriend. I was constantly defending myself by attempting to assure her that nothing was going on between me and any of the girls. She didn't understand that once I took on a dancing gig, I was professional. Plus, I took what I did personal. It was a real stress reliever and my way of fighting back any angel of oppression in my life. I loved what I did. So I would go where ever my skills were called. I would teach kids all over the city of Boston, even in neighborhoods where I was forbidden to go. A lot of guys didn't like me because they thought I was something that I wasn't. I guess anything worth having is worth fighting for.

In preparation to get these girls ready for their upcoming show, I would work with them when and wherever there was time and space. But mostly, right out in the hallway of their apartment building. Although it may not sound glamorous, the hallway was perfect. I used the small space to help them stay positioned and in order. This is a moment where I learned to use less to get big results. There were usually mirrors and a loud sound system in a dance studio, but we had none of that. Just a boombox, my creativity and muscle memory. After a few months, the girls began to love how they looked, and you couldn't tell them nothing. They have fully bloomed into the confidence they needed for the stage. As they should, because they worked hard. Just a month right before their show, they all got together and asked me to perform with them. My first answer was no because it was about them. I felt like I did my part. But of course, I couldn't deny them. They were some "Hood Chicks". In battle, they always have a secret weapon. So I called in another young talented male dancer to help add contrast to the routine. I didn't want to be the only guy on stage with 4 girls. He learned the full routine in only six rehearsals.

One night, while we were walking to practice with the girls. A car with tinted windows passed us. The car stopped and then had made a U-turn in the middle of the street. The packed car pulled up to the curb. With the engine still running, out stepped a couple of guys. Immediately I knew it was a problem, but still, I stood there. Because even if I'm afraid, I just didn't believe in running from a problem. I at least had to get an understanding of the issue. One of the guys asked if my name was Shannyn. I told him it was. He went on to tell me that he heard I had some type of beef with him. I knew then. He was just somebody looking for trouble or an excuse to prove his gangsta in front of his click. In the back seat of the car were more people, but I heard some girls laughing. I couldn't tell who they were because it was dark, but I did hear one of them say to another, "Yea, that's Shannyn".

I didn't know if the guy had a weapon or not, but his body language for sure spoke with that energy. He was serving pressure but never made a move. Even though I felt like a punk in the moment and would get home that night and scream into a pillow for not making a move. I was glad that by this time, I had already adopted the mindset that in any situation, no matter what's said, I only respond to being touched. I always had this gut feeling that someone wanted to be a local celebrity by way of doing me harm. Nothing ever came out of that situation, but there was a lesson that I learned from it. No matter how much you try to stay out the way of drama, try to elevate yourself and do right. The enemy is always somewhere lurking and trying to make you a part of their story.

I realized as we walked away from that I hadn't seen that guy since the 6th grade. He was the same one that came out of nowhere trying to tempt me to come into his world, even back then. After that night, I signed that guy off as just another energy that came with the territory of the environment that I lived in. He was where he belonged. I wasn't.

The show finally came up, and everyone was excited. All of the parents, friends, and family members are involved and supportive of the girls. So we forwarded all the energy leading up to the show and finally took it downtown Boston, straight to The John Hancock Hall Auditorium. It was a competitive Hip-Hop show worth prizes and guaranteed future performance dates from Boston to New York.

We got backstage, and I could see the girls getting somewhat nervous. Even though I suffered from severe butterflies myself, I always stayed calm. But, they didn't know that. What I did know was that I was the leader, and if I showed emotions, then it would make it worse on them. So, I would hide in plain sight to deal with my fears. But, by the time it was showtime I was ready; and so were the girls. When the act before us finished, the crowd got hype. They knew we were up next by the programs handed out upon entrance. Seemed like everybody from Westie, Southie, and Madison Park High Schools were in the building. Yet, this was one of those shows that I told nobody about.

But nevertheless, the show was an absolute success. The crowd exploded as I expected, and their energy was sustained throughout the performance. When we left the stage, we all hugged and showed love to one another. At the end of the show, we placed Second behind a singing group. But the second place still qualified the girls for a prize and to move forward to do more shows. Back stage, the girls gathered their belongings and rushed out to spend the rest of the night celebrating with their rightful friends, family, and boyfriends. I grabbed my backpack, threw on my jacket and out of a side door, I left the building. I began my walk to the Back Bay, Orange line train station. As I was walking, I remember getting love from people that had attended the show along the way.

In the train station, I overheard people talking about the highlights of our performance. That feeling alone was a feeling that has always made my soul tie to what I did. The people, music, creativity, beats, rhythm, body movement and words. This was truly my first love.

On the train ride home, I had already cracked the bottle cap to my pint of Hennessy. I would usually wait until i'm home. But on this night, I felt proud of myself; and the girls for some reason. I was hoping I could've been with my girlfriend that night to celebrate the win, but she never liked to come to any of my performances. She'd rather hang out with her girls.

I finally get home. When I walked in the door, it was silent. My grandmother was on the phone in the living room while Frank was in his usual spot on the couch. The TV was on, but it was on mute. By the look on my grandmother's face, I knew that whoever she was talking to was relating some serious information. I go into my room to put my bag down and get set for a shower. When I came back out of my room, my grandmother hung up the phone with a deeply saddened face and shouted, "Lord my Lord, what is going on with this family?" I asked her what happened, and she told me my cousin Kenny had been shot 12 times. He was shot on the same street that the two guys jumped out of the car on me just weeks before.

Usually, When you hear a person had been shot that many times, your hope is defeated, and you sign them off as dead. But not this guy. He was too mean to die.

The next morning my Grandmother got up early and went over to the Hospital where he was. Kenny's mom; Aunt Linda really needed the support. This situation had made it even tougher on her considering what she had been through in the past year. My cousin Kenny's baby sister; Monique had just passed away only a year before this. She died from complications of Sickle Cell Anemia.

It took me a few days to get up to the hospital to see him.

I was hesitant, for maybe a reason or two. But mainly because I knew that the initial shock of the news would send everybody running up to the hospital. I didn't like to be in that kind of group of energy. But

I also knew that the visitors would slow down after a couple of days. When I finally got there, just like I thought, it was only one person there with him, my cousin Dionne's sister. Not many of the fellas from the family went to visit him due to it being a high-profile case. The police detail around the hospital from the lobby, all the way up to the 9th floor Intensive Care Unit was thick and tight. Everything was being watched.

I remember walking into the room. There were so many tubes, wires, and machines connected to him, you would've thought he was Frankenstein. Endless beeps, buttons, and Oxygen tanks to help him breath. As I heard, he really did look like someone who died and the paramedics brought back to life three times. It's a good thing he didn't have a problem with being over 300 pounds. Because his weight is what gave him a fighting chance. Also one of the ways he intimidated the streets. Along with being a bit of a hot head.

When he learned that I was in the room, he excused the other family member that was there and told me to come close. I walked over to his bedside and asked him how this all happened, and ultimately, who shot him? With a weak voice, he told me that I'd find out soon and that the rest of his homies and boys in the family already knew. Before I could even ask him if he needed anything, he says, "I need you to do something for me. It's important". I didn't know what he was going to ask me right then. But I remember thinking before he did; I sure hope it's not anything outside of my means. Because at this point, all we had was family ties. But I went ahead and asked, "What is it cuz, wussup"? He told me that he was in a predicament and wasn't sure how the BPD would handle the case.

See, whoever shot Kenny, shot him with his own gun. He thought maybe the police would go to his mom's house where he was staying to search the place while he was laid up. So just in case, he asked me to go there and get everything he had out of his stash. That wasn't outside of my means. After he told me where it was, he also told me that he asked one of the other boys to do it, but Aunt Linda wasn't having it. She shut down the whole house. She wasn't letting anybody in. I'm sure her motherly intuition knew something was in the house but didn't know what or where it was. Then I understood why he asked me. She would have never suspected me. Almost every day after school, I would go to Aunt Linda's house to use the restroom before work. I would ring the bell, and just like clock work she'd know it was me and open the door. But only this time, It was at night. I never went there at night unless it was a family gathering. But to my advantage, she was stressed out about her son. So, Seagrams Gin and Grapefruit juice had been in her system all day. When she opened the door, I walked in and gave her a big hug, and told her everything would be alright. I went in the bathroom and sat there for about 10 minutes. While I was in there, the house phone rang. That was my chance to get to the back room when she answered. So I flushed the toilet, checking her alertness. When I came out of the bathroom, of course, she had peeked her head out of the room in suspense to see if I had left out. But I told her I would first get something to drink and leave. She said, "Ok, you be careful out there," and she closed her bedroom door. That was my queue. Because she was drunk and had taken a seat, whoever it was that called; they were going to be a while. I then crept to the back room and went directly where he said. I quietly moved a few things around and pulled out a camouflaged slot in the wall.

I wasn't surprised, but it was quite the stash. He had all the tools needed to get a head start in whatever you wanted to major in at SideWalk University. I hurried and filled my backpack to the brim with everything. I wasn't nervous, but I was a little worried about aunt Linda catching me. I didn't want to have to strong arm the lady that named me all the way out the front door. Plus, I had my grandmother's car that night. The last thing she told me was not to get involved with anything going on with Kenny.

I reset the furniture back to where it was, and I quietly walked out the front door. When I got back to the rest of the fellas to pass off the stash, as I was asked, that's when I learned that the person who shot him stole the gun from him and had been hiding from him. When my cousin finally caught up to him, he approached him. Out of fear of my cousin, that's when the clip was emptied. Come to find out, the person who shot him went to school with me at Hyde Park High. With the way Boston is set up, chances are, if my cousin had died, that person would have been in the midst of us all trying to figure out who did it.

In this class, I've learned that sometimes snakes devour other snakes. But not for any type of nutritional value or even territorial hierarchy. But sometimes, just because it's a snake.

I met a lot of people at the Lee School/Community Center. One in particular that stood out to me was from the projects. His name was Damien. He was older than me and kind of scrappy in his demeanor but pretty cool. We would talk all the time in the weight room as we lifted weights. What we had in common was girls. That would mostly be the topic of discussion. But one day he told me about the time he got shot. A guy tried to stick him up and he tried to fight him off. In the process a bullet went through his hand. The scar was noticeable.

I remember him telling me that he never saw the guy again.

Months later in one of our work-out sessions he asked me when my next show was. I told him that I had one that coming weekend. But correcting the details with letting him know that I wouldn't be performing on stage. But instead, I had a female singing group that I had been working with for a few years that will be. That raised his interest and lead him to ask me more about them. After I told him that they were 3 beautiful sister that really have what it takes to make it in the music industry, he was intrigued to come to the show. He even came to their next scheduled practice with me with plans to invest in them if he thought they were good. By the time we left practice, he told me that he would let me know if he was going to move forward after seeing their performance. He was a street hustler and had money to burn.

The day of the show he called me and told me he was getting ready for the night. He was excited and already hinting like he wanted to go forward with the act. That was a good sign. We ended the call on that note.

When he got to the show, he had 3 other guys tagging along. He was trying to get the guys backstage with him. But I told him that wouldn't be a good idea if he wanted to make a good impression with the girls mother and also their manager. He agreed, then telling his posse to wait for him by the bar. I took him to the back and finally introduced him to the mother of the girls. It was a good first meeting. It looked promising.

The girls finally go on stage and they blew the roof off the place. My work-out buddy was highly impressed and for surely wanted to move forward with the act. When the show was over we made plans to go back to the home of the girls and their manager, Ms. Camille to announce the decision.

Once we left the building I hung around outside with Damien and his posse. We were talking, laughing and of course talking to girls from the dismissed show passing by. In the midst was the 3 sisters that walked over to me with big smiles and excitement; as that was always their energy. I gave them a couple more compliments about their performance and told them that we'll talk more about it when we get back to the house. Right then, one of the sisters asked if I was riding back with them. As I was getting ready to tell them I was going to ride with Damien, that fast there was a commotion. Damien and his crew was savagely beating, robbing and stomping out 2 guys that he seen. Come to find out, one of the guys was the one that shot him 4 years before.

Luckily Ms. Camille didn't see any of that because she already left. But what the girls saw that night was enough to put a dark cloud over the whole connection. So nothing ever came from it and Damien stopped coming to the weight room.

— Past, Present & Future Traditions —

Prom came along, and I was excited about it. I knew that I was going to bring my girlfriend. But I didn't know that Tifani and her girlfriends were all expecting me to invite her. Not many at my school even knew I had a girlfriend. At the prom is where mostly everyone found out. Including a couple of Tifani's friends and family members that also went to school with us. They had her back too. They did everything they could to make my girlfriend feel uncomfortable that night. It was easy to do. She had an attitude already before we even got there. But that was nothing new. She was always upset about something. Overall, I had a good time at Prom. I even left the building as Prom King.

Finally; It's Graduation day. Even though I had to go to night school for the last half of my senior year. It was worth it. I remember feeling accomplished that day, a proud moment for myself. That day I felt something that I couldn't explain then, but now know that I broke a chain that has been on my family since forever. It may not seem like a big deal to most, but I just so happened to be the first one from my family to ever graduate from high school. I will never forget that day. Even though my dad was on a nod throughout the ceremony. Still, It was a good day. Most of my family was there. Including a lady that was my mothers friend back in the day when she was at the top of her game on Seaver Street. She took a liking to me and always had my back for whatever I needed. She was quite gangsta herself.

When they called my name, my family all stood up. And just like at any show, my fellow classmates showed me love. I will never forget looking right at my grandmother as I walked across the stage and received my diploma. Tears were flowing down her face. To me, it was like I finally did something worthy of her approval, even with all of my accolades to this point. This; was what she was most proud of.

I didn't know what I was going to do after high school. But what I did know was that music was an option. That path had always been open. Even though choreography and writing songs for new acts was putting money in my pocket, It wasn't enough to take care of myself and pay bills back at my grandmother's house. Those gigs weren't always consistent, and the pay I was getting at the Community Center had become pocket change to my needs. So, I applied for a driving job at a Graphic printing company out in Newton, Ma. It was a two hour commute each way, every morning starting at 4:45 am. To be honest, I loved it! I took great pride in the job and made great money while doing it. I delivered to the top staff, professors, and departments of some of the most well-known prestigious Universities around the state of Massachusetts.

Harvard being one of them. Along with M.I.T, Boston College, Tufts University, and so many more. In that time, I took advantage of conversations with some of the most intelligent people from around the world. At M.I.T, I remember seeing a barrel full of assorted cell phones, Two-Way pagers, and other gadgets and devices dissected and awkwardly rearranged. I asked one of the engineers what they were doing. He told me that they were improving the future use of the cell phone. I didn't understand it then, but he said that one day soon, we will be able to touch a glass screen to make calls and even improve the quality of the camera on the phone. Telling me that the phone would be like a mini-computer that'll fit right into my pack pocket and so much more. I also saw with my own eyes; a fully operating robotic arm. It was just like something out of the movie "The Terminator".

The engineer was excited to explain what I was looking at that day. He was familiar with me from often seeing me deliver to his department. I remember while leaving out with my two-wheeler in tote; the engineer walking me back to the sliding glass door to let me out by his fingerprint scan saying, "Your future will be quite amazing, my friend". That may not seem like a big deal currently, but back then and in that moment, it was like I had a quick peak into what life would be like today. I got on the elevator and left with my mind blown.

While I worked that job, me and my girlfriend were up and down, and I got to a point where I was finally done. I was gone. Or, at least I thought I was. I did love her. Usually, it was me trying to fix things between us. This time, it was her. We had been broken up for about two months. We haven't even been speaking. Out of the blue, she calls my phone on a Sunday Afternoon. We began to talk. The conversation started off slow. But then she asked me about my tooth that had been bothering me for quite some time. It was ironic because I had a dentist appointment that very next day. She told me it was about time that I finally went. From there, the conversation began to relax and open up a bit. But by the tone of her voice and playful energy I knew just what she wanted. Still, we gave updates on our exaggerated well-being and chuckled about a little this and that. Before we hung up, we established that we missed each other and what other way to prove it by getting a hotel room for the night. We agreed that we'd go to work from the hotel on Monday morning. But I remember feeling like it wasn't a good idea. Like we were really over, and she was just checking back to see if there was any spark left between us. And besides, I had already met another young lady. But it was new, and a commitment hadn't been established.

Still, that night I ended up meeting my now ex-girlfriend at the hotel. Once we were in the room, we talked for a long time. She was doing her best trying to persuade me to get back in a relationship with her. The tears never seemed more sincere. She asked me if I saw anyone, and I was honest with her about it. In return, I asked her the same question. She assured me that there was nobody. That night she was the sweetest she'd ever been. All the promises in the world about how she would change her attitude. I had all the hope in the world that she was for real this time. I took that same spirit of hope along with another shot of Jose Cuervo Gold and laid down with her. As usual, the sex was good. I didn't know what came over her, but she even began to cry amid passion. It all felt different this time. But yet, that old feeling that you long for when you believe that you lost something for good, and you get it back. We fell asleep in the wet spot holding each other. Just like old times.

The next morning, the alarm goes off. We both promptly get up and start to get ready for work. But just that fast, her personality switched. Even though I knew she wasn't a morning person, still, I detected a glitch in her mode from the night before. I tried to engage in conversation, but she was short in her replies. That type of energy would usually agitate me, but I didn't think much of it. I didn't want anything to ruin my morning. So, to keep the peace, I just kept quiet for a bit. But then I started to feel like I was sinking into her world. The kind of world my spirit has no business in. That place that forces me to display the worse side of me. The fool side.

That morning I was doing everything that I could to show her the better side of me. The kind of person who wanted to fix anything or person that was broken. Heal what's hurt. But at that time, I also didn't know that some people aren't broken. Just; they are who they are.

We checked out the room, and to the JFK Redline train station, we began to walk. Still, not much conversation out of her. Not even a hint of what we talked about the night before.

Once we were on the train, there were a few more words between us, including me asking her, "What would you like to see happen between us from here?" Her reply was a little startling. She very short, cut and dry said, "We can talk about it later". It took everything to suppress the anger that I was feeling inside right then. So for the rest of the ride, it was silence between us. Although I felt very awkward, she seemed very comfortable with the energy. Un-bothered. By the time I got to my stop to transfer over to the Green line trolleys at Park Street. As I was getting off, the only thing she said was, "Good luck at your dentist appointment," then rolled her eyes.

I was so mad, that I couldn't even say anything. I just shook my head and stepped through the double sliding doors of the train. Through the glass, I just stared at her while the train rolled off. She never even looked up at me.

Just as planned, I got to my job, and it was a light half of a day worth of work for me. I got out on my route, and I just couldn't seem to figure out what happened from the night before to this morning. So many things were going through my mind. Did I do something wrong? Did I say something wrong? Just how did I piss her off? I just couldn't figure it out. A familiar self conversation that I'd have repeatedly while in the relationship.

But overall, I had come to the conclusion that what we had was indeed done. That old familiar energy had run its course, and I didn't want it back.

Right on schedule, I get back early to the Graphic shop to quickly unload and reset my van so that I can catch the next scheduled bus at Newton Corner for my dentist appointment. I make it in time.

As I'm riding, I remember listening to a mix for another upcoming show that I was hired for. It was a very popular hair show competition that came around annually that the city would be hyped about. But as I'm riding, listening, and going over the counts and routine in my head. I was still totally distracted by the thoughts of my ex-girlfriend and her disposition of character.

Then that day, after my dentist appointment, I decided to go to her job at the hospital to make it clear.

She worked in the Longwood Medical area of Boston, the same as my dentist's office. But she was a phlebotomist over at the hospital.

Since she only worked a block away from where I was. I started walking toward her job. By then, I even figured, since it's almost time for her to get off, we could take a Taxi to have more privacy to talk instead of taking the bus. I really wanted to handle this as maturely as I could.

As I was walking up to her building, I saw a lot of medical professionals and other working-class people pouring out the exits ending their work day. That was normal at that time of day. But what stood out to me as odd was the two younger guys sitting in front of the building on a bench. One had braids. As I walked by them, I made quick eye contact with one of the guys. His reaction signaled me as if we were not perfect strangers. Still, in passing, I subtly nodded my head in greeting. The braided one did the same. When I got to the spinning door entrance, I made a quick eye check back at the two guys right before stepping in. All four of their eyes were looking right back at me. That moment confirmed we had some type of acquaintance. As I'm walking to the elevator, I thought the taxi ride home might not be the best idea. Because of the bulging gut feeling that arose within me, I just wanted to say what I had to say and take off. I pressed the elevator button, and the doors opened. I got on, and went up to the 8th floor. When I got off the elevator, I started walking toward the door to the patient waiting area.

About 8 steps before reaching the door, I heard her voice and her co-workers talking, walking, and saying good night to the rest of the staff. There was no need for me to go through the door because there was only one way out leading back to the elevators. So I stopped in my tracks and leaned up against the window sill. Giving her a moment to come through the door. But, right before she did. I heard the alerting bell of the arriving elevator car. As my ex-girlfriend was coming through one door, the elevator had also slid open and it was none other than the same two guys that was in front of the building that stepped out. Right away, I knew which one was there for her. The extra flashy one.

As surprised as you'd think a man could be in that type of predicament. I honestly can say I wasn't. But, my ex's face; priceless. She couldn't believe what she was looking at. She was in total shock. As for me, my first reaction; It was immediate confirmation. I wasn't even mad. But unfortunately for everyone in the situation, what came out of her mouth next is what contributed to a mindset that I had finally surrendered to.

She didn't say hello. She didn't try to explain. She didn't even think about going back through the door to get her thoughts or story together. But what she did do, was react by yelling out loud, "WHAT THE F*CK ARE YOU DOING AT MY JOB? I DIDN'T TELL YOU TO F*CKIN COME HERE". I'm sorry to say, but that was the straw that broke the camel's back.

Usually, I could have talked that situation down or at least cussed her out and left. I couldn't. I tried. I said 3 words, and the numbing novocain wouldn't let me get it out. I began to slobber and bite my tongue. Feeling a bit embarrassed, and that added fuel to the fire. Then it happened. I felt a rushing rise in my temper. The entire 8th floor went empty. I couldn't see nobody but her and the other two guys. Even my hearing went soundproof. Like, I saw people's mouths moving, but I couldn't hear any sound of words. I totally blacked out. Before I knew it, I had grabbed her by her neck, lifted her off her feet, and then caved the wall with her body. Never losing grip of her. Still, with my hands around her neck, I dragged her across the lobby floor to the elevator. With both of her hands trying to pry mine from around her neck, I pressed the elevator button. I had no clue what I was doing or what I had in mind. All I know is people were screaming at me to let her go while she was crying and gasping for air. I remember a white lady hitting me with an umbrella handle and telling all the shocked and frantic onlookers to call the police. The elevator door opens, and I finally let go of her by forcefully throwing her inside of the elevator. The people who were already on the elevator ran off when they quickly realized the seriousness of the commotion that was boarding. When I got on, I grabbed her by the collar of her blouse and pressed her head to the inner wall of the elevator. Right behind me onto the elevator came the upset white lady, who I believe was a doctor, along with the other two guys. On the way down to the lobby, the white lady was still trying to assist the issue by trying to get my ex-girlfriend out of my grip. As she was in her efforts, my anger went to another level. Because I couldn't believe that the guy she was dealing with didn't intervene by this point. So, with my numb tongue, I said it, "This is the kind of B*tch made ass mutha'f*cka you like. He standing here watching you get f*cked up". Then she did something that took it to another level. She made eye contact with "Ole Boy" and said with tears flowing down her face, "Don't say nothing, I told you him and his family was crazy". So that pissed me off even more and made me smoosh her face into the wall. Because I understood then that I was a topic amongst them and felt plotted on and overall played. Finally, his boy with the braids steps up and says, "Don't be coming at my man like that, Yo". Like a crazy man, I just laughed. Still, they did nothing. Thinking back to that moment; that was probably the best thing.

When the elevator door opened to the lobby exiting floor, I snatched her by the arm, pulling her out. "Ole'boy" finally grabbed her other arm, trying to pull her back in. In that moment, I realized that she had a wrist full of new Gold charms and a necklace that I never seen before. But I got the best of the tug match. I was in a fast step to the front door. Because I knew the police were on the way. I don't know how it happened, but for some reason, with all the commotion going on, it was like we were invisible walking through the lobby. We got outside back in front of the hospital, and I pushed her up the side of a tree. Finally, I said all that I had to say, But added, "Is this what you did with my money I was stashing at your house?" I then ripped all the jewelry off of her, slapped her, and then walked off.

I quickly turned the corner with the biggest heartbreak a man could take. As I was walking, I called my new friend, Draya; to come pick me up fast. I was sure that my description is already circulating within the police presence. So I took off my hat and jacket and walked with the crowd. It was good that Draya didn't live too far from the Medical area.

In the 15 minutes that it took for her to arrive, It seemed like I felt every emotion all at once, feeling ashamed and angry at myself. Ashamed because I allowed someone to have that much control over my emotions, leading me to explode the way I did. And angry because I had to face the fact that Evelyn might have been right all along about the type of girls I would run into.

Because of my mom and dad's lifestyle with one another, along with both of their habits, I had made a promise to myself that I'd never submit to a relationship like that and even stay out the streets. I never wanted to have to put my hands on anyone—nevertheless, a female.

By the time I was picked up and got in the car, years and years of built-up heartbreak and pain had finally took their toll on me. Every man has a line drawn in the sand. I may have not gone straight to class, but I finally accepted my invite to Sidewalk University.

A week later, I was at the after-party for the hair show that I performed. My beeper goes off a few times in a row from my brother Randy. Then, a couple of minutes later, my cell phone rings, and it's my grandmother. I answered. The music in the club was loud, but I could still make out a few words. She was screaming saying, "What did you do, Shannyn? What did you do"? She kept repeating it. I had no clue what she was talking about and at that moment I really didn't care. The Hennessy, girls, celebrities, neighborhood legends and even some of our home town professional sports team players that was in the building had my focus. Whatever she was talking about sounded like it would spoil my night. So I just ended the call. Later that night after the party, I learned that 6 police cars were outside of my grandmother's house. They were looking for me. They came in full force to present me with a restraining order from my ex and a court date appearance. Of course, I knew what it was about at that point, but my grandmother never got the full story. In fact, until now, nobody in my family has ever heard about this.

It was almost 30 days to the day of the encounter at the hospital. I was in court. It seemed to come pretty quick. I can't lie, I was a little nervous about the outcome. But was so ready to be done with the situation. I even accepted in my mind that I was either going to be arrested on the spot or slapped with probation. Whatever it took for it all to be over. I was ready.

I remember walking in the court that day. Alone.

Still holding on to the good boy image, I was too ashamed to tell anyone what had happened, so I had no support. But, my ex-girlfriend did.

That day it was like I had a blank spirit. Like, whatever will be, will be. I didn't even have a prayer to pray.

When I got to the courtroom door, I let the bailiff know that I was there for my appearance. He told me to take a seat in the next room over. I did. When I walked through the door, there were only two people already sitting in there, my ex and none other than "Ole boy".

When I took my seat, they began to giggle and loudly whisper. Love tapping in a childlike way. But they did everything not to make eye contact with me. Somehow that gave me strength. With everything that happened, It was like I finally saw her for who she really was. Every negative thing she ever said to me over the years we were together had lost all power right then.

Finally, the bailiff comes to get her and escorts her into a room. Minutes later, the same bailiff came to get me and brought me into the same room. When I got in the room, she was sitting in the chair in front of a desk with an empty chair next to her. The man behind the desk then told me to come have a seat. I did. He confirmed my name and asked me if I knew the female sitting next to me. I told him yes. He then opened up a folder, and it got extremely quiet for almost 3 minutes as he was reading. So I said out loud, "Do you know what time we're going to see the judge; I just want to let my job know how late I will be?" He looked up slowly at me and said, "I am the judge". I was totally out of my element and thrown off because I didn't see a black robe. I later learned that we were in the Judges office, but still didn't know why we were in there instead of the court room. From there, He started to ask me questions, but nothing about the case. Still, I answered every one of them with respect and authority over my natural character. He had a great poker face, so I couldn't tell if he believed me or not. But that day, I didn't care. All I had was my truth.

Once he started to dig into what had happened on the day of question. I sat back in my chair and became completely calm. But of course, he began with her. He allowed her to say everything she needed to say about that day. Asking a lot of questions that were painting me out to be a horrible person. By the time he finished with her, she had told the story in full detail. Low key; in my mind, I was saying, "She could have left that out. Or, she just wanted to see me locked up". She told everything except for what led up to the matter. But I learned that day that everything that happened before that day was irrelevant to the charges of the case. Strong arm robbery, property damage, Public disorderly conduct, and assault were the problem at hand.

The whole time she was talking, he was writing in his folder. I couldn't see what it was, but I remember thinking he was taking a lot of notes and possibly what my punishment would be.

He looked up and right away asked, "What do you have to say about this, Mr. Johnson?" I took a deep breath, pulled myself up to the edge of my seat and looked the judge directly in the eye, and told him exactly what I needed to say. I told him that we met as young teenagers. We've been together off and on for a long time. We had a lot of good times and good memories. But unfortunately, we also had our fair share of bad times. The bad times started to outweigh the good times, and it all became toxic. I told him that I do still love her very much, but I didn't want to repeat what I'd seen growing up. The judge then grabbed a couple of Kleenex from his tissue box and passed them over to my ex. Because she began to cry. I went on to tell the judge that what she has told him so far is the truth. But that I am very sorry for what I had done. Truthfully, I was. I let him know that I had never felt what I felt that day emotionally towards a woman. It was the first time for me. My reaction may have come off a bit immature. But the actions of my anger were irresistible. The judge stops me and asked, "Do you feel any anger toward her right now?" My head slightly dropped, and I felt that lump in my throat like I was going to cry. I looked back up at the judge, and I told him, "I don't feel anything anymore for her". I went on to tell him that she seems happy now, and I have moved on as well. My ex then began to sob. The judge immediately asked her what is she feeling at that moment. She told him that she was crying because I didn't want to be with her anymore. The judge replied, "Isn't that what you want?" She then turned her head to me, and I looked at her, and she says, "What do you want to do?" I was shocked. But so was the pokerface of the judge. Before I could even say anything, the judge cuts me off and says, "Heres what I'm going to do; since there's a restraining order already in place. I'm going to let that stand for a full year. Mr. Johnson, consider it your lucky day. But, you are not to contact Ms. Bailey and Ms. Bailey, please do not reach out to him. Mr. Johnson, I trust that you understand that you leave the premises immediately if you are in an area that she is in. If not, you will be arrested for violation of the order. Have a good day"! He let her leave the courtroom first. He said that I could leave 10 minutes after. But what happens next I wasn't expecting at all. When she walked out of the office. The judge asked me if I had any kids with her. I told him that I didn't have any kids at all. He said, "That's good". He then comes around the desk and sits on the edge of it. He looks down at me in the seat and folded his arms. He began to speak to me. But in a way as if he was mentoring me. What he said that day left the Roxbury courthouse with me and stayed in my mind until this day. He said, "Shannyn, I've studied law for a very long time, and I have been a judge in this area for almost 20yrs. I've seen a lot of cases of good guys who get themselves caught up in the system and can't untangle themselves out. Sometimes it's drug dealing that gets them, gun possession, or even just hanging out with the wrong crowd. But most of the time, they get caught up with a young girl who clearly doesn't even know who she is yet. Don't be that guy, Shannyn. It's not worth it. No woman is. Don't ruin any possible opportunity of who you could become in the future by a decision that you'd regret in a week. I could tell you have a better head on your shoulders than that,...Right"? I said yes. As he stared at me, he nodded his head and said, "Good".

Soon after, the bailiff came in and told me I could leave. When I left, I was spiritually drained but relieved.

Six months later, I ran into my ex in Roxbury. She was 7 months pregnant. She went into labor 2 months later; giving birth to her first child, on my birthday.

CHAPTER 9

Fame & Torture

— The Choice Is Yours —

It was a cold day but the sun was out. The weekend was here, and I was ready for whatever. But first things first, I had to make my way to the barber shop. The one I went to was in the Codman Square section of Dorchester. I waited for my turn to get faded and lined up. There were non stop solicitors and street salesmen who always had what you needed. From new sneakers and clothes to the latest bootleg DVD of the now playing in theaters and/or even the t.v. to watch it on. Everybody in the hood had a hustle. But the barber shop is also a place where random topics of discussions are being debated. Where constant jokes and "capping" on each other is normal. Also, the neighborhood talent would come to display their work to get approval or a brutally honest critique. Some days it was almost like church the way every ear in the shop would be inclined to the gospel of the OG barbers leaking with street knowledge and wisdom. Myself and the regulars respected and valued their views. They weren't always full-time barbers.

After an hour and a half wait, it's finally my turn to get serviced. Midway through the cut, my beeper goes off. When I looked to see who it was, It was an unfamiliar number. About another 5 minutes go by, and my pager goes off again. It's from the same unfamiliar number. Right then, I thought I should have my barber stop for a break to let me use the phone to call back the number, but I didn't want to interrupt the flow of the service or the conversation at hand with the guys. Then, about another 3 or 4 minutes later, the vibration of the pager goes off back to back. One was from that same number and the other from my brother, Randy. That was it. Before I can even say it, my barber asked me if I needed to use the phone. It was evident that I did. Still with my cape on, I got up and walked over to the phone. I called back the unfamiliar number first. It went straight to an auto-mated service line. It said that I had reached Carney Hospital and gave me options to connect to a choice department. I had no clue why the hospital would be calling me. So I just hung up the phone and dialed my brother's number back. In doing so, my pager went off again. It was my brother again. But this time, he had added "911" at the end of his number. When I called him back, he answered on the second ring and immediately asked me where I was. I told him I was at the barber shop. He said, "Cool, stay there, I'm coming to get you". I asked quickly before we hung up, "What happened?" He said that he had just got a call about our dad. I asked right away, "Is he good?" He just replied, "I'll be there in 10 minutes". By the time he got there, my barber was finished. I left out and got right in the car with him. Right away, I asked him what was going on. He said that he had got a call from my dad's girlfriend. She had told him that dad wasn't doing too well. Right then, I thought, whatever it is it had to be pretty serious. But still, no clue to what it was. My mind started juggling all kinds of possibilities. But I claimed none.

We pulled up to the hospital, and all of a sudden, we both got quiet. The urgency of concern that we both had while in route suddenly became dull. When we got up to his room, my dad was in bed sitting up. My dad has never shown us a spirit of fear over anything until this day. But when we walked in his face revealed that he was ashamed and defeated. But also scared. His girlfriend was sitting in a chair on the side of the bed next to him. In my heart, I always believed that she never told my dad that she contacted us; and this would be yet another secret swept under the rug if she hadn't. So, in that moment, there was a quick awkward silence. She got up and gave us a hug. Soon after, she left to go to work.

When she did, me and my brother both stood at the end of his hospital bed and asked him what had happened. He did his best to explain but didn't do too well. As always, giving us the good side of the truth and withholding the obvious freedom of it. Its like both of our parents didn't understand that their contribution to our upbringing was emotionally preparing us for times like these. Like holding in one breath all of your life just in case a call like this was the day to exhale all worry and anxieties. The doctor then came in and asked who we were. We told him that we were his sons. In telling him that, he asked us to step into the hallway with him to talk. We did, and waiting for us was a priest that wanted to talk to us after the doctor. The doctor immediately began to give us the information that we needed to know. He told us that my dad had a near-death experience the night before. He came into the hospital emergency door, crawling on his hands and knees. He was having a heart attack, along with a diabetic fit, and filled with dope. The reason why he was on his hands and knees was that he had lost feeling in his limbs due to the extreme freezing night cold. On top of that, he had seriously been neglecting his diabetic medicine. The doctor informed us that if he didn't come in at the time that he did; the night before, his life would have been expired. The doctor went on to tell us, that if we loved and cared about dad, now would be a good time to try to talk some sense into him. So that's what we did. We walked back into the room, and I had a few things to get off my chest and knew exactly what I wanted to say. But before we could say anything, the priest jumped in and asked if he could say a prayer for us before we closed the door for some privacy. So out of respect, we all bowed our heads and closed our eyes. The priest began to pray. As I'm listening, I happen to open my eyes midway through the prayer. I looked right at my dad. I remember thinking that maybe we are here for nothing, and the prayer is going in one ear and out the other. Either way, I knew me and my brother was totally over my dad's way of life. Then, I looked over to my brother, and he was also staring at my dad. The face of an upset son who shares his dad's name and so far can't find one reason to be proud of it.

When the prayer was over, the priest gave us a few more words of hope and exited the room. It was needed, but it was time to get serious with dad.

In the beginning, Randy didn't say much. But right away, I went in and began to tell him how we felt about the condition of his lifestyle. And, asking him how long it will be before he really gets the help he needs. Letting him know how disappointed we are in him. Hoping that right there in the bed, he would snap out of whatever traumas that maybe he even had. See what Dad didn't know that I knew already he had a childhood best friend that lived in the same building he did, Jeff. From what I understood, they were inseparable. Jeff was the one that introduced my dad to dope. They were only 14 & 15. But unfortunately, Jeff died of an overdose. You would think that experience would have stopped dad in his tracks and gotten help right then. But sometimes, trauma will make you fall deeper into darkness. After a while, I started feeling like I was pleading with him. It quickly began to take a toll on me because I don't like to feel like I'm begging anyone for anything. Especially about something that is so obvious that they should do. Even though dad was nodding his head like he was taking everything said into consideration. We still didn't totally believe that he would change at all. Hope felt dim. But then, out of nowhere, my brother Randy who is not a man of many words changed the whole direction and narrative of the moment. Tired of hearing my plea and underdeveloped life coaching attempt. He opened his mouth and spilled some information that penetrated my dad's emotional steel wall. He gave it to him raw. "If you want to die like this, then go ahead, thats your choice dad. I don't know about Shannyn, But what you won't do is be in my life anymore". My dad looked up at him. Immediately I could tell that Randy's tone and energy were how dad needed to hear it. My brother went on to drop the bomb on not only my dad but me as well. He went on to say, "All of our lives, we watched and had been a part of you and mom being reckless with your lives. Even try to kill each other, over and over again. Well, from this day forward, if you don't want to do right; you don't have to. But you won't be able to meet or get to know your new grand baby. Ever. I won't allow my kid to be in the company of a dope fein." My dad looked away and straight out the window. When he looked back at my brother, he was choked up and teary-eyed, but puzzled. As if he wasn't sure if my brother was making a statement or giving him an update. Before my dad could even say anything, my brother says, "Me and my girlfriend is having a baby. I'm gonna be a father". With a tear finally falling from my dad's eye, he told my brother congratulations, and that was the best news he's heard in a long time. Me, on the other hand, was in total shock but congratulated him immensely. We talked a little more about it but never lost focus on why we were there. We were only there for about 45 minutes. But before we left, we had a group hug. As we were walking out the door, Randy looked back at dad and said for the last time, "I'm serious about what I said". Dad choked up one last time and said, "I'm gonna get this right, I'ma fix this, Finally." A moment with something bad, came something good. About 2 months later, my dad began his journey toward his sobriety.

— Anybody, But You —

I was sitting outside in front of the community center. There a young guy, older than me, approached me. Nathan was his name. I've seen him before because he worked for the city. So he would come to the community center every now and again. He already knew that I could dance but told me that he heard that I could sing and even write songs. I told him it was true. He told me that he had a strong industry connect. But he didn't have any artists. He then asked whether I ever thought about being a solo artist. Of course, I did. So that's what I told him. He seemed to consider that by saying that he'll keep me posted on what's next.

True to his word, a couple of months later, he did just that. He called me, and we linked up. When we sat down, he told me that he had found a girl artist as well. He bragged on her and was very excited about her look and singing talents. I could tell he wanted to say something out the way of our original conversation but didn't know how to say it at first. But after a while, he let it out. He went on to say that she didn't have any original songs. Also, she never recorded a song, never performed in front of a crowd before, but was wondering if I could write a couple of songs for her and make her the first artist that he'd invest in. I figured since all I was doing those days anyway was dancing. I had the time and energy to at least see where this goes, because I was interested in that industry connect he said that he had. About a week later, he called me and told me that he had some beats from a young local producer that went to West Roxbury High School. He was pretty dope too. Nathan wanted me to meet the girl soon and see if I could catch a musical vibe with her. So we set it up for the next coming Sunday night. He picked me up, and we went to one of his affiliate's home in Milton. Milton was considered a suburban part of Boston, but really it connected to the back roads of Hyde Park. When we got there, Nathan introduced me to his crew and, of course, the little star in the making, April Mays. She was a cute 15-year-old hood chick. Immediately you can tell that she had a rough upbringing. But that wasn't out of the normal considering the part of town she comes from. The well-known Gang and drug-infested area of Bowdoin Street and Geneva Ave. But one thing I could say about her; she really could sing. The toughest part was trying to make her believe it.

After everybody got acquainted and settled in. The guy who lived there turned down the sound on the NFL game, and Nathan introduced him as his partner in this plan that he had. His name was Zeek. He was a cool dude. You could tell he use to play in the streets but had a leveled head. He was smart, and I quickly knew why Nathan had him on his team. Zeek was quick-witted, and business savvy. Nathan was more hood.

Nathan starts playing the instrumental that he got from the producer. After the 4th track went by, I had already heard 2 for myself. But I understood that it wasn't about me just yet. I was waiting to see what April's vibe was. Then, after asking her what she thought so far by the end of the 5th track, her answer was simply, "They're cool". I knew right then that Nathan maybe had a get rich quick type dream. Not understanding that there are a lot of girls out there that are pretty and can sing, but they also have to have charisma and an ambitious mindset about it as well. I realized that's what he was telling me about her from the beginning. So I considered that maybe she's just shy or uncomfortable, being that she was the only girl there with all guys. I tried to get her to sing that first day. She barely got out a full verse to a Song by Monica. All I knew was that this was going to be some work. To be honest, I really didn't understand why we didn't stick to the original plan. With me being the first artist to surround and invest in.

Two months went by and we finally got a song recorded. I chose the track, came up with a concept, and wrote the lyrics. Once she was able to hear her own voice on the track, that's when she started coming alive about the whole project idea. Soon she started gaining a little confidence in herself. I'm starting to think; maybe this will work out.

Not too long after the song was recorded, Nathan called me and told me that his industry connect would be at the next rehearsal. I couldn't wait. But to be a team player, I wanted to have another song ready. So I wrote another song for April. My plan was to teach her the new song that day. I wanted to make a good impression for myself with whoever the connect was.

I remember that day hoping this person wasn't just another local connect to the actual connect. Because one thing I learned early with the music scene in Boston at the time. Nobody really had any solid connections to the industry. Mostly everybody just had an idea and a wish.

Both songs I wrote were very catchy and detailed to her essence.

When we got back to Zeek's house, where we'd usually practice. About 20mins later, in through the door came this big guy with a mini afro looking like he was about to get braids, his name was Veeh. He wasn't flashy at all. Immediately you can tell he was a gentle giant, and his demeanor was very professional. He was young too. Somewhere around the same age as Nathan, 30 to 35 years old.

After Nathan introduced him to the rest of the crew and me. We all sat down and talked. He begins telling us about his music career and background. One of the things that stood out to me while he was speaking was that he got his first check out the music industry when he was 14 and hasn't stopped since then. Right there, I was locked into whatever else he had to say. He went on to tell us why he was in Boston at the time. He was taking care of some business for a project that he produced for a legendary rap group out of Roxbury. Thats when I learned that he was a connect and a song-writer and producer himself. After running down his body of work and a long list of musical celebrities he's worked with. I was glad that I made the time for this project with Nathan. Because now it really seemed worth it.

That night, Everything went to another level when he shifted the conversation onto April and what the plan was for her.

So Nathan told Veeh that he wanted to play the one song that we had recorded with April. When he pressed play. The music started, and at first, Veeh didn't show any reaction or vibe to it. I figured, that's just how industry people do. But when the verse started, he started to groove with it. By the time the song got to the first chorus, I could tell that he liked it. He then said over the music playing, "She wrote this?" Nathan said, "Naw, my other artist did, Shannyn". Veeh turned to me and gave me a high five without even saying anything else until the song was over. I felt like right there, life was bout to change. But instead, he gave critiques. All of which I respected. He then asked Nathan when we'll be back in the studio the next time. When Nathan told him, Veeh said, "I'll be there". Then he asked April to sing live right there at the moment. It took a minute or two to get her to do it. But just like what she did when I asked her to sing, she kind of did the same thing with him. With Veeh's experience, he got her to loosen up a little bit more as the night went on. But for me, even considering both our confidence levels not being as strong. It still wasn't enough enthusiasm or charisma for me. I had 2 other girls that I knew who were just as pretty, could sing, and had the "IT" factor that I know would have taken advantage of all this attention and opportunity. Even Nathan seemed to be taken back a bit by her vibe.

Veeh went into his bag and started pulling out CDs with music that he produced on them. He put it in the CD player and started skipping through the tracks. Every track that I heard was hot without a miss. He was clearly on another level. Once he found what he liked, he started humming melodies until they became words. When he got a line, he related it to her to sing it. She started to get into it after while, which made me relax. But I could tell that he wanted her to want it more.

As we started winding down the meeting. Veeh told Nathan that he still wanted to move forward with her. That was good news to me. The night ended with Veeh Turning to me and saying that I wrote a great song and to keep writing. I left there that night with my hopes up and ready for whatever it was to come next. Long as it meant living out my dreams.

As the months were moving by, Veeh was coming in and out of Boston to handle his business. In one of his pop-in's, just like he said, we ended up in the studio to record with April Mays. It was a great day too. Because I got to learn a few things from Veeh as far as writing a song and how to arrange it better. I was constantly taking notes.

After the song was done, we all left the studio and went on our separate ways. Veeh left town again, but this time was longer than any other time. But Nathan was keeping me updated on everything in that time.

When Veeh finally got back, he came with a different energy than from the times before. He was more serious and very direct with April. He wasn't the producer anymore. He was the businessman.

He came to the practice spot over at Zeek's house, where we all first met. This was also the day we had planned to go to April's house and meet with her mom. What we had in mind was to fill her mom in on how deep April was in with this opportunity and to get her to consider signing a management contract.

But before we all hopped in the cars and took off to go. I noticed that he kept shaking his head no as if something wasn't right. So Veeh stopped everybody in their tracks. He turned to Nathan and told him that he needed a moment to be frank with April. Nathan nodded his head and said that was cool.

242

Veeh looked over at April straight into her eyes and asked her, "Do you want this April?" She stood there like a deer in the headlights and didn't say a word for almost 10 seconds. Before she even said anything, Veeh went on a spill about how her vibe wasn't telling a story as if she really wanted this as much as everybody else around her did. Letting her know that everyone believed in her.

April got teary eyed and started to display an attitude, yet still not even trying to answer the questions. As he was stepping over to his bag. He told her that he could change everybody in the rooms life tonight. But that depended on her. When she did open her mouth she said, "Whats taking so long for it to happen?, Y'all been talkin about it for months". We all chimed in and told her that it's a process and it takes time. But overall it was a telling moment that said that she didn't want it. Veeh went in his bag and pulled out a stack of typed-up papers. He held it up and asked her if she knew what it was. She glanced over at the papers and said no.

He told her that it was a 3 Million dollar contract to sign whoever he wanted. He told her that he was seriously considering her. But he just doesn't see enough excitement coming from her. He looked around the room with frustration on his face. As he put the contract back in his bag, he said out loud, with April standing in the middle of the living room, "She don't wanna do nothing great, cause she's a little Bitch. She think being a little bitch is some cool shit". He threw his backpack over his shoulder, gave everybody dap, and told Nathan that he couldn't rock with that. Ultimately letting him know the deal was off the table. Just like that, he walked out of the door without me ever getting the chance to prove that I would be a great candidate for the opportunity.

— Judgment Of Character —

I don't know what I was going through at the time. But I know that in different junctions of my life up to this point, I would fall into a place of hopelessness. As if giving up was an option.

While in a rehearsal at the Lee School Draya had asked me if I was ok. I told her that I was.

She said ok and left me alone for the rest of practice. At the end she walked over to me while I was gathering my things. She asked again if I was ok and then went on to tell me that she notices something was off with me. She was judging by my vibe. Because usually when I'm in practice I'm in upbeat spirit and keeping everyone else's spirits up too. But on this day, that wasn't the case. I was totally silent and withdrawn from everybody. Draya then says that she notices in the time that we've known each other that I have these moments. Sometimes they're just a day, sometimes they're a week or more. I knew what she meant, but I couldn't explain what the feeling was. So again, I just told her I was cool. Before we left out the back auditorium door, she said, "I don't know exactly how to help you myself, but I do know someone that can". I looked at her like didn't want to know, but went ahead and asked anyway. Who? She said, "My mother". Immediately I frowned on the idea and said I was good, denying her suggestion. But after a couple days, I ended up on her moms couch. I remember not even knowing what I was trying to explain to her that day. Because the feeling was beyond me. But, she understood. I don't know how, but she did. She listened and then gave me some words of wisdom go with. She was very calm and steady with her words.

One thing that stands out from that moment that I have never forgot. She told me one day I will be able to walk on water. All I had to do was stay focused on the man at the shore line.

As much as I wanted to ask further questions about what it meant. I didn't. I just left with it on my mind. But it was enough to make me want to know what that day would be like.

I had got a call from Trevar Michaels. He was calling to find out if I had time to take a choreography gig. He didn't have many details about the gig, but did inform me that he knew the talent manager and that if I took the gig, the money would be good. So I agreed to at least speak to the guy just to get a feel of what would be needed for his act. So Trevar gave the Manager of the act my pager number. The next day I was contacted by the manager; Larry.

From our phone call, we decided a time to link up and go over the details of his vision. Right away, I could tell that he was the kind of guy that didn't take no for an answer. Because in our conversation, he was very persistent as to how soon he wanted me to meet his young boy band. He asked me what my schedule was like. When I told him, he never took any of what I said to him into consideration. Not only was I working with other acts at the time, but I also had a job.

A few days later, I finally met the Boy Band. There were 5 little black boys. Immediately reminding me of the boy band I was 1/5 of. Also fitting the very tradition and culture of some of the most famous and legendary male groups of our time. In the first meeting with the group, I quickly learned that all of the members had different personalities, a fun and high-energy chemistry. Which is important to know if I will move forward with them. But what we all had in common, connecting me the most with them, is learning that they all were from Roxbury. That was my original motivation to take this gig. The group's name was "One Step Above" or "OSA"; a name given to them by their manager Larry. He introduced me to them by lining the quintet up in front of me and having them to sing. And right on cue, in perfect harmony and pitch, a cappella; they sung, "The Star Spangle Banner". I was blown away by their powerful and blended voices. I knew then that I would give my all in doing my part to help these young boys succeed. I just wanted to be a part of something that had a chance. Although the group had a special connection vocally, their footwork and coordination were not synchronized. I learned quickly that I was hired for a reason.

They knew all of the new and popular gimmick dances but had never danced choreographically with each other. I had my work cut out for me. Larry turned to me with a big Don King smile and said that if I could make them dance together as good as they could sing, I'll pay you every week until their first show. I asked when that would be, and he said, "In 3 weeks." I glanced over at the group, and by the time my eyes turned back connecting to Larry, he had 3 one hundred dollar bills dangling in my face and told me there's a lot more where that came from. I took the money and started working with the boys that day. Honestly, I would have done it for $100. Because it wasn't like I actually knew my worth at the time. I just had a vision that this would go somewhere and wanted my hands on it.

Larry had a big personality, a gift-of-gab and demanded perfection. Not so much of a bad thing when you have a vision that you want to bring to life. His energy easily reminded you of the father of the Jackson 5. With his experience in and out of the music industry for years; he knew what it would take to make it. With that being said, that was my connection to him and being loyal to the movement. Because I felt like he knew the way. Also, I figured that because he was related to a few of the band members, he too had a loyalty, passion, and determination to break this act into the music industry by any means. He was always fired up about the group. It was the majority of his conversations. His energy behind this Band idea felt as if somebody told him he couldn't do it, and he was on a mission to prove them wrong by making it come to life. I had a lot for respect for that type of leadership.

Even though he was old enough to be my dad. He built a team made up of young and talented, upcoming professionals from around the Boston area to surround and influence his act with. All of them had the fire and desire to make it into the entertainment world with our own individual ideas of what success looked like.

There were 3 of us. We were the elements. First, there was the quick pen hand of Ken. He came from a boy band background as well. His achievements were much more extensive than mine with Tuff Assignment. Ken, could write a song within 1 hour. Upbeat or Slow, If the beat had a vibe, he had a flow for it. Because I was already aware of him and his musical journey, I was excited and honored to even be on the same team with him. He wrote the majority of the songs for "OSA". Then, there was Zachery. He was a music-producing prodigy. A fluent piano player that had a natural ear for lyrical talent. Singing, rapping, to song writing; Zachery could listen to the song you have in your head and right on the spot make the beat that would perfectly cradle it. Then of course, I covered all of the dancing, artist development, and stage presence for live performances. OSA had everything it needed to be successful. A true dream team.

Three weeks passed quickly, and the first show for OSA was here. Come to find out; this performance wasn't just a show. But a showcase for an A&R out of New York representing a major record label. Larry worked fast.

But unfortunately, nothing ever came from that show or connect.

But the manager of the group didn't stress at all. He had other connections already in the works. He had the eye of the tiger. It got to a point where almost every weekend OSA had a show. It was good for them. With each performance, they got better and better. I would critique every show and break it down to them at every rehearsal until their performance became muscle memory. Creating a dynamic that would electrify their audience.

With every show came more and more popularity of the band, which brung a high level of attention from girls. But this is normal and comes with the territory of any entertainment lane where the male gender is the center of attention. It got to a point where little girls fitting their age groups were popping up at the places we held rehearsals. This happened so much that Larry somehow got it in his mind to find a way to make the show greater by adding female dancers. Overall, I didn't think it was a great idea. But as a young man trying to grasp the idea of business, thought that this would be a great opportunity to make more money. A couple of weeks after mentioning the idea to me, Larry told me that he wants to audition for female dancers. After working out the numbers added to my weekly pay, we got to it. A week later, we all ended up at a dance studio where almost 30 young girls were waiting and ready to audition. I noticed upon walking in that Larry had an unusual amount of excitement and readiness about the audition. But I paid it no mind. Because I was excited as well to get to work. The auditions ended up being better than I thought and was a success. All we needed was five dancers. That same day; right on the spot between Larry and I, we chose the five dancers along with three extra to understudy the routine just in case we lose a dancer for any reason. But if it were left up to Larry, We'd have kept them all.

The following Saturday, I was scheduled to hold the first rehearsal for the girls. When I arrived, there was 8 girls already there with their parents or guardian, as I suggested from the audition. Some were there in support, and others were there as skeptics about the whole thing. Once Larry got there, he had a way of persuading a situation, quickly making non-believers, believers. Never giving a skeptic a chance to have doubt. Then, I met with them. I assured them all that what I was doing is real, and will always be professional. It helped that a few parents already heard of me around the city.

I worked with the girls two times a week for a whole month before incorporating them with the band. In that time, I built trust and respect from the girls and their families. Even though I was just a 20 years old, I carried myself in a mature and stand-up manor. With my experience teaching female dance and singing groups over the years. I already had a high level of vigilance when working with evolving adolescent girls.

After rehearsals, I would go back home or to another gig most of the time. Other times I would go back to Larry's house with the rest of the crew to hang out and kick it with everybody. At first, it was cool, but overtime the girls that were part of the act came more often and began to bring guests. More girls. For the band, that was ok in my book. Because it actually helped them with their swag. But what I began to notice was the energy that Larry had about it. Some of the girls were well endow for their ages where I would notice and keep it to myself and never comment about it. Larry couldn't resist but be outspoken and downright flirtatious about it. Putting feels in the air that would entice the most gullible and curious. That used to piss me off and began my reservations about his character. Because I respected his hustle and brilliant business mind; I thought that he'd be a lot more reserved from that sort of energy. But that wasn't the case. That energy got stronger and stronger as time went on. Especially the more OSA was becoming even more popular. The gut feeling I had from the beginning about Larry quickly came into realization.

There were days that I thought some of the girls were late for rehearsal. But Larry would have picked them up from school, home, or a scheduled location and bring them to practice himself. I thought it was a little odd, but I figured teamwork makes the dreamwork.

Larry learned early that I picked up on his grooming behaviors and intentions. In return, that began his reservation with me. Because people don't like you when you represent a sense of "Know Better/ Do Better" energy in the presence of their mischief. Before long, I started noticing a change in the girl's energies toward me. But, not as

if they were being mean or didn't like the rehearsals. But they began
to be a little more vulgar in their approach with me. I wasn't too much
older than them, so I knew a couple had their young girl crush on the
older dancing guy. I get it. But I never gave it any energy or attention
to blossom. I could always tell what girl he had tried from the crew.
Some he would conquer, and then others were really there to dance
and be a part of something great.

Every now and then, out of nowhere, while in that time working with
the girls I would get a call. They would call with curiosities about
my relationship with the crew. It would be one of the girls asking
things like, "How long have you been choreographing for OSA," Or,
"are you and Zachery cool?" But the main question would always be,
"Why don't Larry like you?" I would simply give a quick humorous
or watered-down answer to keep from adding to any gossip by saying
something like, "Because I could dance better than him". Making
light of the situation. But most times, I would change the subject or
interrupt the call altogether.

In one particular situation that I remember, I asked, "What makes you
ask me that?" The girl said that Larry would speak so negatively about
me every time that I wasn't around. As if he hated me. Telling me that
all the people in the crew would sit around and laugh at everything
he'd say about me. Believe it or not, I wasn't shocked at all. When it
came to situations like this, even then, I was wise enough to know that
some people can't help who they are. Like one time, after a rehearsal.
It was Friday, a pay day. Like usual, Larry would have my money in
cash. Being the very braggadocious and arrogant person that he was.
In efforts to impress the same girl that called me, in which was with
him that day. Larry had pulled out a wad of cash and begin to peel
back money, gathering my payout, and said out loud, "If you're such
a great dancer, then you'll be able to pick this up with your teeth".
Then he slammed the money on the floor of the dance studio. In the
same motion, he walked out the door of the Ballet studio laughing

as if it felt good to do such a thing. As the girl's face cringed as he was walking out, I was frozen, staring at the back of his jacket as he bent the corner out the door. He never looked back at me to even read my facial expression. With her jaw dropped, the girl made quick eye contact with me and stared off. In shock of this display of total disrespect. She grabbed her bag and walked out behind him without saying a word. As for me, It wasn't like I couldn't believe it. Because at this point, I didn't put anything past this man. I stood there in a silent rage for about 3 minutes. A thousand different scenarios and ungodly thoughts ran through my mind in that time. But eventually, I calmed myself down.

Even though I needed that money and worked hard for it, I grabbed my bag, turned out the lights, and walked out of the studio, leaving $450 in the middle of the floor. The following Monday evening back at rehearsal, I overheard the black lady that owned the studio say that one of her Tap Dance students found 450 dollars in the studio. She said she took the money and told that child's parent that the next month of lessons were free. I never spoke up or told anyone about it, because in my book that money didn't belong to me. To ease my anger I was pleasured at the idea of some kid and family having some extra cash that they might've needed more than me.

One day in rehearsal, one of the girls came out her mouth with something inappropriate that she would like to do to me. Everybody in the rehearsal laughed and made their oohs and ahhs. It felt like they were all trying to provoke me into something. But I wasn't having it. So, the first thing I did was shut down the whole vibe. I told the young lady that she was out of pocket and to check herself. I made sure that she understood in front of everybody there that if she ever talked to me in that manner again, I would be letting her mom know about her behavior. I had to make an example out of her and let it be known in front of everybody that what some other crew leaders may have thought was cool, I didn't co-sign. She was embarrassed and, of course, rolled her eyes at me but still straightened up right on the spot. Everybody else just snickered and giggled. I didn't have any more problems out of her after that. In fact, even though their involvement with the shows as backup dancers didn't last very long. The rehearsal with me were taken even more seriously until their last show.

Over the years there was a disgusting rumor about me floating around the city. It wasn't true at all. I didn't know how to handle it at first. But I tried. Because of course, the first time you hear something about yourself that isn't true, your first reaction is anger. Then you try to figure out who or where it came from. Secretly, you begin to question yourself, which turns into critiquing yourself in areas of your life that you never needed to.

Every time I heard it, or was even asked about the rumor. I would look at people like they had two heads. Because it was like people who would bring it up was so convinced by what they've heard. I was so messed up about it that I even brought it to Trevar Michaels attention. After talking with him it led me to create a ready-made defensive reply to protect my character and image.

I valued his views and thoughts. Especially on this matter. I was hoping that his years of mentorship would help. But, his only advice was simple. "You're a dancer Shannyn, and you live in the hood. You don't have to explain yourself to anybody. There are those who matter, and those who don't. Some people are born just to misunderstand you. Believe me, I know". I can say that what he said didn't solve the problem or what I was feeling at the time, but it helped. Because from that day, when I would be asked or told about my sexuality. I would be ready. I would say something like, "Because I'm a dancer and so passionate about it; and I don't have a rough and hardcore demeanor, I see how that could be easy for someone to make that assumption". But most of the time, after that being said, I would walk away still wondering if that person believed me. Hating the fact that that was even a question about me, yet accepting that they didn't. Even though I knew what was said about me wasn't true, It made me begin a love/hate relationship with my talents. I'm not saying that people who are homosexual are less than anybody. I'm just saying that I took pride in being a dancer without being homosexual. Considering the number of guys around the city that was. Where family and friends once adored me for imitating Michael Jackson and dancing; it seems now it has become a taboo. I wish that I knew then that what other people thought about me was none of my business.

It wasn't until many years later that I found out where the rumor came from.

One day, a few of the girls from the backup dance crew ended up back at the house of Larry. A conversation arose that was entertained about who the girls might have a crush on from OSA. One of the girls said that she didn't have a crush on anyone from the band. That struck an interest with Larry and the rest of the girls there. So then the question was asked, "If not from the band, then who do you have a crush on?" At first, the young lady was hesitant with her answer. But then, after some gossip provoking. The young girl finally blurted out, "Shannyn". A couple of girls smirked and agreed, and then there were a couple who had already been mentally well-groomed by Larry's perceived notion of me.

The conversation goes back and forth for a few minutes. Then, the plot seed was planted. In efforts to manipulate and persuade the room, Larry asked the girl in front of everybody, "Why do you like him?" Everybody instantly got quiet, yet excited to hear what she'd say. When the girl replied with her answer filled with daydream like desire and lust, Larry quickly grew annoyed. It drove him to a devious state of mind pushing him to gain dominance over the room. That energy led him to drop the bomb. He told a room of 5 young gossiping girls among other company that I was homosexual.

To add insult to injury; He went further into it by prompting the girl to get a confirmation for herself by crossing the line to strongly flirt with me. Inciting her to believe it was ok to do. In the back of Larry's mind, he knew I would turn her down. Obviously because she was an under age 13yr old girl. She was the same girl that flirted with me in the rehearsal that I had to check in front of every one about her behavior. My reaction that day painted a picture to the rest of the girls that what he said about me might be true. It wasn't long before The girl back-up dancer season was over. But all those girls grew up around the city of Boston believing that I was something that I wasn't. That was a tough time for me. Because I had no clue where it came from.

I learned in that situation that sometimes in life, the people who need you the most are the ones that have the least amount of interest in your well-being. Your value will never exceed the service you provide them. The sad thing is that you usually never know how they felt about you until the damage is already done.

— Its Go Time —

For the longest time, I wondered if any of the parents even picked up on any out of the ordinary vibes from either Larry or their child. But I realized that fast talkers and money flashers can blind some parents. Also identifying with the hustler in Larry, I guess you can say that I'm guilty of knowing something wasn't right. Yet, I was only concerned about my check. Adopting the mindset that none of it is my business. Just worry about myself.

A couple of months in, I'm back to working with just the band. Because Larry had connected with a high roller in the music industry out of New York. He was highly interested in OSA. This was a big deal so I had to have them tight. One of the days we were off, I was at Tifani's house on the couch watching TV. A call came through. It was sort of surprising. Because the call was from one of the parents of a former backup dancer. She started off the call with small bubbly talk. But it wasn't long before the energy changed. All of a sudden a heaviness came over her voice. I didn't know if she would ask me for some money or if she was heartbroken. The next words out of her mouth was, "Mr. Shannyn," and then about a 8 second pause right after. Right then, I had an idea of what the call was about. She began by telling me that she and her husband thought highly of me regarding my talent and professionalism. I thanked her. But I knew that was just a warm-up. There was something more to this call. She brought up her daughter. Telling me that both her and her husband have noticed a big change in her. She hasn't been making her curfew at night, and when she does, she's not there long. She would be up early in the morning and gone before her parents and younger siblings woke up. She came home with new clothes, money, and a new cell phone. She even gave her mom a couple of hundred dollars. That's what raised curiosity with the mom. But she couldn't ask her any questions because doing so would turn into a big argument. The concerned mom informed me that her daughter had got a job as well, but she knew that what she made hourly didn't cover her newfound lifestyle make-over. It all sounds familiar to me as she tells me all of this and more. I remember sitting there with the phone to my ear, thinking, "Of all the people that were around, Why am I the one being called right now?" Yet still, Because I was the type that would go down with the ship. My loyalty tried one last time to defend the situation. Knowing that the young girl was hot and fast anyway. Right after I said it, I felt stupid with saying, "Maybe she got a new boyfriend. Or, she's not comfortable living in a shelter anymore". I knew I was out of line for that with the background I grew up in. I thought the mom would have took offense, got angry and the conversation would have heated up leading to an abrupt ended call. But the mom never broke her humble spirit. She then said, "Mr. Shannyn, I know we are not doing too well right now. But my husband and I are doing the best to raise and protect our children. Maybe one day when you have kids of your own, you'll understand". That totally struck a nerve, and I got where she was coming from and respected it. She then told me that her and her husband was riding around talking about their daughter's sudden change. She asked if it was ok if they could stop by my house because they had a very serious question to ask me. I told them it was ok, but I wasn't home. They didn't care. She said, that the matter was very serious to them and they would take a ride to where ever my location was. So I agreed. About an hour later, they pulled up. I went downstairs and got in the van with them. We talked a little more about random things, but no more than five minutes. I could tell the mom was anxious, so she got right to the question at hand without wasting anymore time. She outright asked, "Is that man F*ckin my baby". I just dropped and shook my head. Because I knew this was going to be the question.

But just in case they had any type of recorder somewhere in that van, I never gave them a straight yes or no answer. But I did go forward with saying, "You called me, you burned gas and drove all the way out here to ask me a question like this. What does your motherly intuition tell you"? The dad was visually angry. Maybe wanting me to give a strong confirmation. The mother just cried while repeating, "She's sixteen, she's sixteen, she's sixteen". As if she was trying to mentally relieve herself at the idea of her daughter being old enough to make that decision. On that note, I exited the van walking back toward the building door. Out the window of the van, the dad told me to keep doing what I do and that God would bless me one day. As I watched them back out of the parking spot to pull out of the apartment complex. I stood at the top of the stairs, stuck on what I just witnessed from the mom repeating her daughters age. Sixteen, the age that my mom met my dad. I immediately had inner Questions. I was trying to figure out what mattered more. Her being mature enough or not, to make that decision, or the age difference between them?

But what hit me the most and scrambled my mind was the thought that if my own mom had been obedient as a young girl and did right by everybody else's standards, would I even be here? I went upstairs and rolled the fattest blunt ever and sipped from a fifth of Hennessy bottle for the rest of the night.

After almost a year and a half, none stop rehearsing, recording new original songs and performing. It turns out that the guy who had high interest in OSA made a deal with Larry, and the group finally got a break. That deal included a major recording contract with one of the biggest record labels in the industry. I was more than excited for them. All of that hard work had paid off.

After all the contracts were signed. Everything started moving quick. The band began to go back and forth to New York City regularly. From elite photoshoots, Magazine interviews to working with some of the hottest music producers in the industry. Everything was heating up.

Because of the momentum and the obvious near destiny of this band. I began to speak up on other talents that I had, one being songwriting. Because I overheard Larry on the phone say that the record label was accepting song submissions for OSA to record. Believing that I could write a song for the band's debut album; right away I brought the idea to Larry. But of course, he curved me on the idea. But I admit, he didn't say no. So I brought the idea straight to Zachery. He was initially open to the idea but told me that he wanted to run it past Larry first. Nothing was wrong with that. But I couldn't help but feel like that wasn't going to go good considering the nonchalant energy Larry had given me just days before. I always felt like anything mentioned about me to Larry was an automatic no. So I was doubtful. But, a week later, Zachery called me. When I answered, he had excitement in his voice, letting out his traditional brotherly like chant by saying my name; "Flip-Ouuuuut"(Flip-Out). A name I adopted over the years as being a choreographer.

On that call, he told me that he had made a few new tracks that he thought would be perfect for the band's new album. He wanted me to hear them and let him know what I thought and more importantly, if I wanted to help him write lyrics that night. He never told me if Larry was cool with the idea or even how the conversation went between the two. By this call, I assumed that it was cool, and besides that; Zachery already knew I had some writing skills.

I played it off cool, but he didn't know that I was ecstatic. I never had a problem with giving credit to whom it's due, and Zachery was a beast with the music production. So of course I was down. Thats what I wanted. Shortly after we hung up, Zachery pulled up to my house. I hopped in, and from there, we drove around the city vibing out to the tracks until we was done writing one whole song. We both were hyped about it too. We had every reason to be. We were both young and part of something that our talents made room for.

Zachery and I had previously collaborated making reference and demo songs for my own personal music project before the band got the deal. Because my dreams were alive and kicking. It was great music. But writing songs for OSA felt different. Maybe because if the songs were good enough. They would make it on a real album with the machine behind it, a real outlet for the material. The way I've always seen it for myself.

Before I got out of the car that night, Zachery pressed eject on the car stereo system and handed me the CD that we were riding and creating to. He said that there were two other tracks available with no concept to them on the disc. He told me to see what I could come up with. I told him, "Cool". We gave each other dap, and I got out and closed the door. 48hrs later, I had a whole new song for the band. But I wasn't so quick to tell him. I waited. Only because I knew the band would love it. But with me being the only writer of the lyrics, I also knew Zachery had a way of putting the idea on the back burner or just plain'ole shutting down on the concept.

One day, after a show. We were all in the Limo Van, heading back to a hotel. It was just me, the band, and one of the band member's mom. This was my moment to introduce the song to them. But they were still hyped up from their performance. I was in the back of the van and had my headphones on going over the song. With my pen and pad in hand, I said out loud, "This is gonna be dope". Because their adrenaline was still pumping, It seemed like nobody heard me. But as I was spilling the lyrics and melody. One of the band members in the seat in front of me overheard me. He was usually the cool and laid-back one anyway. He then turned around to take a quick peek at me. What he saw was me in a full charismatic head nodding knock. His eyes squinted as he smirked asking, "That's Zach's beat?" I told him it was. He didn't even have to ask if I wrote it because the band had already caught wind that I collaborated with Zachery anyway. By the time we got in our hotel rooms, the whole band was already humming the song's melody. A few weeks later, they recorded the song. Needless to say, both songs were approved by the record label and made it on the album sequence. I felt accomplished.

Larry had bought a house about 45 minutes outside of Boston. The house was big enough to hold rehearsals for the band in the basement. That's what I ended up doing. One day after practice while getting ready to leave to go home. Larry had reiterated that he wanted me to have the guys sharp and tight. Because "One Step Above" had just been added to a major tour lineup. He told me we only had a couple of weeks to be ready. As usual, I told him that would be no problem. He then grabbed a CD off the kitchen countertop and handed it to me. He told me that it had a 15 minute show sequence on it. I was puzzled because just a week before that, we agreed that we would go in the studio with Zachery to create a sequence that would allow me to present an impactful performance for new upcoming shows. He's the one that suggested for me to be there. So I asked him why didn't he call me. His answer was, "You wasn't around". Yet, he never called me. I knew it was an excuse. But at this point, It was nothing for me to get angry about. Because I had accepted how this man works. I stopped taking things so personally. Because I've seen how he treated his own family. Plus, the way I thought then; he held the key to a door that I've always wanted opened in my life. So I made the most of what I was given to work with, and I kept my peace.

The next two weeks passed quick. To be honest, I couldn't believe I was going on a real tour. We had taken convoy-like road trips in the past to different surrounding states for spot date performances. But I wasn't quite sure how we would transport from state to state and city to city this time. There were so many dates yet with hundreds of miles between the locations. I didn't know what to expect, but I was ready. The night before we were set to get on the road, I remember my 2-Way pager going off saying that one of the parents was on the way to pick me up to take me out to Larry's house. That's where we were all leaving from. I wasn't quite finished packing, so I began to rush. As I was leaving out, I felt as if I was leaving something. When I got in the car, I still had that feeling, but I just couldn't figure out what it was. I got to Larry's house, where the whole team was lounging around. Then I realized, It wasn't that I forgot anything back at the house at all, but I forgot that I told my cousin Wiz I would kick it with him that night. I could've very well canceled with Wiz, but we had planned to link up a few weeks prior, and we haven't hung out in a long time. Besides, Wiz was always into something. One way or another, it was either some girls or money. I was always down for that.

Even though Larry had a big and expensive luxury vehicle, he never haste to throw anybody the keys to it. Long as he didn't have to drive. I took advantage of that. So I told Larry that I had forgotten my wallet back at home. Without any further questions, he just threw me the keys and walked away. I guess when some things are meant to be, the time will always be right. I hopped in and took off fast. Because usually, when that engine starts, everybody wants to hop in. It was a big flashy truck.

I got on the highway and called my cousin Wiz. He told me to meet him at a hotel in Downtown Boston. When I got there, just like I thought. He was in a room on the 6th floor and had two girls from out of town with him.

Wiz wasn't the type to tell you his business. He kept his accomplishments and endeavors to himself. His demeanor was evident. He demanded respect and lived by the thug life culture. He was the type that didn't mind you getting money with him. But he wasn't going to teach you anything. Either you understand the flow, or it wasn't for you to know. No matter how tough or money-motivated you think you were, It would be no time before you would have to show and prove with Wiz. Either keep up or keep back.

The two girls were about our age, both beautiful and sexy. I had my eye on one, but I held back just to feel the vibe of the room.

Since Wiz introduced me to the girls I wanted to first see who he had his highest interest in. Because you never want to impede but in this case, Wiz was taking too long. So as usual, I took a couple of Hennessy shots to push the reveal along. But something happened after I took the shots. Usually, I would be ready to turn up a too laid-back vibe. This wasn't that type of night.

While I was talking to one of the girls, I began to incline my ear to what Wiz was saying to the other girl. The lingo was familiar, though. There was an older guy back in my old Hancock Street neighborhood that always had money and a lot of women. For some reason, when I saw him, out of all the kids my age that were around, he would always tell me about what he did to make money with them. Wiz was riding that wave and had this girl's full attention. Where we once used to just say what we had to say to get in between the legs of some random girls and kept it moving. This night, his own sexual pleasures was at the least of his thoughts. This time around, the conversation was about the price of pleasure. Continuous intense questions, one right behind the other that dominated the insecurity and intellectual level of a 20yr old girl who didn't know which way to reply. All she knew was that she was pretty and most likely just came out to have a little fun. But learned quick that she wasn't in a room with the average sex thirsty guys like I was sure she was use too. To be honest, before I walked in that room. I didn't even know I wasn't sex thirsty. It was a new program, but I caught on. Quickly I learned that night that I had a natural gift to coach and motivate outside of dancing.

Understanding totally what my cousin was up to, my conscience began to push and tug within my mind. That night, I began reminiscing back to my own self-encouraging words. Trying to talk myself out of making a decision that just might not totally be for me. On the other hand, I fully gained confidence because I never forgot what Evelyn told me. Planting that seed with telling me to make those girls pay me. That, echoed in my mind. Still, fighting against the wave with remembering all the times I promised myself that I would stay positive and never get involved with anything in the streets. All because I saw up close and very personal what it had done to both my parents. This was also a lane that my dad played in as well.

I took a lot of pride in not being a follower. And up until that day, I wanted no parts of it. But unfortunately, my pride was weakening to the conditions of my pockets and status. Therefore it was clear that Wiz was on to something. It made sense. Why resist a hustle if it keeps presenting itself to you? From the outside, looking in on Wiz's lifestyle and the convenience of doing anything he wanted because hard cold cash was flowing in daily; I needed no more evidence that it worked. It was obvious that dancing wasn't making that kind of money. So, this was an influence that made sense to me. Without knowing what the lifestyle would do for me or to me. The idea of tax-free money was attractive and irresistible. Comparing what I had to go through to get paid for my talents; this was a wave I knew I had to ride.

While in the room, I don't know if something came over me or finally came out of me. But I turned to the other girl that was there and began chanting game at her. She had no chance of leaving that room the same girl she came in as. It was like every pickup line, con artist, or hustle man vernacular I ever heard activated and was beginning to take form within me. Then, it all started spewing out of my mouth. The crazy part is, everything I was saying made sense, and most wasn't far from the truth. Except for the lie that I owned a big luxury truck sitting right outside. All the while illuminating big confidence and structure of an alpha male. I looked into her eyes and could tell that my passion of the conversation turned her on. For a couple hours, I didn't even sound like me anymore. But I instantly liked it. She did too. I think I even shocked Wiz that night. Before I knew it, every question I asked her, she replied with either a passionate "yes," or "I feel you," or "makes sense to me". Every yes began to drag me in deeper. Building up a sense of false confirmation that this is what I'm supposed to be doing. Like a dope fein, the first few times plugging their vein. It just felt good.

I didn't know it then and it may even sound weird, but because life up to this point has always given me a bunch of "No" in areas of my life that I truly desired something financially; "yes" became an addiction. It was like my gemini twin found his long lost second face in an instant. Realizing now that I was more like the environment I grew up in than I thought I was.

I finessed this girl until she was excited about what she's never done before. To the point she was ready to get started that night. She even picked up the keys to the truck and said out loud with excitement, "Lets go, now". We all just laughed. But Wiz looked over at me lightly, nodding his head yes and smirking. I always imagined that that moment for him was like a proud mentoring moment. Because everybody, whether you know it or not, have their own vision for how they see you.

But the girl's head was on fire and was ready for the world.

But not only did I motivate her, I was putting a fire under my own ass at the same time. To be honest, to some degree, I probably needed it. With the adrenaline I had running through my veins that night, I was also ready. But it was 4 am, and I had to leave. Because I was going on tour in a few hours.

Later that morning, back at Larry's house about 8:30. I awaken from a quick 2-hour nap from the sound of Larry loudly waking everybody up and telling us all to get ready. He was wired on coffee and super excited. As I gathered my stuff, he yelled out, "Everybody get outside". So we all began to make way. We were all puzzled when we got out there. Because nothing was going on. But then, a couple of minutes later, his phone rang. Whoever it was, he started giving direction toward the house. But I paid it no mind. After all, I was still sleepy from a night out with Wiz. Then, It happened. One of the band members, while looking toward the top of the street, yelled out,

"Yooo," in complete shock and excitement. The rest of us looked up at once, and coming down the street was a tour bus. It had just got real for me. It was big, It was luxury, and it was our ride for the next month. Not only was I excited for the band, I was happy that I had something to contribute to this movement.

About an hour later, everybody hopped on the bus and began our journey onto our first city.

Up and down the East coast, we went, and every show was a progressive success. Every now and then, the team would bump heads, but we executed our assigned duties at the end of the day. For the most part, I loved every moment of it.

— Setting The Stage —

There were a few times that stood out to me that were life changing. Now I've been on stage before and had every crowd reaction that comes with the territory of being an amateur entertainer. From being boo'd off stage to rocking a crowd as if I was a celebrity. One of the highlights is audience participation with knowing the words to your song and singing along, the greatest feeling ever for a music artist. Even though it wasn't me on stage as the performer. It was an awesome feeling to hear a crowd of 8 to 10 thousand people sing along lyrics that I wrote. Also, going to a city I've never been to before, and people already knew who I was blew my mind. Because at that time home internet connection was in its baby stages. Not many people I knew had that cringy world wide web online dial-up. There was no Instagram, twitter, Facebook or nothing. Apps weren't even a thought to anybody. At best, MySpace was just touching the surface.

One day, the bus pulled into the pavilion at Hershey Park in Hershey, Pennsylvania. Usually, I would get off the bus with the band, because I would have their mics and costume luggage. But this particular day, when I got off the bus. As expected, I heard the fanatics at the gate screaming the names of OSA members. But what snatched my attention was the sprinkle of voices in the midst of it all saying my name as well. It was noticeable enough for everybody to hear. Even Larry. Where we would usually go straight into the venue and get ready for soundcheck, this day was different. Larry told the band to go to the gate and greet the fans. As they began making way, I started walking towards the venue door to do my job and set up for the group in their dressing room. But then, I heard a voice that shouted out over the pandemonium of OSA getting closer to the gate saying, "Flip-Out, my daughter is a dancer and she is a big fan of yours". There was no way for me to deny what I heard, and I damn sure couldn't just keep walking. So I put the bags down, and I too began making my way to the gate in my Kobe Bryant number 8 jersey. When I got to the gate, it was a middle-age white lady and her 13-year-old daughter. It was true, her daughter was excited to see me and told me that she liked the way OSA danced. I needed to hear that. I charged that to my confidence level, hope, and motivation for my own vision. Before I walked away, I took a few pics with the people out there, just like the band was. Right before I stepped back inside the gate, My curiosity arose. So I turned to the lady and asked her how she knew who I was. She said, from the Nickelodeon website. I didn't even know I was mentioned at all. After that, I continued on to do my duties. When I got backstage, Larry was already there waiting for me and told me not to talk with OSA's fans, because I wasn't part of the band. I heard what he said, and it did agitate me. But I had got to the point where I adopted paying him no mind. Mostly because it became obvious where his energy was coming from. That night, after OSA's set was over. I left our entourage and walked out into the audience by myself. I watch the rest of the show headliners as a consumer for the first time. It was big lights, familiar songs, and non-stop screaming. I wanted to see what I could take in; add to the enhancement of the artist that was growing inside me and my professional repertoire. Even though I learned a lot at the community center doing plays and halloween productions over the years. This was another level for me.

I was also hoping to pick up something that I could apply to OSA's opening performance. Of course, some acts was better and stronger than others. Making me further believe that I could do this for myself. Because I knew I was better than a couple of the acts I saw that night.

But what stood out to me while observing each performance was that they all had someone to come out and introduce the next act. Right there, it popped in my head to create a new mission for myself. So at the next show somewhere at a county fair. I took it upon myself to pull the sound man to the side at soundcheck and tell him, "Before the show starts, turn on the red-tagged microphone and wait for me to introduce the band". Without asking anybodies permission or even a pause in reply, he simply said, "Fine with me". He was cool. That night, OSA got dressed, went over the routines, and then began making their way to the stage. Once we prayed, I put them in their show start positions. Like clockwork every night at 7:05 pm, the lights went off, signaling the show was about to start and the crowd begins to rumble in excitement. I quickly gathered my nerves and what I would say on the spot. I stepped out into the stage spotlight and spoke into the mic. Out of the arena speakers, I heard my voice saying, "OHIO....., Are you ready for the show" and the crowd went wild. I then told the crowd to repeat after me and just like a cheerleader for a team; I made them chant the initials of the band name all in unison. After the third cycle of the chant, I got louder and louder until the crowd went berserk. They were ready. All there was left to do was introduce them. "Ladies and Gentlemen, I bring to you, O-S-Aaaaa". The sound man couldn't have been more on cue. He started the music, and the group came out more hype than they ever had, taking their show energy to a new height. Something that they didn't have on the tour up until that night. They kept that energy throughout their whole set. When they came off the stage, they was glowing like real entertainers, finally. The whole crew was proud of them.

Nobody from the team knew I was going to do what I did. But they all were glad that I did, including Larry. After that night, introducing the band was part of my duties. What they didn't know was that that was my attempt to try to get discovered by somebody, anybody. I was still that Roxbury kid "live" from my mothers living room on the 7th floor, fighting for my chance the best way I knew how in a situation that should have been fruitful, not only for me but for everybody.

The next show, Camden, New Jersey. After OSA's soundcheck was over. I went to catering to finally eat for the first time that day. That whole morning I had been low-key and too myself, not talking much to anyone. I wasn't in a bad mood at all, but at times, I go into deep thought, and I just need some time alone. Especially with what has been going on behind the scene within our crew. As I was eating and watching TV. I heard Larry all the way from the back door of the venue loudly calling my name and quick-stepping; "Wheres Flip-Out, Have you seen Shannyn"? I heard somebody tell him that I was eating. So Larry bent the corner into the backstage kitchen with this big'ole Koolade smile on his face and said, "Leave that, you can come back and finish, somebody wants to meet you". My first thought was that it would be some type of prank. But it wasn't. When we came down the hall toward the back door, I saw an old school car like Doughboys from the movie "Boyz N' The Hood". It was nice and shining. When we got to the door, I stopped while Larry crossed the threshold. Again, in what felt like an awkward moment because I was a little skeptical of his fetch for me. He turned around and just looked at me in the doorway with the Don King smile and excitement on his face. So I asked him while peeking through the door. Who wants to meet me? He then told me to come out and look on the other side of the opened door. So I did, and lord and behold, It was the legendary

Queen Latifah. No lie, I was in shock. She looked at me and smiled. I extended my hand to shake hers as she said, "So you the one, huh?" Stunned in amazement of the rapper turned movie star, not knowing what she was talking about, I said, "The one for what?" That quick, at the moment, I thought Larry had a change of heart about me and had referred me to her as an artist. But that was, of course, wishful thinking. Because all she was referring to was the soundcheck and a run-through performance of a couple of songs that she just saw from OSA. Telling me that they looked good and she enjoyed it. She asked me how old I was, and I told her 21. As we stepped over to the bus for her to take pics with OSA and the rest of the crew. She planted a seed by telling me that I should keep pushing toward my dreams and never give up. I took that in, and held on to it as long as I could. After that, I walked back to the kitchen and finished my food in a new spirit. I needed that. Because what she said led me to push myself even harder as a solo artist.

The next day we had a day off, so we ended up in New York City. Now I've been to New York plenty of times before, but not at this level. Larry had a meeting at the record label with the executives. He took us all along with him, myself, Zach, and the group. As we were going up the elevator, I got a flashback of the time my former boy band Tuff Assignment and I went to Laface records by ourselves. We were in Atlanta on our own little tour and tried to perform in the lobby. They kicked us out. Now with the right representation and situation, I have access. Larry even allowed me and Zach to come in the well-known executive's office and listen in. At the end of the day, this is what I respected about Larry. The vernacular, confidence, and savvy to go back and forth with the big wigs. The kind of influence and exposure I needed.

It was a quick meeting. When it was over, the "Executive" sent us over to the office of the A&R responsible for the band's schedule.

This was her first day meeting OSA. After shaking all of their hands in greeting. She began to update them about a couple of things that were happening for them in the coming week. For one, they would be recording a new song for the album produced by one of the top production teams in the music industry at the time. Everybody was excited about that, including Zach. And second; they were going to be shooting their first music video. We were all excited about that too. But then, she dropped the bomb. She asked them if they had met the choreographer? Everybody was puzzled. Then one of the band members started laughing. As if he was insinuating that my job was cut out or my services were no longer needed. To be honest, that was a thought that crossed my mind.

To gain an understanding, the woman asked who I was. I told her that I had been the choreographer for the group so far. She then said, "Oh, I thought the group made up their own show routines". Then quickly changed the subject and pulled out the photo's from their last photoshoot for them to see.

It wasn't until that night while OSA was in the studio recording radio drops that I had a conversation with the guy that originally made the connection for the record deal. Somehow, it came up that he didn't know I had choreographed all the songs that the group had been performing either. He asked me if I was getting paid, and I told him I was. He then asked how much, and when I told him, he took quite the pause without saying anything and just stared at me for a few seconds. His face never implied that I said anything wrong. But my immediate discernment revealed a vibe off of him. Even though I'm not known to play card games, I read his poker face pretty easily. We talked a little more, and then he left. When he did, I sat there watching OSA record through the glass for a few more moments. But at the same time, I was thinking about whether I said too much or too little. This is New York, so you never know.

The guys were going to be a little while, so I decided to go to the store. When I got downstairs in the lobby, I ran into one of the assistants of the management team for the boys. We began to chop it up too. He was a real cool Muslim brother. Before we parted, he asked me one question. "Why won't Larry invest in you"? I told him that I didn't know. He said, "You do want to be an artist right". I said yes. Then he said, "If he was smart, while he's breaking OSA he could start working on you right now. You got the look, it's obvious you can dance, and I heard you can write a song". Right after that, he asked me a question that I didn't know where it originated from. He asked me why was I jealous of Ken? Suddenly I squinted my eyes and jerked my head in disbelief of the question. Looking straight at him, and asked him, "Why would I be jealous of Ken?" He chuckled a little bit and then said, "Naw, I just heard you was jealous of Ken". While standing there confused about the question, I went on to tell him that I thought Ken was a dope writer and that I respected Ken. I don't know where that came from, but that kind of energy was always floating around within our camp. He said, "Ok" and lightly chuckled again. The conversation ended with him telling me to stay focused and keep doing what I'm doing. We dapped up and went our separate ways.

The next week, after performing from Poughkeepsie, NY to Wilkes Barres, PA to Baltimore, MD, and back to New York City, finishing the tour. It was finally time to get into rehearsal to prepare for OSA's first professional video shoot aired on 106 & Park. But it turned out that I ended up being the assistant to who was hired by the label to choreograph the video for their first single. A song that Ken wrote.

I was first given the option to go home. It was momentarily a thought. But the Muslim brother showed up at the hotel and gave me some words of advice from his years of music industry experience and wisdom. After telling me who the choreographer was and her resume. He thought it would be in my best interest to stay and take notes from someone of that status. Telling me that you never know what could happen and that New York is about network and relationships. So I stayed thinking I would just watch. But then the group's loyalty kicked in, and they began to complain that they didn't understand or get the counts she was giving. So right on the first day of rehearsal, the guys walked over to me and asked me to show them the technique she was giving them. So I showed them.

After recognizing there was a slight disconnect from keeping them enthused. She came over to me and asked me who I was, and I told her that I've been working with OSA from day one. She stepped back and took a quick surveillance of the chemistry between us and right then on the spot told me to fall in line and learn the routine with them. I did. By the time we got toward the end of the song. She told me to take it away and give them my style, creating a masterpiece between the both of us. On the 3rd and last day of 10 hours straight of closed rehearsals. There was a knock on the studio door. While we were tightening up the routine with the boys, in through the door came a short light skin lady, and she had a couple of guys with her. I didn't know who she was, but she looked really important. I didn't think she was there for me, but I was wrong. She said Flip, can I see you in the hallway. So, of course, I stopped what I was doing, and I stepped to and through the door behind her and the guys she had with her. She was straight to the point and very frank. She said, "I don't know how you guys do it in Boston but this is New York". From that, I had thought I did something wrong. She said that if I wanted to be in this business, I'm going to need a lawyer and people looking out for me. She then went inside of her coat and pulled out an envelope with a check in it and handed it over to me. She said, "This is the other half of the money that belongs to you for the choreography that you've previously created for OSA, don't tell anybody, that's yours". Before she walked away she looked me straight in the eyes and told me not to get used to somebody reimbursing me money that was taken from me. Because that doesn't happen. On the spot forcing me to open my eyes to the fact that It's a business about talent. I told her that

I understood clearly. Then the question was asked, "Just one more thing; did you ever receive your tour jacket?" I told her that I didn't. Without breaking eye contact, I could see that her wheels were spinning with the confirmation that I'm being eaten alive. She urged me to find representatives at this level to protect my talent. The lady didn't come right out and tell me exactly what was going on. That wasn't her responsibility. But at this point, I took it as she already did more than she had to. Come to find out, Larry was receiving the budget for his team and was giving everybody what he wanted to give them. He was taking full advantage of what we didn't know. From what I understood, Zach didn't get treated fairly either. As far as the tour jacket, I later found out that he gave it away to some girl he was trying to impress. I even remember asking him about it. He said that the Label never sent one for me.

A day later, It felt good to be on a video set with a 6 thousand dollar check in my pocket. The video shoot was a success. It was such a big production. I got a chance to see how a record company markets their product. There were magazine interviewers there. Photographers, make-up artist, fashion stylists, and too many industry hustlers to even count.

When the shoot was over, we got back on the road back to Boston.

After a couple of weeks off, I was ready to go back. I loved the lifestyle. Even though I didn't understand the business side of it. But I'm sure if I stayed in New York, the continued trials and tribulations would have created a beast. Just like everybody else there. Fool me once, shame on you; fool me twice, shame on me.

— It's A Wrap —

Once I got back to Boston and settled in. I figured, let me get back up with Wiz and pick up where I left off. So I called and paged him a few times, but I never got an answer. So one day, I took it upon myself to just stop by his crib. When I did, a girl answered the door. She knew who I was, so she let me in. When wiz came downstairs, he seemed agitated, not necessarily about me but something else altogether. That wasn't out of the normal for him. Wiz was on edge and moody regularly. I didn't want to go straight in on the topic where I left off at the hotel before I left to go on the road. So we picked up some small talk, just kicking it. But after a while, I felt the vibe was off. I didn't think nothing of it. I just took it as if it's just not a good day. So I decided to take off. As I began stepping toward the front door, I heard a key in the lock. Somebody was coming in. It was none other than the girl that I was kicking it with that night. When she stepped through the door, her eyes lit up but then quickly told a story that the opportunity was gone. I said wussup, she said wussup; and with nothing more being said walked right past me going up the stairs. There was nothing left to do but turn around and give cuz a fist bump and leave. I didn't necessarily feel bad on the ride home or even get upset at my cousin. But he did teach me a valuable lesson. Opportunities don't wait, and you can't hate who's ready for it. I shrugged it off.

So when all else failed; I went right back to working with other acts around the city. One being a gospel group at a church in the Mattapan section of Boston. It was one of the first mega-churches in the city. I can't say that I was very spiritual then. But I know now that I was called there for a reason. But at the time, money was the calling for me. So twice a week, I was at the church. At least until it's time to get back on the road with OSA.

About a month later, I got a call saying that the boys are back over in New York, and they're going to be on 106 & Park premiering the video. I called all my family members and friends and told them all to watch. Everybody was excited—especially the local music community.

That same coming weekend while OSA was still out of town. I had planned to go out with one of my homies and turn up. I felt like I deserved it because I was teaching like crazy and busy with everything else all over the city. From being present in the Boston Public Schools, judging talent competitions, and even up early on Saturday and sometimes Sunday mornings to teach since I had been back.

But this particular Saturday, It wasn't going to happen.

Because that Friday night, I had plans to go out. I got ready, and my boy had picked me up. It was good that he did because I had all plans to get wasted. As we were riding the back roads from my grandmother's house in Mattapan into Dorchester. I took a swig from the Hennessy bottle I had been pregaming with since an hour before he pulled up. As we were going through the intersection crossing Blue Hill Avenue, I got a 2-Way pager alert. It was from somebody that I really didn't expect. It was the choreographer that was hired for OSA's video, Madelyn. All the message said was "Call Me".

So without letting any time fill the gap of us speaking, I had the phone ringing. Not knowing what the call would be about, I had a little nerves, but the Hennessy was working already. After the second ring, she answered. "Flip-Out, what's up, you still in New York"? I said, what's up, but told her that I wasn't. She said, "That's too bad". Because of my mood at the moment, I just thought she was calling to invite me out to party. She told me that she had just got hired for another big gig and was short one male dancer. So I jumped the gun and asked her if she needed me to come. She said that it depends on how far I am. She had forgotten where I was from. So I reminded her that I was in Boston. Playing down the distance between us. Still, she became indecisive, saying, "Man, you're too far". So I redirected the energy and asked how much was the gig. After she gave me the rate, she still sounded unsure. Because the next thing she asked was, "Would you even have a place to stay once you're here?" I told her I would work something out. Right then, I had made up my mind that no matter what the gig was, I was in. Because along my journey, I've learned that you can't leave any space to let anyone doubt you. Especially when you really want something. I wanted this. So I wouldn't let this call end without me being locked in. She took a quick pause, and said, "Ok let's do it". After a quick silent, fist-pumping cheer of celebration for myself, I asked her what the gig entailed, and she told me it was for a rap music video. After giving me the rest of the details, before she hung up she said, "I will see you at 12 noon tomorrow". My jaw dropped. Because the earliest I thought that she wanted me to come was the following weekend. But that wasn't the case at all. It was pure dedication, determination and drive for what I do that agreed to go before I hung up the call. With it already going on 11 pm at the time, all I could do was tell the homie to make a u-turn and take me back home, canceling a night of partying. Because I had to make some very quick arrangements in order to make it to New York City's Port Authority within the next 12 hours. He was one of my best friends and totally understood.

Sure enough, by 6am, I was boarding a greyhound at South Station in downtown Boston bus station. Back to the Big Apple I go. This time, alone.

Even though I was sleepy. I was more excited than ever. Everything happened so quickly that I didn't even get a chance to tell anybody that I was going. It wasn't even until the bus was going through Connecticut that I started arranging a place to stay for the next 3 days. In which I ended up staying at an ex-girlfriends family member's apartment. It was my only option besides my grandfathers house whom still lived over in Newark, NJ.

Luckily when I arrived at the port authority station in New York City. The studio was only 5 blocks away. That gave me enough time to get something to eat. So, as usual, whenever I go to New York, I stop and get a chicken Gyro from one of the food trucks. I loved those. When I finished eating, I picked up my duffle bag and began making my way toward the studio. I arrived with 20mins to spare. When I walked in, there was 2 girls on the floor stretching and talking. I introduced myself, and the energy was good from the beginning. One of the girls looked very familiar too. When the other male dancer came in he was cool too; Travis. We dapped up and kicked it. While we was stretching, I could tell he was a hustler in the conversation. Yet, ruff around the edges. Braids to the back like mine, focused, and could dance his ass off. Dancing in videos wasn't even his dream, just another hustle for him.

Then, It was time. Madelyn called us all to the mirrors and told us that we only had one day to learn the choreography and have it locked in by the next day. And, the rehearsal was scheduled for 12hrs. That was intimidating. For a couple of reasons. For one, even though I use mirrors in my own teaching sessions. I've always started teaching the routines without the mirrors. Using them only at the end of rehearsals or when I'm done creating to tighten up the formations. But everybody has their own way of doing it. Secondly, I didn't even know what the song was. She was teaching so fast that I wasn't picking up the counts. As I looked over at the other 3 dancers, they were flowing with her. My nerves started turning up creating tension within me. Because I immediately started talking down on myself. Thinking that I wasn't good enough. Yet, where I got stuck, I would ask her how to do this or that. She would stop and teach it to me again, but after 4 or 5 times, I could tell she was getting frustrated with me. I was getting frustrated too. Feeling a little embarrassed as well. My inner voice telling me that I was only good enough for the Boston local talent climate. Even at one moment thinking I should just tell her thanks but no thanks, and give up.

For the whole first two hours of the rehearsal, I went through this. Then suddenly, it all turned around.

She said, "Let's run through what we have so far one more time, and then try it with the music". When we did the run-through, she was counting out loud. An area of teaching I wasn't as strong; using counts. It was good. But still not feeling confident about it. As we reset to start again, she yells out, "Shannyn, you gotta pick it up". Nodding my head yes, knowing that I did. When she pressed play, and the familiar beat dropped in. I felt a new vibe and energy come over me. Everything started to click, and my wheels were spinning. Feeling the discouragement peeling from my spirit.

After that run-through, I started flowing in the routine as if I was creating it myself. For the next 10 hours, I was on it. When I left there that night, I was pleased with myself. Madelyn was too.

As we were getting ourselves ready to leave the studio. Me and the other dancers started talking. Mainly trying to figure out what everybody was doing for the rest of the night. One of the girls said she was going straight home because she just had a baby. The other girl said that she was going out with her girls. So Travis said that he was going to the club. One of the girls asked him, which club? After he told her she continued to gather her belongings. Then, he asked me if I wanted to go. So I said I did. His next question was, do you smoke weed? Even though I did, I was always skeptical of telling new people whether I did or not. Because I knew I couldn't smoke with everybody.

Travis, had to use the restroom. As soon as he walked out the door. One of the girls walked over to me. She asked me a question that threw me off. She asked if I was gay. I looked at her sideways and told her, "Hell naw, why what's up?" Without changing her energy or tone, she looked me straight in the face and said, "Because you didn't seem like you were". She flowed right into the question, "Did you know Travis before today?" I told her that I didn't. She went on to inform me that she did. She then told me that the club I was just invited to was a gay club. I wasn't even shocked. Or mad. Nobody surprised me anymore at this point in my life. When he came out of the bathroom, he went to try to give me the address. But because my coat tail was yanked, I declined the offer. He did seem a little disappointed about it.

As he grabbed his bag walking out the door, he gave a quick look of salt at the girls. He knew they tipped me off.

The next very early morning, Madelyn picked me up and we went over to the Bronx. The Bronx is where the video shoot was set up at Fordham University, in the gym. When I got there, I didn't see the rap star at first, but I did see quite a bit of television and film stars. There was a lot of mixing and mingling of everybody. Being that I've always been a people watcher; I kind of stayed in one spot and observed it all. Always being aware and in control of the energy in the atmosphere. Letting whatever is meant for me to come and what's not, pass. Then, I was asked to move because the set designers needed the space I was in. So that lead me to a new spot. A folded seat at the end of the basketball court. There is a lot of wait time when filming a professional music video. So I sat there for quite some time. After a couple of hours, in came the rapper. Not only him, but an entourage and a few other known music artist too. As time slowly ticked well into the afternoon. The Rapper got bored while waiting and walked over to the basketball court with a few crew members. They grabbed the ball and began to shoot around. One of the members began to instigate a 3 on 3 pick up game. When they realized they were short one man, they looked to me sitting at the end of the court. The rapper steps over to me with a crew member close by and asked if I could play. Before answering, the crew member abruptly asked me where I was from.

I told them I was from Boston. The rapper redirected his first question to ask me what I was doing there. I told him that I was dancing for him in his video. He then nodded his head yes saying, "Aight, then you on my team then". I didn't do nothing much but pass the ball. But when it came down to the next point win. Fat Joe passed me the ball, and I hit my only shot in the game for the game win.

He said with an excited loud yelp, "LARRY BIRD…". With all the basketball games and shooting around at the community center I grew up in; I knew a thing or two about shooting 3 pointers.

We all dapped up in a quick mini celebration, and I returned to my seat. I didn't see the rap star no more until it was time for the director to say, ACTION. At the end of the day, the whole experience was awesome and a success.

About a month later, the video premiered on BET's 106 & Park. It wasn't until I was standing in front of the TV watching that episode that I learned that the song and video belonged to a movie soundtrack. That was good news. But the bad news was that I never heard from Madelyn again. But the hype off of the video created another burst of choreography work for me around the city of Boston. I lived off of that for as long as I could. From Boston College to Harvard University campus, I ran with it. I continued to use my vision and skills to image and develop new up-and-coming performers, rappers, solo-artist, more singing groups, and of course dance crews. I was really trying to build a name for myself.

— Flight Plan —

OSA's album was finally done. But the only thing left to do was get a release date from the record label. That was the news I depended on for myself. Because I just couldn't wait to get back on the road again. But in the meantime, I was back to rehearsing with them as normal. Still getting paid. I got a call from Larry saying that the boys was scheduled to do a taping for the very famous tv show, Soul Train. He asked me if I would be available to go. Of course, even if I wasn't I would have made it possible in my schedule. This is Soul Train. A show that I grew up watching and also daydreamed of me performing on. This program was just as famous and important to me as the Apollo. Before hanging up, Larry told me that he would be getting back to me with the flight details within a day or two. That was fine with me, because it was all the time I needed to tell as many people as I could. Some people were happy with me about it. But then there were those that take your good news as bragging and tone it down for you. I've learned that not everybody is clapping for you.

The night before the OSA entourage was set to fly into LAX, I got a call. It was about 11:30 pm. It was Larry. He called to inform me that something has come up regarding my ticket. The record label only paid for an undisclosed number of tickets and hotel expenses, and unfortunately I was going to have to sit this trip out. I can't lie, I was a little disappointed about it. But of course, still excited for OSA. Since my grandmother was in Florida at the time taking care of some business. For the rest of that night I just took advantage of having the apartment to myself. So I invited a young lady over and sipped on some Hennessy until we got carried away for the rest of the night.

The next morning about 8:55 am. My brother Randy came in the door amped up. He still had his keys to my grandmothers apartment. Even though he had moved out, got married and started his family.

I heard him yelling out, "Yo, Shizz; get up, get up. We under attack"? I had no clue what he was talking about. At first, my woozy head thought he was talking about some drama in the street. But then he said it again, "Yo, get up, come look at this". So me and the young lady got up and rushed to the living room where he had turned on the TV. When I looked at that floor model TV screen, I couldn't believe my eyes at first. But I knew right away that what I was looking at was real and very serious. We flipped the remote control dial through every basic cable channel we had, and it was on every channel. A few minutes later, what we watched went to another level of excitement and confusion. As we all were standing in the middle of the living room floor watching and debating if it was a mistake or not. A catastrophic confirmation of war was deliberately flown into the south tower of the World Trade Center. All three of us screamed on impact. We were all in shock. Then my brother said something to me that really woke me up.

He said, "What time was your flight supposed to be today?" Then, I broke down emotionally, realizing that the first flight that hit the North tower was the flight number that OSA was on. Flight 11 out of Boston Logan, Airport.

All 3 of us sat in silence for about 15mins. We had no other choice. Because all incoming and outgoing calls and pager messages were all down due to the high call volume on the entire east coast. Later I learned that that was a tough moment for both my grandmother and Mom in Florida. Because the last time my grandmother spoke to me, she said, "Have a safe flight, and I will see you when we're both back". They both had thought I was on the plane.

But fortunately, the next day, my 2way started going berserk with incoming notifications. It was all of the backed-up messages from the day before. A lot of them saying things like, "Please tell me you wasn't on that plane," "please reply back," "Shannyn are you there"?

The same kind of messages I was sending to the OSA team. I replied back to everybody promptly.

Then, I got a message from one of the band members. That was a total load off of my conscience. He told me he would call me when they landed in California. Turns out, when the team arrived at Boston Logan Airport, Larry had got a call from the Record Label saying that they found cheaper flights for the whole entourage to be able to board the same flight. But the only difference with that flight was that they had to layover in Minnesota. But when they got to Minnesota, of course, the military was there waiting to escort all passengers off the plane and to the nearest hotel. Before they grounded all planes. The crew made their next flight out the next day, continuing on to California. The band made it to the Soul Train studio and taped their first recorded TV performance.

For two days, I did nothing but sit in my room and try to put this whole tragedy together in my head. For the first time in my life, without anybody nudging me or even bring up in a conversation; I had a question in my mind about who God was. I was all in my head about it. Almost obsessed about why I was invited to go somewhere, but then denied my seat. Still, when the time came, it was already agreed that I would sit out for this trip. Yet again, at the last minute, the label found a budget for a few more people to go. I just couldn't put a finger on it. The only question I had in the back of my mind that kept replaying was, "Is that God?"

That Thursday of that same week, I ended up at Jubilee Church in Mattapan, where I was putting together choreography for a gospel singing act. But on this day, I wasn't there to teach. I talked to the man who hired me to work with the gospel act. He was all I knew to go to because I didn't have anyone in my life at the time that I knew lived a holy lifestyle. This man was. He was very knowledgeable of God, and I had questions. When I walked into his office the first thing he asked me was, "I thought you went to California?" Just as soon as he said it, his eyes stretched and it was noticeable that it dawned on him that I probably didn't go because of the attacks. He then asked me to have a seat in front of his desk. When I did, he immediately asked me if I was ok. Because it was quite evident that I wasn't in my normal headspace or my usual upbeat, spirited self. Mentally I couldn't fathom any thought or anything that was outside of the question, "Is that God?" Because the question had taken root in my psyche, I didn't hesitate to open up and begin telling him the whole situation that had just occurred. And of course, ask him this burning question I had. Because I needed to know. We sat in that office for almost two hours, going back and forth. For every question I had, this man had an intelligent biblical answer. Totally ministering to me, raising my awareness of God and true in his attempt to make me a witness.

But the answer to my question. He broke it down to me in a way that I could understand. He first grabbed his bible and then my hand next. He told me to bow my head because he wanted to pray before he gave me an answer. After he prayed out loud. He grabbed the Bible, sat back in his chair, and began to flip through the pages. Once he found what he was looking for, he read it in silence for about 20 seconds. Then he looked up at me and told me that the answer was right there in the book. Then he asked me a question to my question asking, "Did you know that God knew who you was before you were born?" I realized right at that moment that everything that I did know about God was by the legend of the stories I've heard. Also from the songs I learned from the time my grandmother made me sing in the choir when I was a little boy.

The question put me at a crossroad where I didn't know if I believed that God had that much insight on me. So it raised a couple more questions. But I just went ahead and simply asked him, how? He then showed me a scripture in the book of Jeremiah. Chapter 29, verse 11 to 14. He basically told me that God had a plan for me and wanted to prosper me in my future. Further telling me that it is impossible for God to lie and that I have some type of favor because he picked me. I don't know why but when he said that, I immediately thought back to what the Lab professor at M.I.T. said to me about my future. All through my life, little random things like that would stick in my mind.

Before we wrapped up, he said, "You may not get it right now, but God doesn't stop giving signs and wonders to the ones he love, but only when you start believing, you start receiving". As if he knew what my struggle was. Then he asked me if I had a bible of my own. I told him that there's a bible at my grandmothers house. He laughed and said, "That's your grandmothers; might be time for you to have your own".

We left out of his office right then and we walked up to the church book store and he bought me my very first student bible. He prayed over it, signed it, and then sent me on my way. After that day, no matter where I traveled, that bible was part of the trip.

It wasn't too long after that that my work relationship with OSA started to fade. After months had gone by, Larry tried to get a release date for the album. Things came to a screeching halt as we learned that "One Step Above" had been dropped from the label. It was a devastating blow to the hope and vision that I had. Not only for them but myself as well.

So it was back to the drawing board for me. I submitted to find a new job. It was a while before I landed something solid. So, for the time being, I continued to do what I knew best to make money. Dance. For two years straight, that was my only hustle. Even though I had the skill of dancing, I knew the money would eventually be inconsistent with paying any bills, month after month. So I did get a little worried about what my near future would look like; and it didn't help that my grandmother just announced to the family that she was moving back to Florida after her now husband; Frank retired at the end of the following year. To be honest, I didn't know what I would do. But I knew I was tired of my fate depending on other people. At that time, I even fell into a depression that nobody even knew about. But that was my fault. Because I tend to smile even in times of pain.

— First Semester —

Out of the blue I got a call from an employer. I had filled out the application months before they called. But thank God that they did, because it was right on time. They asked me to come in for an interview. When I did, they hired me on the spot. It was an orphanage in West Roxbury. I lived in Boston all my life and drove past this place plenty of times and never even knew what it was. It reminded me of how I felt all my life up until that point. Invisible in plain sight.

They assigned me to a dorm with 7 & 8 year olds. I immediately fell in love with the job, becoming a star worker. I connected to the job because it was about people. It also reminded me of the summers I ended up being a summer camp counselor at the Community Center. Except this environment was way more intense. There might be 3 or 4 kids at the community center that might have it tough at home. Maybe showing out and displaying some trauma here and there. But at the orphanage, It was non-stop. From the time you begin your shift until the end, there were fights, nervous breakdowns, cries out for mommies and daddies, and little boys that pissed the bed. Mothers trying to kick their drug addictions and legally get their kids back would come and visit, while I would have to stand there and watch. Because the courts required that all visits with their own kids be supervised. I always applauded their efforts. Because that was something that my mother never did for me and Randy.

There was one kid that I remember. He stood out to me. You can tell he didn't come from the typical neglected home situation. He was more of a well-kept kid. I remember him because I identified with his pain to a certain degree. He glowed in a way that said he didn't belong there. In which none of them should be. His parents weren't addicts or abusive to him whatsoever. They loved him and spoiled him. The night he came in, he had on the newest of everything. A diamond earring, a gold bracelet and necklace, a bubble goose coat, a pair of timberlands, a fresh haircut and a hand held video game. But he was crying and scared. When I learned his story the next day, I found out that he came from some parents that were kingpins and scammers. They weren't substance abusers at all. Their only addiction was money and taking care of their only son. But they both were sent to prison, and they didn't have any family that was in a position to take him in. He wasn't scared of the other kids, and for the most part, he was friendly. But every now and then, I would find him staring at the other kids playing while his face sat with frustration and confusion. Other times I would find him looking out the window and crying. Reminding me of the times, I would sit in the window on Shawmut Ave and cry when nobody was looking.

One time I asked the kid if he was ok. He looked around the dorm while another kid was being restrained on the floor and said straightforwardly, "I don't belong here. My mommy and daddy would be mad if they knew I was here". I felt that. Because I knew what it was like to feel out of place or in a situation that I shouldn't be in with everything being above my reach to change it. A few months later, that kid was picked up by his grandfather and never returned to the orphanage again. Sometimes I wonder where those kids are today. Hoping that they've all fixed their stories.

The time began to wind down toward my grandmother moving. With the money I was making, I wasn't confident about finding a place of my own. But something had to happen. Because, either way, Ma was surely leaving soon.

At the time, Me and Draya wasn't necessarily a couple yet, but I tried to make something out of our connection. Draya use to be one of my dancers. I met her about a year after I graduated at a show. I was wearing the color red as a theme to my outfit and even my Timbaland boots were red. That was the focal point for her as I was getting ready to walk out of the double doors. I knew the girl she was standing there with so I stopped to greet her. Draya looked me up and down and then boldly made a pass at me complimenting my vibe. She took a serious liking to me. At the time I was well into my player ways although I did have a girl friend at the time. But that never stopped Draya from her pursuit of me. Even though she was slim and tiny. Her big heart and noticeable ambitious ways were unstoppable.

With that being said, Draya was still a little immature for what I needed at the time, especially where I was mentally. But, what I did know was that she was a rider. She was smart. She wasn't a street chick but definitely understood her surroundings. We started off as a fling, but survival pushed me to ask her for us to move in together. Of course, she was down. Right away, we started putting our money together to purchase all the stuff we needed. Still not 100 percent sure if this is what I wanted to do. Not because she wasn't a good girl, but because I knew the option was always open for me to go shack up with Tifani. But even she wasn't mature enough or mentally strong enough to handle what I was going through. Tifani was very loving, caring, and nurturing. But not a fighter, and what was coming next for me, I needed a fighter. Draya was a fighter. She even punched me in the face one time. As angry as I got that day; It's crazy how I recognized that as real love.

After a few months or so, we finally moved to a new place. It was a great feeling and accomplishment. My first Condo with my name on the lease.

Everything was going smoothly for a while. Then Draya started complaining about her job. She hated it. She had taken a job doing an overnight shift. I can't lie, I saw it all over her. The job was breaking her down. The hours were tough. She was coming home every day with a new complaint about it. She also hated that when she was coming in from work, I was on my way out to work. We'd miss each other all through the week.

I was always in my head about situations that didn't even happen. I began to panic a little bit about the thought of her quitting. Leaving me to be responsible for all the bills. I started obsessing over the thought. Fueling me to do something anxious. Because I realized that this time when all else fails, now I don't have my grandmother's house to go back to. That was something I got used to over the years, moving in and out.

The only time my mind would seem to be at peace was when I was at work. The pay wasn't the best, but it was the job I had, and I was going to work it until it worked for me.

There was a girl that happened to work there. She only worked part-time, so I would see her here and there every other shift. She was cool, and I could tell that she liked me. Even though we didn't talk much, her face would light up when she saw me. But to be honest, I thought she liked every black guy that worked there. But for some reason, she was drawn to me. Overall I believed she just wanted to have sex and keep it moving. I was cool with that too. But little did she know, I had another idea for her. We went out together one night and had some drinks. For some reason, I knew by her personality that she was the adventurous type. She wasn't necessarily wild, but she was intrigued by everything. Totally open. Before I dropped her off home, I pulled over at the Jamaica Way pond. We had a great vibe, and the conversation was flowing. It was the kind of night that you didn't want to end. Not at all like I was falling in love, but I just felt good. As we were going back and forth, something she said triggered me to step to the plate on the idea that I had in mind while talking. She told me that there was a guy back at the job that has been interested in her, and he's been coming on strong. She told me that she gave him her number, and they've talked a couple of times. I knew exactly who she was talking about. I asked her if she was just as interested as he was. She said that she wasn't. When she said that he wasn't "mentally stimulating," I took it as an invite to be all the way me and real about what I wanted and had in mind. About 10 minutes more into that conversation, My twin showed up. That vibe that came over me in that hotel room with Wiz that night came alive. This time he came fully prepared and ready for the new opportunity. Way more serious about it than I was that night. At this point, feeling like I had nothing to lose but everything to gain. I began to tell her what she was and was not going to do, and she never had a rebuttal. She picked up right where the other girl left off and started giving me yes after yes to everything I asked. It was almost like that's what she had been waiting for me to say. At first, I didn't believe she totally understood what I was saying. So, to make sure she was locked in, I told her to delete every guy's phone number in her phone. Without hesitation, she went into her phone settings and hit the hard reset button. Blanking her phone. She looked over at me and told me that she wanted what I want. Telling me before she got out of the car that night; "I got you". The following weekend, we were off to the races. My first turn out paid me $600 for one hour of her time. I officially entered my first class at Sidewalk University.

CHAPTER 10

Before Graduation

— This Can't Be My Life —

Being a good boy has opened doors and has brought me some good memories in my life. But after feeling that money and the flow of it coming in, I came to the realization that being a good guy had been a lot of pressure too. Pressure to be mediocre. Especially growing up in an environment that doesn't seem to respect it. In some way, in almost every situation you're expected to compromise, turn the other cheek, let disrespect ride, or just be the better person. Just downright accept having or being second choice to everyone and just about everything. At all times. I was spiritually exhausted with that. Even though I was just turning 23 years old and time was still on my side. I didn't see it that way. I had already begun feeling like a failure at life. Microscopically looking at all that I didn't have or didn't accomplish instead of recognizing my gifts and being grateful for what I did have. Comparing myself to everything and everyone on a financial level. Never considering that the level they were on wasn't too much better than mine. Emotionally locked into not only what everybody else expected and thought about me, but how I viewed myself as well.

Because I felt like I put all my eggs in one basket and it didn't pay off. Having nobody to be mad at but myself. For letting opportunities slip through my fingers out of a disability that I now call "being too loyal". Always finding a reason or excuse to be a good guy to people who would never return the gesture. With that misunderstanding; all of that; now, as an adult, it set an "tick-tick boom" energy within my spirit.

Fear had begun to take root in my life. A panic fear of dying without ever fulfilling my dreams. Fear that I would be the drunk "has been" that everyone starts to laugh at for chasing my dreams. Like so many that I've seen coming up as a local artist. Harshly learning that people believe in you temporarily. But also, the messengers of the town talk that couldn't be trusted anyway would sometime be added to my already unstable spiritual and mental state of mind.

All these feelings that I had, became a quiet depression, high anxiety, frustration, anger and even suicidal thoughts. What do you do when you're mad at God and yourself? The torment of not knowing how to explain that feeling and Nobody that I felt safe enough with that I could tell was heavy. But it Fueled me to become what I needed to be to get to wherever I was going by any means. But because I didn't know the exact solution or path; I never wanted to bleed on anybody that didn't cut me.

— Breaking Point —

For a few months, I tried my best to stick it out with Draya.

But I knew that what I was doing, she wouldn't understand. All she knew, was that I had more money than I usually would have from a bi-weekly paycheck. For a little while, I did my best to keep it all a secret. But that feeling of being a good boy started digging in my side, fighting to come back. I didn't like him very much at this time, almost hating him. So I sat Draya down and finally told her what was up. Because one of the pressures of being a good boy is to lie in order to save a woman from a broken heart and being left with more work to do by trying to keep up with the secret. Still what I told Draya wasn't easy for her to hear. She met me as a good boy, that's who she fell in love with. And that's what she was expecting for the rest of her life.

Her understanding of it could only reciprocate that Marci was just another woman trying to be in a committed relationship with me. So, of course, that would spark up tension. It did for a while. But then Draya got comfortable with the money aspect of what I was doing. Learning quickly that money does muzzle the attitude and mouth of a woman, even though she didn't agree with how the money was being made.

Before I knew it, Draya had quit her job. So for two months, I paid all the bills. To be honest, I really took pride in doing that. But in that time, Draya had become stressful to me. Because since she wasn't working, she expected me to spend more time with her. But I didn't have the time. The way the money was coming in, I didn't want time for anything else. To be in the streets and be successful was to be more attentive to your hustle more than anything else. Depending on how focused you are; even a relationship would have to take a backseat. And I was driven.

Draya was trying to find another job. But, in the back of my mind, I really didn't want her to. Because that meant that she would stick around and contribute her portion of bills again, and her emotions and clingy vibe would intensify. So one day, I asked her what she had in mind to do next. She told me she had made up her mind to enter Hair School. That was a great idea, except that the hair school was one mile away from where we lived. My agitation was growing.

Because I wanted to do things my way without considering anyone else's feelings in my life, for once.

Something had to change. Because almost every little thing Draya did quickly became a major problem to me. Not that she was truly doing anything wrong out of the way for a 22 year old girl. But her presence began to devastate my mission. So I got to a point where I narcissistically started to look for any reason and excuse to make more space for the life I wanted.

It was a Saturday, and we went food shopping.

When we got to the Malden Center grocery store, we grabbed a cart and started going up and down the isles throwing everything we want and needed in it. Because I knew I would be out all times of the night and there was only one car. I grabbed the groceries that were quick and easy to make or microwavable so that she didn't have to try to cook. After filling up the baskets. We stepped to the checkout line and began to throw our items on the belt. As we are in motion, I noticed that some items that I knew were surely out of Draya's cooking experience. There were two batches of collard greens, ham hocks, sweet potatoes, and more Sunday dinner items. Even though I was baffled by this, I was still going to buy it. But something twisted my spirit and made me snap. The moment when Draya "happy go luckily" pulled out a pack of turkey necks, I stared at the package for a few seconds. Then instantly my temperature boiled. I picked up the turkey necks looked at her, and asked, "Why are you getting this stuff?" With the good boy not being so far gone from my spirit, I even gave her the benefit of the doubt by hoping she would say that her mom was coming to cook or something like that. But when she replied with, "Because that's what I want to eat". I couldn't hold back anymore, and I said out loud in the middle of the grocery store, "Well, who the f*ck is gonna cook it?" Embarrassing the both of us, Draya, looked at me and went on to say, "Don't you know how to cook?" That added fuel to the fire.

In a perfect world, that would have been funny. But that did it. That was the nail in the coffin, with totally gaslighting the situation.

I took all unnecessary stuff off the belt, paid for the rest, and rushed out the door. I was pissed.

Once we got in the car, I was home in the next 15mins. After arguing and fighting for hours about it, that same day, before the sun went down, I had called Draya's mother and told her I was dropping her off with all of her clothes. Draya was hurt, and of course, thought that I used her. But that wasn't the case or ever what I had in mind at all. It was simply because a financial door opened, and I was with it; she wasn't. Truth be told, I really wanted Draya to be ok with what was going on. But she couldn't find it in herself to do so at the time. That was the deal-breaker for me. That day I learned that people just don't go around compromising what they really want or feel. Even in a relationship. They stand on what they want, win or lose. So I figured that was the day I'd stop compromising what I wanted. Therefore, "Love me or leave me" was birthed in my spirit.

That night I dropped Draya off at her parent's house, and I didn't speak to her for a while.

Once Marci learned that Draya was gone, she got even more in tune with what we were doing. She was excited about it, and business was booming. As much as we were together, you'd think that Marci would've moved in with me. But she didn't. It really was just business between us. So much that Marci called me one day and told me that she quit the job we worked at together. She chose me over the job. But I still worked there for a couple of months longer. I wasn't ready to step all the way into the life. Understanding that scared money to don't make none; I was making just enough to be satisfied. Always keeping in the back of my mind that what was going on wasn't forever. Because my life has surely showed me that the streets will never love you back, or protect you as much as you'd think. So I made a promise to myself. First, I set a time for how long I would do this. Then I set a marker for how much I wanted to make and stack up. Promising myself that no matter how much money I had by the set time was up. I still had to forfeit the game.

Of course, my first plan with the money was to fund my music career. Yes, I was still fighting for that vision. Because I knew that underneath it all, that's where I'm at my best. So still here and there, I continued to work with different producers around the city and had come across some of the best up-and-coming MC's from around the city. Doing my best to musically lead them in the right direction. After all, it was my reputation. And the way the music game was changing, it kind of went hand in hand with this new lifestyle that I adopted. Everybody wanted to be "Big Time".

Around that time, I first thought of making my own tracks. I had never done it before. Up until then, I was just a Choreographing, song-writing, singer. It was my first swing back at cutting out the middle man. Or, shall I say, the scavengers and savages.

I remember being on Mass Ave one day, and I walked into a music store. It was right across the street from Berkeley School of Music. When I walked in, I went straight to the back where all the instruments were. I would go over to the Piano's, keyboards, and synthesizers. I felt like a kid in a candy store. I started to play with all the sounds in them. I found one that I really liked. It was new on the market at the time. A Yamaha Motif 7. I felt connected to it. So much that I ended up being in there for almost 2hrs playing with it. I asked the store rep all kinds of questions about it including the price. When he told me it was $2800, I gasped. But the crazy thing is, I had about $3500 in my pocket at the time. I realize now that I gasped out of a natural comfort zone and mental condition of being a "have not".

Still, I walked out of the store by telling the store rep that I'd be back to get it. Not because I couldn't get it then, but because I had to go and talk myself into investing in myself. About two weeks later, I made it make enough sense to go back and get it. So I did. When I got there, the guy gave me $300 off the original price just for keeping my word.

Once I got that thing in my possession. I was on fire about figuring out how to make music with it. At first, I had a hard time with it. But I wouldn't stop hitting buttons and reading the manual. After about a week, I was already frustrated with it. But, when all else fails when it comes to electronics. I took the machine over to my brother Randy's apartment. He and his new little family had moved into my grandmother's old apartment. After leaving it there with him for one night, he had it figured out by the next day. No matter how much attention was on me, I always thought my little brother was a genius. Once he showed me how to do it. It was on from there.

Now because my Condo had become a place of meeting and a spot to impress more curious girls about what I had going on, I didn't exactly bring the Keyboard there right away. I brought it to Tifani's apartment because even though we had our differences, I never stopped loving her. The way she'd always believed in my musical talents made it easy for me to keep her around. Whenever I was working on putting together my beat patterns, those were the times she wouldn't bother me at all. For hours, and even days. I think she was just more content with knowing where I was by being there. Although, at times, she'd piss me off just as much as Draya. And, with everything that was going on with me mentally and emotionally at the time. I attracted the question of a lifetime. Can you love two people at the same time? It became a question that I carried in the back of my mind for years. But I was too focused and had begun adapting to an immature, selfish heart. Not even trying to attempt to answer it.

Tifani's genuine support for my vision outweighed our differences. Even with what I had going on with Marci. Although I will say, It took me a little while before I told her. The reason being, Tifani was a bit of a gossiper. She couldn't hold water in pot. It was normal for me to keep secrets from her. But in the beginning, after I did tell her what was up. Tifani wasn't as cool about Marci either. Once again, just not understanding that angle of my mission. Also standing up for her position with me and that Marci was just another chick trying to be "wifey". This was a side of me that she never met either and didn't know that I was willing to do whatever I had to do to survive.

It wasn't until one wee hour of the morning that I went to her house after a long night of moving around with Marci. I was too tired to go all the way home. So I instead went to Tifani's crib. From the time she moved into this place, I always had a key to it. When I walked in the door, she got up and, like always, started to ask me all kinds of questions and insinuate in a sarcastic way that I probably came thereafter I just dropped off some girl. She was right. But it was her family tradition to start an argument. That night, I was so tired. All I had was enough energy to take all the money I had from both of my pockets and throw it at her. Telling her to shut up and count it; and let me know how much it was. Her face was priceless. I then laid down across the bed and fell fast asleep. Later that morning, I woke up with all the money neatly in a stack on the dresser. I didn't even hear her leave out for work. From that day forward, Tifani never had another complaint about anything that I was doing. For some women, showing and proving yourself will cause them to submit. No matter what path you take to win.

— New Heights —

One day while at home cleaning and listening to some music. I looked in the mirror, and I knew that I was changing. Becoming more confident and relaxed about what I was doing. It was the first time outside of music that I realized that I liked myself. Not to be misconstrued with loving myself. Because I was a long way from that. But I began to be more boisterous about what I want. Allowing this newfound sense of confidence to splint my backbone to a new level of strength and dominance. Nothing over the top, but just enough to go a little deeper into the life. So finally, I quit my job. I figured, how can I be a boss if I had a boss.

After I left the kids behind, I had way more time on my hands. So, more time meant more money. Mentally getting too big for my britches.

With that being said; I stepped into another side of the streets. Even though I had all the connections I needed within my family. I figured I wanted to be independent and also keep the chatter down amongst the family. So I stepped outside of the family line and purchased my first pound of weed. Now that may not be a big deal to anybody. But it was a big deal considering that I always said that this was something that I'd never do. So today, I know better than to say; what I'd never do.

But I had a plan. After I broke the bundle down and got it ready for sale. I established a little operation. Nothing major; but very incognito. At least I thought I was. I had three people in mind that I figured would hold me down.

The first person I called was none other than Chubbs AKA, Randy; my brother. At the time, he delivered mail in the hood. After I told him the idea, he was all for it. Underneath his good boy image, a resting kingpin was in cue, ready to come alive. I always knew that if I didn't happen to be his big brother, chances are, he probably would have really been a real kingpin. After all, his Godfather was in pretty deep. And Chubbs, his mind worked like that. But thank God, he looked up to me above all and valued my earlier example. Because, let's be real, it wasn't like mom and dad showed him the right way to live either.

After him, I called Draya. Even though she was still mad at me, she was with it. If she had it her way, this was how she'd rather me get money anyway. And lastly, I told Tifani. But I had to give her special instructions. Because she knew plenty of people that smoked weed. Knowing that she had been sheltered from this type of thing all her life. The people around her knew it too, and I knew they'd try to take advantage of her if they knew she was holding anything. After things got rolling. It turned out to be pretty smooth for a while. It was working.

In the meantime, while that was going on, I continued to allow myself to free fall into the game. Accepting the opportunities that fell in my lap. Finding out that I didn't have to chase women to get involved. Most of them saw what was going on and chose to ride for me, and then others allowed their curiosity to push them over the edge.

Outside of shows and afterparties or even an occasional invite. I didn't usually go to clubs to have a good time. But I'm making money now, and on this one night, I wanted to hear some loud music and have some drinks. So I ended up at a club in Boston, "Venue". Like everywhere else I went after my brother got married, I decided to go alone. As the DJ is rocking out and playing all the latest hits of the time. I was having a ball. I even ran into a few old friends from middle school that night and kicked it with them for a little while. About 12am I looked up and seen that the club was packed. Everybody looking their best and shining. Before I knew it, I had been back and forth to the bar 4 to 5 times. After that last trip, I found a new empty spot that I could post up in the now crowded club. But as I was standing there sipping my drink, all of a sudden, my good mood changed. Almost like a 180. From where I was standing, it allowed me to have an eye-level view of the tops of everybody's heads on and off the dance floor. I instantly went from the vibe of celebration and feeling good to who the hell do I think I am and why I am here.

The trigger for the mood change was everybody that I ran into that night had on something that represented Boston. Not that this was a bad thing at all, because I always have and will always love my city. But it was something about seeing all the caps and jerseys, Antonio Ansaldi Vest and Timbaland Boots. When I stepped back and checked my own style, I too had on an oversized Celtic Jersey, with the matching hat, Some Antonio Ansaldi Jean, and Timbaland boots. Something about that didn't sit right with me and I immediately felt like I was no different from anybody else in the place.

So I finished my drink and left.

On my way home, I took the long way. From time to time, I did that. While in route, I pulled up to a traffic light. On my right side, pulled up a white Mazda 626. I happened to look over at the driver. She was pretty but had looked like she'd been crying. So I rolled my window down as if I was going to ask for directions. Once she rolled her window down, I calmly asked her, as if I already knew her, "What's the matter". That was some game I learned from my uncle Bryce back in the day. He was super smooth with the ladies.

She said that she's been having a bad day. So I told her that I was sorry to hear that and went on to ask her where she was going. Before she could answer, the light turned green. She seemed like she wanted to talk so I told her to pull over at the next intersection in a closed McDonalds parking lot. Of course, she was skeptical, but she agreed. When she pulled in front of me I noticed she had out-of-state tags. But that wasn't strange at all. Because Boston is a college city. Once we both parked, I got out and walked over to her car. I asked her name and she told me Ava. The first thing I noticed was all of the stuff she had in the car. It looked like she was in the middle of moving. Come to find out, that was almost the case. One of her girlfriends from Boston had hooked her up with a guy. They'd been talking long distance for a while. It was going good. So good that she had moved to Boston from the Midwest to be with him. When she got there, he had flaked out on her. So for two weeks, she'd been sleeping here and there and, of course, in her car. I can't say that I felt bad for her. But I did immediately see how her situation could work out for me.

After she openly told me her dilemma. I continued the conversation by asking her what she had planned for the rest of the night. She reached in her bag and pulled out a sandwich bag with an 8ball of cocaine in it. She told me that she was on her way to revere beach to dust the bag off and see what happened. Right then, I took charge and told her that there'd been a change of plans. When she asked me what I meant by that, I told her that I would get back in my car, and she was going to follow me back to my house so we could talk more. She looked up at me with an unsure face and like she wanted to say something to pass up the opportunity. So I bent down to her eye level sitting in the car, and asked her, "Do I look like I have nothing to lose?" She said no. 35 minutes later, she was sitting in my living room.

She loved my place when she had walked in. Her first question was do I live alone. I told her, "Yes I do". From there, we really kicked it off well. Besides the fact that she sniffed a line or two every 10 minutes. So I rolled a blunt and set the tone early with her. Letting her know that if she was going to be around, she had to handle her noticeable habit. Also giving her a disclaimer, that being if she ever offered me anything stronger than weed, there would be a consequence. Because I always believed that the person who offers someone hardcore substances with extreme addiction powers somehow was a miserable devil. Especially when it's evident that its not their vice.

She had no rebuttal and got where I was coming from instantly. My tone of voice, body Language, and direct soul-piercing eye stare did the trick. It was easy for me to be that way with people I didn't love.

After about 3 weeks of kicking it with her, I could tell that she was intrigued by what was going on. But what she was trying to do was redirect my mission toward seeing her as my girlfriend. So, I ended up telling her that if this is not what she wants, I'm going to have to fall back from her. I can tell she didn't like the sound of that. But I didn't want to waste anymore time with her if we wasn't getting to the money. Because I didn't have any other interest in her besides adding her to the same mission that Marci was on. She started asking me more questions, but I told her that I couldn't go any deeper with her about the game if she wasn't about it. But girls will be girls, and she asked me, "How do I know if I want to do this If I don't know how it works?" I laughed at her and said, "You see enough to understand if this is what you want to do or not; don't play games with me". I went on to ask her If she knew what a heart surgeon does. She said that she did. So I asked if she wanted to be a heart surgeon. She said that she didn't. When I asked her why, with a silly smirk on her face, she scrambled to come up with an answer. But couldn't find the words or some slick reply. We laughed because it was evident that she knew just enough about it to know she'd never go over to Cambridge and enroll at Harvard and further learn how to do it. Ultimately, she knew that she observed enough to know if she would or not. She said nothing else and went on to sniff the last line of Cocaine from that sandwich bag. Playing dumb to camouflage how smart you are is never intelligent.

That same night I met up with my cousin Wiz and some of his friends at an after-hour lounge. So I let Ava tag along. Which is not a good idea to bring a girl around the kind of guys affiliated in the game prematurely if you know the girl isn't committed. Because there are levels to this. But this was my last night with her one way or another as it stood anyway.

When we got to the lounge,everything was cool. A couple of Wiz's friends was out alone. But one of guys had one or two ladies with him, including Wiz. When I stepped to the bar to buy a couple of drinks, Wiz had stepped over to the bar as well. He asked me who Ava was.

So I introduced him. His next question was about her affiliation. "Is she friend or Go"? I didn't want to lie, so I told him that I'm working on it. He asked me how long has it has been. Because he had seen me out with her once before. When I told him, with a hint of playfulness, he said, "3 Weeks? And she been staying the night at the crib too? Naw cuz, f*ck that." This was a moment of truth. Either she was with me, or she wasn't.

Wiz turned to Ava and asked her, "Do you Like my cousin?" She told him that she did. He told her that he could tell she did. Wiz put his drink down on the bar and bent down to her ear, yelling in it, saying, "B*tch, what the F*ck are you waiting for, you think my cuz got time to play wit'chu?" She was stunned by his tone. You can tell the coke had her head spinning. She looked at me, looked at him, then looked up and saw what kind of environment she was in. When she glanced over at the stunning girl with Wiz standing next to him, in which, it was very noticeable that Ava admired her status. Wiz's chick was looking back at her unbothered, smiling, sipping her drink and lightly shaking her head, yes. As if she was welcoming Ava to the game. Right then, I handed Ava the drink I ordered and told her to stand at the end of the bar and don't talk to anybody. She did. After approximately another hour of kicking it with Wiz, I left with Ava right behind me. By the time I made it back home, she had her mind made up. The next day, Ava was off to the races.

After Ava got into the flow and now her and Marci are vibing. For months, everything flowed with ease. I had no worries about anything. Because of my praise of the mighty dollar. I even exceeded the money marker that I set. So, since everything was good, I figured I'd just set another marker. But this time, it was like hitting a mental switch resetting my motivation using the idea of being completely unsatisfied as fuel. Therefore, aggression was born, but now in a fully narcissistic way. It was like everybody owed me; Something. I was still not totally respecting the level I was on and comparing myself to my peers.

But every now and then, I would run into a situation that would stand out to me, letting me know that I was either doing good or it was time to quit. But when you're young and full of testosterone. You can be blind and dumb to the signs.

One Friday night after the girls left out. My brother called me and said he wanted to get out the house. He was a hard worker and very hands-on with his family. Sothat was no problem for me. I would stop and drop what I was doing for him anytime. Truth be told, he knew me best and knew everything going on with me. When I picked him up, we went straight to the liquor store to buy a bottle of booze for the night to sip and kick it. When we got there, it was some guys standing outside that we knew from the neighborhood and high school. Some of them gave up on their lives and talents soon after high school, and the others who was still scratching and surviving. At the end of the day, we all was.

When my brother and I came out the store. One of the guys stepped over to my car and kicked it with us for a few minutes. He was one of those guys that talked real big about himself and looked at everybody else as if they were lower than him. The "nobody is on my level" type. This was a "Wish a MF would" moment for me in the back of my mind. At this point in my life I wasn't accepting disrespect from anybody.

As we were talking, he brought up a hustle that he was on. The hustle being that in which I had my hands in already.

But, of course, he didn't know that. He went on and on explaining to me how it works and how big his status was. We just sat there and listened. Because we did already know that he was involved. But to what degree, I didn't know.

My brother began to crack the seal on the bottle to take a sip. The old friend then came out of his mouth and said something that confirmed where I stood in the food chain. He said, in a slightly condescending way, "Shan, you need to get you a couple of riders and level up. You'll be on your feet in no time and make $800 a week, and get like me". As my brother tried to get the first sip from the bottle down his throat, it reversed on him, spitting out the liquor in a hysterical laughing fit. My face; priceless. The old friend chuckled but never caught on. Noweven though to someone else, that would have been a sign of disrespect and also an opportunity to break this guy's spirit, I never did. Because for me, it was really no need to. It just directly confirmed to me that I wasn't at the bottom of the food chain. That was enough for me.

My only come back to what that guy said to me came with a hint of sarcasm. As I turned to my old friend, giving him dap. I simply told him that I could never be like him.

As he walked back over to the guys, I got in my car and pulled off.

My brother was in the passenger seat, still giggling at what had just happened.

He looked over at me and said, "$800? You just made that in the last hour doing nothing". I learned two things from that situation. First; Mindset makes a big difference toward achieving your goals. Second; Listening defeats ignorance.

— A Place for LeRaun —

For years my mother had been fighting with her sister Nellie for the returned custody of my baby brother, LeRaun. Years ago, after the childcare worker took him from the hospital. Malina, (the childcare worker) was trying to keep him in foster care in efforts to permanently get LeRaun adopted. Where chances are, we'd never see him again. But luckily Aunt Nellie stepped up to take him in, just like Aunt Breena did for me and Randy.

But by this time, my mom had left the state of Massachusetts and had been clean for years. But for some reason, aunt Nellie didn't care. As my mom went back and forth from Florida to Boston for court appearances numerous times. It became very stressful and expensive. Me and Randy wanted my mom to get LeRaun back too. We really wanted to see if she'd do a much better job with him than she did with us. We both were in her corner. She never stopped trying to get my baby brother back. Even after she moved from Florida as well.

Even though my aunt Nellie swore to give LeRaun back to my mom once my mother was drug free; it seemed like she reneged. Pushing my mom into a constant agitated mental space. The situation got so nasty between the two of them that I use to think that my Aunt was paying my mom back an old vendetta for something my mom did to her when they were little girls. But as time went on, I started to realize that my aunt and her husband fell in love with LeRaun as a baby and he had become a special part of their family. To be honest, that was understandable too.

But my mom wasn't having it. She wanted her child back. Causing an uproar with everybody she spoke to about it. Almost splitting the family in half over where LeRaun should be. Over those years, I even ended up in court with my aunt and uncle because I defended my mom's honor. Leaving me to be charged with property damage on my aunts house. Although everybody thought I might have been a mama's boy, I really wasn't. But at the end of the day, she was still my mom. After my mom slapped aunt Nellie in the grocery store while my mom was in Boston for one of those court dates, it solidified that LeRaun was already home with my aunt and her family forever.

— I'm The One —

We've all heard it before, and it's true. For every level, there are new devils. Despite my good fortunes, I ran into another situation. But this time, the situation quickly put me in my place.

A Rapper friend of mine that I made music with introduced me to a young lady. She was a bit older than me, but she was a beautiful and sexy white girl from Danvers,Ma. She took a liking to me immediately. She wasn't a bad person but you can tell she was into a lot. She came from a good family but was addicted to the fast life. She was introduced to a life by the father of her bi-racial son. She was a hustler though. When she learned what I was into, by way of eavesdropping on a phone call from Marci. She immediately started telling me how many girls she knew and how they'd be down. My intuition told me that she was telling the truth about that, but on the other hand, I was skeptical of her "Diddy-Boppin" like energy. The kind of girl who mix and mingles amongst various crowds and every guy she knows is her boy or homie. So I told her right then and there that I didn't want to meet anybody she knew until she got down first. She said that she didn't get down like that with a rapid reply. So I said, "Then let's not talk about it at all". Then quickly changed the subject. Just to reassure her that it wasn't a conversation to play with. So we didn't. But I could tell that she was bothered by the way I wasn't thirsty for her fiery and seductive ways. Leaving her totally turned on in the moment, raising her interest in me. So she reset her approach. It was like she simply pushed a defense mechanism off button. Yet, the conversation carried on, and surprisingly, it was good. So much that we really got kind of tight with each other after that and we began talking on a regular basis. So much that one late night while I was at Tifani's house, she called me. The house was quiet, and Tifani overheard her say something sexual to me. So that led to us arguing all night.

A couple of weeks went by, and my new found friend called me to let me know she wanted to come by my house and kick it with me. She had been telling me that she wanted to talk to me about something anyway. I didn't have any plans for the night so she called at the right time. She rang the bell, and I let her in. This was her first time coming. But she also had a guest with her, another beautiful girl and a bottle of Hennessy.

Upon walking in, I noticed her vibe was off. But still, she introduced me to her lady friend. They looked around and started admiring. She told me that I had a lot of class, and for some reason, she kept saying, "You're the one". I couldn't figure that out. But overall, she was judging by the way I had the pad decked out and how clean it was. She even told me that my place was the cleanest and well put together out of all the guys she knew. A "Diddy Bopper" for sure. But I figured she was just trying to finesse me or gain some type of brownie points. The other girl didn't speak much, but I could tell something was off with her too. At first, she just seemed a little tipsy. While the other girl sat in the living room, we finally stepped into my bedroom to talk. She wanted to tell me that she was a woman of her word. She Brought the other girl to prove what she had told me the first night we met. I can't lie, I was with that. Ready to go back into the living room and start that conversation. After 20 minutes of talking in the room and right before I opened the door to walk out, she said, "I have one more thing to talk to you about". I asked her what was up. She said that she knew when she met me that I was the one. Telling me how smart and smooth I was. How I wasn't like everybody else and for that, we can win together. Telling me that I was her style and type, as if I was her first option. She was trying to seduce me by her plead to be a team. It almost worked too. Because this white girl was bad. She had a body out of this world. But when she took me into her arms and looked up at me, she told me that she had the connect for dope and wanted me to invest in a big package. She lost me right there.

Still, I listened to what she had to say. How she had it all figured out, without me ever having to touch anything, just get paid. Before leaving the room, I told her I would think about it. But I knew wholeheartedly that I would never cross that line. We left the room, and I went straight to the kitchen to pour myself a glass of Hennessy. I rolled a joint and then sat on the sofa and lit up. Thats when I realized sitting directly across from me, on the other couch, that both girl's whole vibe was that of dope feins.

I sipped my Hennessy, smoked my joint, and watched them have sex for the next hour until I kicked them out.

For the rest of that night, I sat on my sofa alone and truly thought about what was asked of me. But not in a way that I was considering at all. Because my mind was made up; that wasn't for me. Even though some of the people I know would have thought I was crazy for passing up that opportunity. That's why I never told anyone until now. But while I was sitting there, a thought came over me that made me proud of who I was. Allowing me to shake it all off. It was something about my decision to not move forward and deeper into streets. In some way, somehow, I felt like by denying the offer, I stopped a new generational curse or cycle from going any further in my family. I sat there and thought about that until the sun came up. Then, I put on my sweat clothes and headed back into Dorchester to teach my waiting dance students at 10 am. Because, no matter where I was or what I was going through, on Saturday morning I showed up for the kids.

Believe it or not, on the way in town, I got a random call from my dad. He called me to tell me that he had got a new job. He told me that he liked it a lot and gave me the details of his duties. I was truly happy for him. Actually proud of him for sustaining his sobriety. But what he said next blew my mind. He said, Do you know where Jubilee church is ?" I told him that I did. He said, "Well, that's where I work at now. But what I can't understand is why everybody at the church knows you"? When I told him my affiliation, he was shocked. He told me that the gospel singing group I worked with just performed at the last Sunday service and blessed him. He then asked, "You did that?" I told him, "I'm The One".

— Friend Or Foe —

I knew I was getting in too deep when one day, after my dance class. One of the mothers of my students approached me. She asked me what I had been up to lately. It was a normal question. So I answered her by giving her that same ole bland and uninformative answer that everybody gives. "Nothing much". She laughed and said, "That's not what I heard". So as I'm gathering my things, I just looked at her and asked her what she heard. She replied with, "C'mon Shan. You know what I'm talking 'bout". Truly I did, but still, I tried to play it off as if it was nothing major. But she didn't let up. She kept going. Suddenly, her energy changed, and she got quite serious. She then frankly said, "Shan, You know this is Boston, and the streets is always watching". She was a real one. So I told her that I knew what she meant. She went on to tell me that because of my image, I should better protect it by letting her join me. I can't lie. She was a hustling ass chick. But at the end of the day, her image was a little too rowdy for me. I figured her energy would bring way more attention than I ever wanted from this lifestyle.

The conversation didn't last that long. So we ended it with me once again denying another offer. The last thing she said before we left the community center auditorium was, "You smooth with it, Shannyn, but be careful out here tho. People talk. Call me if you need anything".

She wasn't the only person that said that to me. But I always read in between the lines with everybody. You just never know who to trust. Because enemies can appear as friends.

— The Discovery —

I would go food shopping every other week for my house. But I would also go food shopping for Tifani's house as well. Because I did spend a great deal of time at her house. I figured since I didn't pay her bills, I still came and went as I pleased; the least I could do was make sure she had food. I would pull up to her house while she was at work and drop off the groceries. I would put the refrigerated items away and leave all the other items in the bags. Then I would take back off. I was always in a rush and had something to do. When she got home, she would put the rest of it away herself.

As many times that I've been to her house. I never checked the stash or even asked her about it. Of course, she would never bring it up either. To be honest, I didn't really expect her to have even touched it. I kind of just wrote it off as a rainy day stash.

One day while dropping off the groceries, I just so happened to randomly check to see if she even budged with it. But when I pulled it out of the stash spot, there were only six bags left, but only $180 in cash. At first, I got really angry. But I quickly toned myself down and gave her the benefit of the doubt. Telling myself not to jump to conclusions and forced myself to think; Maybe she needed the cash for something important. But either way, I needed to hear the story behind my discovery. So later on that night, after she got home, I went back to her place. She knew that I had been there earlier because of the groceries. So she was sweet to me when I walked in the door. Thanking me as she always did. But, I didn't get straight to the question at hand. I actually showed her how to cook a dish that she'd been asking me about. I wanted to see if she'd bring up the shortage I found in the stash. After we ate, I went back to the stash and brought the box out to the living room and sat it in front of her, and stared at her. As soon as she saw it, I could tell she was trying to quickly pull her story together in her head. But before she could say anything, I asked her, "Where's my Sh*t?"

I was so hoping that she would say that she needed it for a bill; or something like that. But she gave me the answer that I was dreading, saying that a family member and their friends said they would pay her back. I flipped out. Totally blew a gasket. Raging with some of the foulest and disrespectful things you could ever say to a woman. Breaking her spirit by attacking every insecurity she ever had. In the moment, I felt like she deserved everything I was doing and saying because I specifically gave her instructions to protect herself from this happening. Because I knew how the people around her would be if they ever found out that she was holding. So to me, by her not following my directions, she showed me that she couldn't protect my mission. Making me feel like she was yet another person that I loved but couldn't trust. The same anger that I was displaying reflected what I felt inside about myself. Stupid for expecting this girl to get it. At the time not knowing any better myself that just because a person loves you, doesn't mean they automatically get you. Before I walked out, I asked one last question. I asked if she really believed that they would pay her back, and she said that she did. I just shook my head in disappointment because I knew the real answer to that. I told her that her lack of loyalty made me question her love for me. That sucked because I really did love her. I grabbed all of my music equipment and left out the door. It was a while before I saw or spoke to Tifani again.

— 99 Problems —

One day I stopped by Draya's house to check on her and see what the business was doing on her end. Come to find out; it was better than I expected. When I pulled up in front of her house, she got in the car with me. Before she gave me the cash, she had a disclaimer, telling me that the amount I was expecting wasn't going to be accurate. I quickly jumped to being frustrated, and I asked her what happened? She told me that my bags were too fat. I asked her what she meant by that, and she went on to explain that she opened up all the bags and pretty much broke them all down in half and was reselling them. I was expecting $500, and this girl gave me back $850. Of course, I wasn't mad at all at that, and we just started laughing.

That same night we had went out to eat, and when we were done, I decided to go have a drink down on Newbury Street, downtown Boston. It's a very popular area.

I haven't heard from Marci in about three days. That wasn't out of the normal for us. But what was out of the normal was her not answering my calls when I did call her.

Even Ava told me that she hadn't been answering her calls either.

Once me and Draya got to the bar. We ordered drinks, talked, and laughed. Good vibes. We stayed until the bar closed. We left out and walked back up Newbury Street to where I parked. We got right in and pulled off. As I'm passing the same bar we just left from, I saw Marci. It seems as though we've been inside the same bar for the past hour and a half and didn't see each other.

She was standing outside the bar talking to some guy. I could tell he was a square and was just trying to get her number. So I pulled over and double-parked. Before stepping out of the car, I turned to Draya and told her not to get out. I walked across the street and in between two cars onto the sidewalk. I stealthily stepped up behind her. When she turned around and saw my face, it was like she just saw a ghost. Like she knew this was about to be a problem. I never acknowledged the guy. I just demanded her to step away and talk to me. So she did. When I asked her what was up and why she hadn't answered my calls, she had all kinds of excuses as to why she didn't. But I knew she was lying about something. So that sparked a confrontation, and our tones escalated. Before I knew it, I had grabbed her by the collar and yanked her toward me to tell her a few choice words to set the situation straight. The guy she was talking with looked and saw what was happening and yelled out, "Hey, What are you doing M'f*cker"? All while stepping towards me in his "Captain Save'em" attempt. I turned to get ready to square up with this guy. But from out of nowhere, in between 2 cars parked 25 feet back towards where he was still standing, came a scrappy Draya who stepped in front of the guy screaming, "Don't walk up on him like that". The guy was stunned by her sudden appearance and stopped in his tracks. He then asked her who I was and what was going on? Draya told him to "mind his F*ckin business". He was drunk and confused. He looked over at me and Marci one last time and just walked off.

After that, I put Marci in the car with me and pulled off. I dropped Draya off back at her parent's house and drove around with Marci into the wee hours, talking and trying to figure out what's been up with her. Come to find out, she was extremely jealous of Ava and the time she'd been spending with me lately. Letting her emotions get the best of her and struggling to understand that I didn't plan for our team to just be her and I. She was also upset because she had seen how Ava jumped in and started moving fast and without any other overhead but me. Marci still lived at home with her parents.

But what I knew about Marci was that she was super competitive. She felt like she wasn't keeping up. That caused a lot of frustration within her. But how my mind worked back then, I really didn't care how frustrated she was, yet instigated her emotions as new fuel to get more money. Underneath it all, Marci just outright disliked Ava. Everything she said so far was minor to me. Because I knew It all came with the territory of the lifestyle. But what raised my concern is when Marci mentioned that her family started questioning her whereabouts more lately. With all of the late nights and early mornings she was running out of excuses. Right then, I asked Marci if she wanted to move in with me. She said that she would, but her parents would want to be too involved with her making that decision, which would raise their curiosity about me. We both agreed that we didn't want that to happen at all. Even with that being the most serious of the conversation that night. She kept bringing it back to Ava. I had to reiterate repeatedly to Marci that it wasn't just about what she could do for me alone. Telling her that Ava was there to pick up the slack where she couldn't.

As I finally pulled into her neighborhood, she looked over at me and said, "I guess teamwork makes the dream work, Huh?" I replied and told her that there was no other way. By the end of the conversation, she was back on track.

But what Marci taught me in this situation is this; some people only want to help you or be there for you under the condition that they are praised as your superhero.

A few days later, Marci called me like nothing was ever a problem. She told me that she had a few things lined up in Maine. I usually would just let her take the car and go. But what she didn't know was that Ava had a few things lined up in New Hampshire. Considering that Marci wasn't feeling Ava at all, I decided to go for the ride in order to keep the peace between them. We ended up being gone all day and night. After I dropped them both off, I went straight home. I was feeling good too. It was a good night. When I pulled into my driveway, it was about 4 am. I still remember Jay-Z's "Can't Knock the Hustle" playing through my speakers. I backed into my assigned parking spot as I always did. But as soon as I turned off the car, a weird feeling came over me. It was eerie. For the first time, I was spooked. The first thing I did was turn off the radio. I then leaned my seat back and started pan-gazing over the other cars in the parking lot. Without taking my eyes off the other cars, I leaned over into my passenger seat, grabbed my money, and stuffed it in my jacket and pants pockets. From the position of my car, I could see up to my condo windows on the second floor. All the lights were out like I left it. But right when I got the thought that I was just bugging out. I went to grab the door handle to get out of my car. But the weird feeling intensified, and all I could do was turn the car back on and take off, screeching back out of the driveway.

I ended up at a friend's house. She thought I came to have sex like usual. But that was the furthest thing from my mind. Still, with my clothes on, I just laid at the bottom half of her bed thinking about what I just felt back at my house. I just knew I was being watched.

— Gone —

A year later, my 25th birthday has come and gone. Teaching at the community center hadn't even been a thought at that time. I wasn't doing any shows, but I was still making music here and there. I was totally frustrated with the local music scene. One day, I got a call from an old friend who asked me if I could help develop a new band. But this time, a girl band. When I found out who was behind the idea, I quickly lost interest. I told them I couldn't do it. Because it was a team that I've worked with in the past. I felt like I knew what the outcome would be. Some people feel like sometimes the second and third time is a charm. But at this point, I was definitely feeling like it would be insanity for me to try to do the same thing expecting a different result. Overall, that had become my spirit about everything. It just felt like my life was missing something, but I just couldn't figure it out. I felt myself becoming numb to everything going on around me. So I started to keep more to myself. I needed it. It was my first attempt to put my best foot forward to identify who I was. Doing my best to create good memories for myself. Finally, the thought came to try and make my life about me. Searching for that selfishness that others seem to be born with. Something I knew I needed if I was going to be out in the streets. But in my time alone, the reality of what I found was heartbreaking. Because while I was looking for an equivalent match of deceitfulness, narcissistic, untrustworthy, scamming, broke and flashy, poverty-stricken, angry, fake loving energy within myself. I just couldn't seem to find the "Real Nigga" in me. That part of me that says I am what I've been through. I am what this society and environment says I am.

I began to feel unworthy of all the proper front row seat grooming and upbringing that my family and community invested in me. But there was nobody to blame because everybody was true to who they were and led by example. So it all boiled down to me deciding if I would make everyone proud or not.

Even though Marci finally disappeared on me for the final and last time, I didn't stress about that at all. Because the show must go on. She was replaced before she went missing back into her normal life without her ever knowing. That didn't matter at this point. Because I told the girl I replaced her with to find her family and never call me again. Ava was on her way out too. She had relapsed back into not only sniffing coke, but now using even harder drugs.

One late night I got home, and upon walking in, I never turned the lights on or did my usual walk-through to see if anything was out of place. I did that because Draya still had a key, and the last time she was there, we had a fight, and she threw a knife at me. That caused a serious scene with the neighbors. Because the cops came and all. On the other hand, the way young drug dealers had been getting kidnapped and held for ransom around the city was getting out of hand.

But on this night, I was drained and just went straight to my room. I took all of the money from my pockets, put it on my dresser, and laid across my bed with all my clothes on. This would probably be the 30th time I've ever slept in my own bed.

The next morning, I woke up at about 7:30am. I laid there staring at the ceiling for about 20 minutes. My mind was racing with so many thoughts, good and bad. Like they all were struggling for a position to be focused on. When I sat up, I planned to do my usual and go into the bathroom and wash up. But when I did, I couldn't stand up. Not because something was wrong with my body. But because the thoughts got heavy and began to sink into my spirit. I was just staring directly into my closet. I remember feeling like I lived so many different lifetimes already. Before I knew it, I had been sitting in that same spot on the side of my bed for about an hours. I finally started to look around the room at everything that I had. It was all expensive and looked very nice. Finally, I stepped down off of my bed and walked into the living room. I never saw the sunshine through those bay windows as bright as they did that morning. I must have stood there for another 5 minutes. Then, a feeling came over me that was familiar. But this time, it didn't spook me. So I pulled out a chair from my dining room table and sat down. The silence over the condo was somehow refreshing. It gave me a chance to look at all that I hustled up in the last 2years of my life. Allowing me to be proud of myself. But then thinking how much more I'm capable of.

But, those thoughts didn't last that long. Because, all of a sudden, a voice popped in my head and simply changed my life with one word saying, LEAVE.

Immediately I took offense. I even said to myself out loud, "Hell no". Spiritually, I tussled with that word all that morning. Forcing myself to think that I could do more or how I've only just begun. While on the other hand, the spirit within me was beating me down with truths that I didn't understand. It wasn't until I walked over to one of the windows and looked out that I came to grips with the fact that if I stayed, this would be the highest level my life would go. But from that time on, if I stayed, I'd be responsible for whatever comes my way. Ready to accept the fact that cycles and more trauma was for certain.

Of course, I had thought that since I've been through everything that I did and survived, that I could make it through anything else that came my way. To help solidify that understanding, I also thought; where would I go? Without having a direct answer for that, I started to feel like I was just bugging out. Easily resorting back to the comfort of my thinking. Trying to force myself to believe that nothing could be better than what I got going on right now. As if what I've always known and had was winning the fight.

But then, that voice of LEAVE came back, and this time with authority. I couldn't shake it, and I had no other comeback after the mighty blow. It started as a whisper in the back of my mind. Then it got louder and louder. "For he knows the plans that he has for you, and to prosper you in your future". It repeated in my mind for quite sometime. Then I went back to my room and got my phone. I don't even know who I was going to call. But when I got the phone in my hand, I dialed my aunt Breena. When she answered, I didn't even know I would say what I did. But I told her that she can have all of the pieces of art and vases that she had once said she liked. When she got a moment, she could come and get them. She said ok, and we talked for about another 5 minutes, and we hung up. When we did, that's when I realized that I was leaving.

The very next person that I called was my Mom. I had talked to her about a month earlier. But I remembered the last thing she said to me was that she really liked the new city she moved to. Charlotte. She went there to help my cousins with their kids while they were busy getting there business off the ground. That day, I didn't tell her anything that was going on or even where my head was at the time. I just wanted to know a little more about where she was. She volunteered information about one of my younger cousins who just moved down there from Boston a year before and had her own apartment. I saw that as an open opportunity for me. Because the idea of living with my mom wasn't an option. Before we hung up, she told me that

I would love it there and spoke highly of Charlotte. All I said was "maybe one day I will find out". After that, we hung up. The last and final person I called that day was Tifani. She was excited to hear from me. I told her that I would come by her house later to kick it with her. When I did, she was saddened by the news. I had made up my mind to move to Charlotte. Even though she didn't like that idea, she was super supportive.

Within 2 weeks, I paid off my lease to the condo, moved out, gave away most of my furniture, put the rest in my God-Parents basement, and totaled my car for the insurance money. After the word had got around to the family that I was leaving. Something happened that still to this day, I don't know if it was a good thing or bad thing. Because as we know sometimes, with everything good comes something bad.

I got a call from my Aunt Nellie. She said, "You leaving, huh?" I told her that I was. She went on to tell me good luck, and she hoped it works out for me down in Charlotte. But jokingly, like everyone else, she said, "You'll be back". We laughed at that. She asked me what day I was leaving. When I told her the date, she said something that blew my mind. She told me very simply and calmly, "Before you get on the road, come and get your little brother and take him to your mother". I was shocked. At that point, I had already accepted that she would raise my little brother until he was old enough to be on his own. I believe the whole family thought that. After we talked for a while about it, I agreed.

After telling Draya about my decision, she wasn't as excited but was ok with it. I could quickly tell that her wheels had begun spinning immediately. But I knew she'd be ok.

My brother didn't give me any pushback about going either. But I couldn't help but feel like he thought I was going because I was a "Mama's Boy". Not fully recognizing that I had my own demons to face and workout at the time. But long as he was ok, I was good. And besides, his wife, Carla and their new growing family had him wrapped around their fingers. He ended up on the right track for sure.

A week before I left, I got a call from that old friend that I used to booty call. She started the conversation with small talk. But then, she changed the vibe. She asked me if I still lived in the same place. I told her that I didn't. She asked why? I just told her that I had moved to a new spot. In which I did. I temporarily moved into Tifani's apartment. But I didn't tell her that. I asked her why she asked. She didn't answer right away. Instead, there was a pause as if she was getting her words right to reply with. When she finally said something, she disregarded my question all together. But went on to ask me why don't I hang out with my cousins or have any dudes around me? That was kind of odd. But I did answer, and it was simple. "My cousins be busy". Believing in the back of my mind that if I ever needed them, they'd be there. Then I told her that I don't feel safe when it comes to keeping a lot of guys around me. Usually, your biggest enemies lurk in your crew. I just felt safer by myself. She told me that she understood that. Then, the conversation took a turn.

She told me that she had something to tell me and needed to listen to her. She sounded serious and sincere. So I asked her, what's up? She took another pause and then began to tell me about how she was out at a bar the night before she called me. She was there to meet one of her girls for a couple of drinks and talk. But before her girl got there, she was approached by a guy that was obviously trying to flirt with her. She said he offered to buy her a drink. So she agreed to that and he did. As they were talking, another guy walked in and stood next to him. It was obvious that they knew each other. The guy that bought her the drink told her he needed a moment to talk to his friend that just got there. He went on to tell the bartender to get her whatever she wanted until he was done and put it on his tab. He then turned his back to her and engaged in his conversation with his boy. As she was sitting there somewhat alone, her friend finally walked in. They begin to talk as well. But girls being girls, they started to eavesdrop on the two guys' conversation. Because it seemed pretty serious, yet mysterious and secretive. About 10 minutes into their conversation, she said that she overheard one of the guys say, something like, "What's up with the dancer?" She said, that struck her as odd because the two guys didn't seem like they would be acquainted with a dancer. But she didn't think too much of it and went on to order another drink. But whenever one of the guys said something to the effect of, "We gotta play it cool cause I know his people". She said that was enough to incline her interest, until the guy that came, left. Further details that she told me from the call were quite interesting. She said that the moment she knew they were talking about me was when one of the guys referenced the dancer in Fat Joe's Music Video. Also about how they knew the town I lived in outside of Boston and how they figured I had an extraordinary amount of money.

Before we hung up, she told me that I should be careful. Again telling me that maybe I should consider hanging out with my cousins more. That way, I'd have a fighting chance at the attention that obviously seems to be coming my way. I told her that I would and thanked her for calling and pulling my coat tail. Thank God that I had a lot of trust issues at the time anyway. Because sometimes the messengers don't mind having bloody hands. It was always strange that she couldn't remember the guy's name who bought her drinks all night. So we hung up without me even telling her that I was leaving.

I stayed at Tifani's house for a whole week, counting down the days. I didn't go anywhere. I was empty and had nothing left to give. I was mentally and spiritually exhausted. Just tired. To be honest, I really didn't know if leaving would make a difference. But what I did come to realize was that what I already knew didn't do well compared to what

I didn't know. So instead of being stuck in a comfort of dysfunction, changing my environment was necessary if I ever wanted to grow and heal. Because trauma after trauma on top of more trauma without ever being healed leads to a crazy cycle of pain.

The day came for me to finally go. I rented a van. I stopped by Draya's one last time. I gave her the longest hug and left her with a kiss. She didn't say much, but her silence said enough. I got back to Tifani's house, and she was sad. But still, she was packing me a few sandwiches and snacks to go with. I packed the van with everything that I was going to bring. A TV, a DVD collection, clothes, a shoebox with cash in it, and an aero-bed. After I got everything loaded up, I then gave Tifani a hug and kiss and told her she could come and visit as soon as I got settled in. She said ok and that she was going to miss me. Then I left.

But before I got on the road. I had to make one last stop. I pulled up at my aunt's house and got my little brother, LeRaun. I watched him hug my Aunt Nellie and the rest of her family goodbye. With excitement, he jumped in the van with a backpack and one big suitcase. I remember before I pulled off just looking at him in the passenger seat. I could tell he was scared and didn't know what he was getting ready to walk into, because he didn't know our mother that well. But also what he didn't know was that I was just as scared. Because I knew nothing about a Queen City.

Right at midnight, I pulled out onto I-95 South.

Charlotte, North Carolina; Here I come.

With over 5 thousand colleges and universities in America alone, I can only hope that you change the trajectory of your family traditions by leading by example. Allowing them to see that the only way they can graduate from Sidewalk University is by falling short of doing the right thing, and committing to the possibility of consequences that come with making bad decisions. Even if you took a couple of classes as I did. Apply what you did learn to the areas of your life that it fits best. Because what you did observe was enough to help a freshman transfer his/her credits before they get a chance to graduate from Sidewalk University.

— THE END —

A Letter To The Wanderers

One of the most heartbreaking things to see is a person that is living beneath the calling and purpose on their life. With understanding that not everyone finds out what it is right away; I believe that its never too early or too late to seek out what it might be. But then, there are those who don't know any better to do so, becoming a wandering soul, completely uninformed of their own truth. Letting life in this world torment you in cycles. Getting beat down in a slaughter because you have no idea of what weapon to use to defend yourself. Either from your own self and/or the enemy.

This is why I believe it is important to be prayerful over your friends and loved ones. A prayer that sets them free from un-forgiveness, the comfort of their dysfunctions and help lead their minds to a full understanding of their existence.

Although what every human being on the earth has in common is, for sure death. It's the sight of the ones you love in a self inflicted speeding process that hurts the most.

I admit; People who have a relationship with God are not perfect either. But Because we (should) know better; don't run from a word that might set you free. Allowing God to swallow up an early death in his Victory.

—Author/Shannyn Casino

In Memory Of

Raykim Q. Jackson

Ephesians 4:22-24

22You were taught, with regard to your former way of life, to put off your old self, which is being corrupted by its deceitful desires;23to be made new in the attitude of your minds;24and to put on the new self, created to be like God in true righteousness and holiness.

About The Author

This, creator, writer, artist, actor, mentor and empowerment speaker of life; A.K.A Shannyn Casino, has over 30 years of displaying his gifts on a multitude of platforms. From his adolescent years to adulthood, Shannyn has evolved these gifts into a light of hope that draws people from all walks of life.

Shannyn Casino was born in the infamous Roxbury section of Boston, MA. He has worked with a number of music artists and groups both professional and amateur, traveling the U.S. and abroad bringing his clients to another level with his influence. He has also acted in both independent and big budgeted film projects. With the inspiration of the lights and camera; Shannyn founded his own film production called The Social Maximus. Shannyn's vision and creativity is considered a jack of all trades. And now, he has added author to his lists of titles.

Shannyn Casino exudes charisma, determination and perseverance. He takes extreme pride in his work and is relentless towards succeeding. Nevertheless, obedient to God's plan.

He now resides in Charlotte,NC.

THANK YOU,
TO THE CITY OF BOSTON.
EVERY FAMILY, EVERY FRIEND!

Brown Family, Toney Family, Minnifield Family,
Johnson Family, Moore Family, Bryant Family,
Suell Family, Allen Family, Farrow Family, Camillo Family,
Higginbottom Family, Variste Family, Tyler Family,
Vaughan Family, Brigham Family, Haith Family, Bibby Family,
Ortega Family, Mendes Family, Dickerson Family,
Stephens Family, Brooks Family, Martin Family,
Haynes Family, Gunn Family, Jemmott Family, Wilson Family,
Szpiech Family, Donald Family, Jackson Family, Battle Family,
Cannady Family, Durant Family, Stinson Family, Ward Family,
Bland Family, Humphries Family, Hill Family.

—Shannyn Casino